VIKINGS IN THE EAST

MARTYN WHITTOCK

VIKINGS
IN THE
EAST

FROM VLADIMIR THE GREAT
TO VLADIMIR PUTIN

THE ORIGINS OF A CONTESTED
LEGACY IN RUSSIA AND UKRAINE

\Bᵇ\
Biteback Publishing

First published in Great Britain in 2025 by
Biteback Publishing Ltd, London
Copyright © Martyn Whittock 2025

Martyn Whittock has asserted his right under the Copyright, Designs and Patents Act 1988 to be identified as the author of this work.

All rights reserved. No part of this publication may be reproduced, stored in a retrieval system or transmitted, in any form or by any means, without the publisher's prior permission in writing.

This book is sold subject to the condition that it shall not, by way of trade or otherwise, be lent, resold, hired out or otherwise circulated without the publisher's prior consent in any form of binding or cover other than that in which it is published and without a similar condition, including this condition, being imposed on the subsequent purchaser.

Every reasonable effort has been made to trace copyright holders of material reproduced in this book, but if any have been inadvertently overlooked the publisher would be glad to hear from them.

ISBN 978-1-78590-905-4

10 9 8 7 6 5 4 3 2 1

A CIP catalogue record for this book is available from the British Library.

Set in Adobe Caslon Pro and Trajan Pro 3

Printed and bound in Great Britain by
CPI Group (UK) Ltd, Croydon CR0 4YY

To Steve Tamplin.

What a great person to have had as my first head of a history department. Thank you for that and for our ongoing friendship.

CONTENTS

Map of the Rus lands — ix
Acknowledgements — xi
A note about spellings — xiii
Introduction — xvii

Chapter 1	Go East!	1
Chapter 2	Evidence for Vikings in the eastern Baltic: Trade and settlement	23
Chapter 3	Vikings of the rivers	39
Chapter 4	East meets West in the world of the gods and goddesses	57
Chapter 5	The creation of the Rus state	67
Chapter 6	To the 'Great City': The lure of Constantinople	85
Chapter 7	The making of 'Holy Rus'	99
Chapter 8	Vikings on camels	115
Chapter 9	A new Slav state and the last hurrah of the Vikings	131

Chapter 10	The eclipsing of Kyivan Rus: The calamitous thirteenth century	147
Chapter 11	Contested lands, 1300–1654	165
Chapter 12	A persistent legacy, 1654–1783	181
Chapter 13	The absorbing of 'Little Russia', 1783–1917	191
Chapter 14	From the Russian Revolution(s) to the 'end of history'	209
Chapter 15	An independent Ukraine and the return of the Vikings!	229
Epilogue	Back to the future? Where next for the 'deep story' of the Rus?	249
Notes		253
Index		267

MAP OF THE RUS LANDS
NOTE: NOT ALL DETAILS SHOWN WERE CONCURRENT.

ACKNOWLEDGEMENTS

I wish to thank Robert Dudley, my agent, and James Stephens, Olivia Beattie, Ella Boardman and all the team at Biteback for their encouragement and assistance.

I would also like to record my thanks to Jessalynn Bird, at Saint Mary's College, Notre Dame, Indiana, US, for permission to quote from her very accessible adaptation of the earlier translation of Ahmad ibn Fadlan's account of Scandinavian merchants on the Volga in 922, by Albert Stanburrough Cook in the *Journal of English and Germanic Philology* (1923).

Peter Bull, of Peter Bull Art Studio, produced the map giving the context of the Rus lands.

I am grateful (as always) to my family for the interest they take in my work and for the support shown to me as I embarked on yet another 'Viking journey'.

It goes without saying that all errors and interpretations are my own.

A NOTE ABOUT SPELLINGS

Russian and Ukrainian are closely related languages. As a result, there are Russian and Ukrainian versions of place, river and personal names. So, *Kiev* is the Russian form of the city's name, while *Kyiv* is the Ukrainian. *Vladimir* is the Russian form of the name of the ruler who accepted Christian baptism (into the Orthodox faith) in the late tenth century and *Volodymyr* is the Ukrainian form. *Dnieper* is the Russian form of this river's name and will be found in many published and online sources; in Ukrainian it is *Dnipro*.

Until Ukrainian independence in 1991 – and for some time afterwards in many publications – it is usually the Russian form of names that one encounters. This was due to Russification across the lands ruled by the tsars from the seventeenth century and later by the Soviets. Consequently, it was these forms that entered common usage internationally and which were widely found in the English-speaking world.

What to do about spellings now? This has become particularly freighted with controversy as Russian pressure mounted against

Ukraine in the twenty-first century and especially so since the Russian invasion of Ukraine in February 2022.

In the case of Kiev/Kyiv, *Kiev* was the generally accepted English-language spelling throughout the Soviet period and into the first years of this century. But it is now associated with the Russification of Ukraine. The same is true of a number of place, river and personal names. The transliteration *Kyiv* was legally mandated by the Ukrainian government in 1995. However, this new spelling only started gaining traction a few years ago, when the Ukrainian government mounted a campaign to secure international approval for the name of its capital city.¹

Due to the huge number of available published sources that use the Russian form of names, in this book the older (Russian) forms will generally be used to refer to rivers, places and personal names, unless these have traditionally appeared in their Ukrainian forms globally. This avoids changing spellings in published works which are quoted and because these forms have become very well known. So, the more familiar form of the river names *Dnieper* and *Dniester* will be used, because these are the forms most readers will encounter in other published works and online. *Vladimir* the Great will appear in this Russian form for the same reason and for its synchronicity with *Vladimir* Putin, who bears the same form of this personal name. The use of these Russian forms is for clarity and simplification and in no way conveys any disrespect for the Ukrainian language. Where Vladimir the Great is referred to in modern Ukrainian sources, the form *Volodymyr* will be used, while making it clear that readers are more likely to come across him as 'Vladimir the Great'.

A NOTE ABOUT SPELLINGS

However, there is one notable exception. While the form *Kievan Rus* has traditionally been used to describe the Norse–Slav state that emerged in the tenth century – and is the form that will be encountered in most written sources that appeared in the English-speaking world before the last decade – I refer to them as the *Kyivan Rus*, as this form is now becoming the one more frequently found and it makes it clear that the place in question is the city now referred to, in most sources in the West, in its Ukrainian form. All of this is a reminder of the complexity of the area of culture and history that is the subject of this book.

In a less contentious area, where Old Norse terms are used, a simplification of letter forms (avoiding ones no longer used in modern English) will be deployed. For example, we will use the term *Aesir* to describe a family of Viking deities, rather than *Æsir*. The term *Garthariki* will be used to describe the mixed Norse–Slavic settlements of northern Russia, rather than the Old Norse form *Garðaríki*. This is because the letters used in the latter (and older) forms will be unfamiliar to many modern English-speaking readers. However, usually the Old Norse form will also be given, in brackets, as this form often also appears in published sources.

INTRODUCTION

'Without Ukraine, Russia ceases to be an empire.'[1]
— US national security adviser Zbigniew Brzezinski,
March 1994

'Ukraine is the biggest European country and is rich in natural resources. Its capital, Kyiv, has long-held ideological meaning for Russia. It was where the population of the Kyivan Rus was consecrated by Volodymyr the Great in 988. In his article about the unity of Russians and Ukrainians, Putin wrote that these two nations and Belarusians spoke one language (Old Russian), had economic relations, and one religion: the Orthodox faith. Then he continued with pseudo-historical facts about Ukraine. One sentence said, "Modern Ukraine is entirely the product of the Soviet era."'[2]
— Lieutenant Colonel Denys Yurchenko, Ukrainian military cooperation officer specialising in NATO–Ukraine cooperation, July 2024

This book is about 'deep stories'. I first came across this evocative phrase when researching a very different book on another modern political and cultural phenomenon, entitled *Trump and the Puritans*.[3] That was in 2019 when it seemed that the worst that Vladimir Putin might do to Ukraine was the seizure of Crimea. Things have moved on since then.

It was while writing about the US and Trump that the phrase first caught my imagination. It was not that the concept was new to me. Anyone who studies history will know that it is constantly being quarried to define contemporary perceptions and identities. What was so striking was the way in which the phrase so powerfully conveyed both the process and the outcome of this interaction between the present and the past.

The context within which the phrase crossed my radar was an examination of the extent to which the US Tea Party ideology and programme had captured the imaginations and loyalties of Louisianan Republicans, well before the rise to prominence of Donald Trump. This Tea Party support later morphed into support for Trump in 2016 (and later in 2024). The support for the Tea Party – and later for Trump – was largely centred on a small-state, anti-federal government, anti-National-Environment-Agency-intervention stance. This was despite the poverty, pollution and poor health troubling the state, its dependence on federal assistance and its apparent need of federal protection to safeguard its natural resources. The question of why so many Louisianans embraced an ideology whose outcomes undermined the physical well-being of its supporters was sensitively documented in Arlie Russell Hochschild's 2018 study, entitled *Strangers in Their Own Land: Anger and Mourning on the American Right*.[4]

What emerged was the conclusion that both the Tea Party and Trump appeared to speak to the 'deep story' of these voters, as they lived in a bewildering US that was changing around them and in which they increasingly felt marginalised and cut-in-on by others as they queued for access to the 'American Dream'. That the policies of the radical right, arguably, were little inclined to assist such people – who were often damaged by the actions of the oil industry and inadequately served by private sector health provision – was as nothing compared to the right's ability to articulate their anxieties and engage with their 'story' (regardless of its inaccuracies) of what the US used to be like, currently was like and what it might become again. In short, such stories appeared to make sense of complicated issues, reassured its adherents of their identities and the rightness of their hopes and promised a way forward which would validate them.

Such an outlook is rooted in the history, society, traditions, values and perceptions of any given group. And it may or may not accord with hard facts. But being rooted in the *past* is the key to the attraction of the phenomenon. It is seen in slogans produced as part of the process: 'Make America Great *Again*' in the US; 'Take *Back* Control' in Brexit Britain; appeals to *historical* Hindu culture in opposition to 'foreign invaders' in Bharatiya Janata Party strategies apparent in India; *backward-looking* references to Great Patriotic War tropes and anti-Nazism as justification for Russia's invasion of Ukraine. The present is framed in the context of a perceived past. That is a 'deep story'.

Deep stories will prove crucial in explaining many of the phenomena explored in this book. And deep stories exist on both sides of the current conflict between Russia and Ukraine, as they do on both sides of the polarised US and in all other nations seeking satisfying (even if misleadingly incomplete or at times delusional) history-based clarity and affirmation in a turbulent present. Different deep stories can produce different outcomes.

Increasingly, I have become fascinated by the concept of such deep stories and the way in which they are deployed. This was a feature of my book *Mayflower Lives* (2019);[5] the co-written *Trump and the Puritans* (2020);[6] has become a lethal feature of Putin's Russia (as I explored in the last chapter of *The Secret History of Soviet Russia's Police State*, 2020)[7] and has accelerated since February 2022; is seen in the political use of end-times beliefs, as I explored in *The End Times, Again?* (2021)[8] and *Apocalyptic Politics* (2022);[9] and is highlighted in the use of the Norse in areas of modern radicalised politics in the turbulent US, as I explored in *American Vikings: How the Norse Sailed into the Lands and Imaginations of America* (2023).[10]

In *Vikings in the East*, the Norse adventurers are once more being deployed to justify modern outlooks and actions – but this time in the East rather than in the West. This is hardly surprising, because Vikings have an ability to stir the imagination through their combination of heroic exploration and muscular free enterprise. For they could be both state-destroyers and state-builders. And it is in that latter capacity that they play such an important role in the bitterly contested origin myths of both Russia and Ukraine. The Vikings are a historical unifying factor that has – paradoxically – become deeply divisive.

INTRODUCTION

As we shall shortly see, over a millennium ago, Viking adventurers founded the Norse–Slavic dynasties of the Rus, which are entangled in the origin stories of Russia, Belarus and Ukraine. Furthermore, because the Rus were the first community in the region to convert to Christianity – in its Eastern Orthodox form – this confers sacred significance on what could, otherwise, be an origin myth simply of medieval trade and violence. They are at the heart of the concept of 'Holy Russia'. That affords a special profundity and significance to the history of which they are part. This hugely affects how they and their formative actions are perceived.

In the middle of a savage contemporary argument over whether Russians and Ukrainians are two distinct people or constitute one historical community lies a common origin story and the beginnings of Orthodox faith that can be both a unifying and a divisive phenomenon, depending on how it is deployed. And deployed it certainly has been! That is why the full title of this book is: *Vikings in the East: From Vladimir the Great to Vladimir Putin – The Origins of a Contested Legacy in Russia and Ukraine*. It is a place where history collides with the present.

This is not a detailed history of Ukraine and Russia. Many other excellent books provide that. While an outline of Ukrainian and Russian history will give structure and context to the flow of this book, what follows is primarily an exploration of how the actions of Viking – and then Viking–Slav – people played a formative role in the history of the national communities which later emerged. And how this role has been understood and disputed in later times; none more so than in the present. History can have 'attitude'. That is clear in recent, and ongoing, events.

The use – and the abuse – of history is an ever-present reality in the modern world. It was ever thus. As someone once said of the outlook of confident ideologues: 'Only the future is certain; the past is always changing.'

Martyn Whittock

CHAPTER 1

GO EAST!

READING THE RUNES...

An enigmatic Viking Age runestone in Sweden signposts a story which unites the ancient past with the turbulent present, the early medieval period with the twenty-first century, tenth-century Vikings with the Russian invasion of Ukraine in 2022 and Vladimir the Great of the Rus with Vladimir Putin of the Russian Federation. It points towards a 'deep story' concerning the contested origins and myths of both Ukraine and Russia. The runestone in question reads: 'Tóla had this stone raised in memory of her son Haraldr, Ingvarr's brother. They travelled valiantly far for gold, and in the east gave (food) to the eagle. (They) died in the south in Serkland.'[1]

Understanding the significance of the story behind this Viking Age memorial takes us into more than simply an extraordinary period of medieval history. It also opens a window into a past that continues to reverberate in modern mythmaking and in bitterly conflicted national identities. It is history with attitude; it has a legacy that is lethal...

THE VIEW TO THE EAST

Popular culture commonly views the Viking Age as being fundamentally a Western European phenomenon. This is not surprising, given the Viking impact on communities either side of the North Sea and the English Channel and across the British Isles. From here, the story extends westward to Iceland, Greenland and even to North America. In all these areas, the Viking story has become deeply entangled with the cultural DNA of modern communities.[2] However, it also had a crucial eastern aspect.

The eastern aspect provided a key factor prompting the start of Viking raids in the first place. Changes taking place in the distant Islamic caliphate, in the Middle East, in the 740s and 750s, led to the centre of political power shifting from Damascus to Baghdad. This turbulence disrupted the flow of silver to Scandinavia. For years, Islamic merchants and their middlemen had carried silver to northern Europe. There they traded it for slaves, furs and amber. Political conflict and changes in the caliphate disrupted this trade. The flow of silver northwards dried up; Scandinavian economies were destabilised. Silver, which had allowed Scandinavian elites to engage in traditional gift-giving to cement social relationships, became scarce. Facing this change, raiding (going 'viking') offered an alternative way to get their hands on precious metals and slaves.

So it was then that changes, emanating from as far from Scandinavia as Baghdad, rippled out like a stone thrown into a pond.

These changes triggered the expansion now known as the 'Viking Age'. It was an extraordinary example of the law of unintended consequences – and it started in the East.

At the same time, the forest products of the eastern Baltic and the supply of slaves from there drew Swedish Viking adventurers eastward on the *austrvegr* (the Eastern Way), as it was known in Old Norse. For several reasons, the Viking phenomenon always had an Eastern Front. This is their history and an exploration of why its legacy still features in the turbulent and contested deep stories of both Russia and Ukraine in the twenty-first century.

THE 'LITTLE GREEN MEN' AND A STRANGE CLAIM BY VLADIMIR PUTIN

In 2014, the pro-Russian Ukrainian President, Viktor Yanukovych, finally accepted the inevitable, when months of popular protests toppled his government. During 2013 and 2014, these protests in Kyiv (Russian: Kiev), now frequently referred to as the Euromaidan, leading to the Revolution of Dignity, had eventually culminated in the overthrow of this pro-Russian Ukrainian President, who had halted the Ukrainian development of closer ties with Western Europe – primarily the 'association agreement' with the EU – after intense pressure from Moscow. At the culmination of the uprising, Yanukovych fled to Moscow. Prior to this, Yanukovych's riot police had brutally dispersed protesters, and its snipers shot dead seventy-six people in three days in February 2014.

It seemed that Ukraine was now ready to resume its development of Western connections. Membership of the EU might be possible in time, once some significant issues in the areas of governance and civic society had been dealt with. Beyond that – and even more contentious – there might yet be some kind of relationship with (maybe one day even membership of) the North Atlantic Treaty Organization (NATO).

It was following the Euromaidan that Russian special forces – euphemistically referred to as the 'little green men' (Russian: *zelyonye chelovechki*) or 'the polite people' (Russian: *vezhlivye lyudi*) – led the way in a Russian seizure of the peninsula of Crimea from Ukraine. Although their kit lacked unit insignia, everyone knew that they were there on the orders of the Kremlin. The deniability was of the kind familiar from other acts of Russian aggression, such as the Salisbury Novichok poisonings and a myriad other examples.

While the linguistic issues are a little complex, basically Russian has two words for truth. These are: *istina* and *pravda*. And it has two words for lies, which are: *lozh* and *vranyo*. Of the two latter words, it is the second that is most interesting. *Vranyo* means 'to lie', but it often conveys a rather more nuanced and dismissive tone. A fairly recent comment on Reddit summed up the potential meaning of *vranyo* rather well: 'You know I'm lying, and I know that you know, and you know that I know that you know, but I go ahead with a straight face, and you nod seriously and take notes.'[3]

The initial Kremlin narrative – as embodied in the 'little green men' – was a classic example of the use of *vranyo* as statecraft. As we explore more of the tangled history of Ukraine and Russia, especially in its latest form, we will come across a lot more *vranyo*.

But back to 2014. The Russian action in Crimea was an open act of aggression against another sovereign state. As recently as 1997, when the Russian Federation had been granted an extended lease on the port facilities at Sevastopol for its Black Sea Fleet, it had affirmed Crimea as Ukrainian territory. That 'guarantee' clearly had a much shorter shelf life than anyone had imagined in 1997. A lot has happened since then.

As we shall see, Crimea has a complex history. Written references and archaeology reveal Greek settlers there. In the tenth century, it was the place where Norse–Slav rulers (central to our exploration) accepted Christian baptism. Until the middle of the fifteenth century, it was divided between the Khanate of Crimea, Genoese coastal colonies and the Byzantine Principality of Theodoro. For three centuries after this, it was a protectorate of the Islamic Ottoman Empire. Russia invaded Crimea in 1783 as part of the expansionist policies of Catherine the Great. Crimean Tatar communities were several times forcibly expelled by Russia in 1783, 1856 and 1944.[4] The last mass expulsion was for alleged collaboration with the Germans.

Crimea has also had a rather complicated history since 1945. It was transferred to the Soviet republic of Ukraine (within the then USSR) in 1954. In 1991, as the USSR imploded, Crimea was (once again) made an autonomous republic within the Soviet Union, but with the formal dissolution of the USSR in December of that year, Crimea was eventually incorporated into the newly independent Ukrainian state as the Autonomous Republic of Crimea (ARC), the only self-governing region within Ukraine. It is significant that in the referendum of 1991, on Ukraine's independence from the USSR, 54 per cent of Crimea's population voted for an independent Ukraine.[5] This was perhaps not surprising, since it had been part of the Ukrainian republic since 1954. The ARC had its own constitution, Prime Minister and Parliament; its constitution protected the special status of the Russian language. From the mid-1990s, strong pro-Russian tendencies within some areas of the Crimean population led to political tensions and this was a situation encouraged by some Russian nationalist politicians before the presidency of Putin.

The official Ukrainian census of 2001 revealed that 60 per cent of the population of Crimea consisted of ethnic Russians, 24 per cent were Ukrainians and 10 per cent were Crimean Tatars.[6]

Despite these historical complications, and the size of the ethnic Russian population, Crimea constituted a part of the new state of Ukraine, whose territorial integrity was guaranteed by the Russian Federation. In 1994–96, Ukraine gave up its nuclear weapons and the Budapest Memorandum of 1994 – signed by Russia, Ukraine, Britain and the US – promised that none of these nations would use force or threats against Ukraine.[7] All would respect its sovereignty and existing borders. That guarantee, like that integral to the 1997 port-lease, had a shelf life that did not last beyond twenty years.

To return to 2014. Russia seized most of the Ukrainian fleet while it was in port, and the HQ of Ukraine's navy was relocated from Sevastopol to Odesa (Russian: Odessa). Although some of the Ukrainian ships were later returned to Ukraine, others – including the Ukrainian navy's only submarine – were absorbed into the Russian Black Sea Fleet.

This illegal Russian action was followed by a vote (not recognised internationally) by which Crimea seceded from Ukraine and joined the Russian Federation. It is hard to say, due to Russian control of the vote, but there *may* have been a majority in favour of this. This is open to question, though, as opinion polling in May 2013 revealed that 53 per cent of respondents wished to keep the peninsula as part of Ukraine. In this polling, only 23 per cent wanted Crimea to be united with Russia.[8]

What is clear is that the 2014 vote was on a low turnout and certainly not the 82 per cent turnout – with 97 per cent in favour of unification with Russia – as claimed by the Kremlin. There is reason for believing that the turnout was in the region of 30 to 50 per cent.[9]

The West imposed (limited) sanctions and Putin's domestic popularity soared. Even Alexei Navalny, who was a strong critic of Putin and died in an arctic labour camp in February 2024, was initially favourably inclined towards the return of Crimea to the Russian Federation. A lot of Russians viewed it this way at the time, not just the ultra-nationalists.

It was, though, of huge and worrying significance as it constituted an act of territorial aggression deployed to change the borders of an internationally recognised state by force. It had echoes of nineteenth-century geo-politics or the reordering of Eastern European frontiers in the aftermath of the Second World War. It was certainly not what was expected of a 21st-century European state. If the end of the Cold War had seemed to indicate the 'end of history' (to quote the title of Francis Fukuyama's over-optimistic 1992 book), in 2014 'history' had returned! And there was more of this 'history' to come – a lot more. History was back with a vengeance.

All of this provocative behaviour by Russia was consistent with an increasingly bitter narrative from the Kremlin which deeply resented the eastward movement of both NATO and the EU since the end of the Cold War. The Kremlin felt this contravened verbal guarantees that this would not occur (commentators disagree over whether these were given) and was determined to prevent Ukraine becoming part of either the military alliance or the political and economic union. This was also complicated by Putin and his allies making their own contribution to 21st-century 'culture wars', as they promoted what were termed 'traditional Russian values' in opposition to 'Western liberal values'. So far, the Russian action in Crimea can be viewed as a predictable outcome of an increasingly fractious relationship between Putin's Russia and the West. It was a relationship which had gone steadily downhill since the halcyon days at the beginning of the millennium, when it really had seemed that a new relationship between the West and Russia was possible.

However, there was more to it than that. Something a lot older was also in the mix. Something a lot more visceral and fundamental. Something that the West had never understood and even now views with puzzlement. In 2015, when Putin justified his recent annexation of Crimea from Ukraine, he asserted that Crimea has 'sacred meaning for Russia, like the Temple Mount for Jews and Muslims', and, furthermore, that Crimea is 'the spiritual source of the formation of the multifaceted but monolithic Russian nation'. He added: 'It was on this spiritual soil that our ancestors first and forever recognized their nationhood.'[10]

This statement will have left many Western commentators scratching their heads and wondering what Putin was talking about. Like the Temple Mount in Jerusalem? What was that all about? The answer lies in a heady and toxic fusion of nationalism and Russian Orthodoxy which had clearly occurred by 2014, along with a very particular (and highly questionable) interpretation of the arc of Russian history.

It sounds like the kind of cynical pseudo-history beloved of authoritarian rulers. But in this case, there is more to it than this. Whatever the genuineness of Putin's commitment to this reading of Russian history, his determination to make a connection with ancient roots (however unconvincing) was, and is, very real. Tucker Carlson discovered this, in February 2024, when he was treated to a half-hour-long 'history' lesson by Putin.[11] The Putinist history in question reaches back to a very ancient past – an ancient past which forms the contested origin myths of both Russia and Ukraine. And in this quest, his 2015 statement was not an isolated example.

ENTER THE VIKINGS...

In Borovitskaya Square, in central Moscow, stands a monument 17.5 metres (57.4 feet) high to St Vladimir the Great (Grand Prince of Kyiv/Kiev from AD 980 until his death in 1015). He is credited with the introduction of Orthodox Christianity to Russia and his life and achievements form part of the deep story of both Russia and Ukraine and their common historic Orthodox Christian faith. The figure, holding a giant cross, was erected in 2016 on the initiative of the Russian Military Historical Society and the city government of Moscow. It was unveiled by his namesake: Vladimir Putin, President of the Russian Federation.

The erection of the statue was immensely controversial because St Vladimir – called St Volodymyr in Ukrainian – is claimed by both Russia and Ukraine as a founding father and many Ukrainians considered it a provocative gesture. It was highly significant that the statue was unveiled on National Unity Day in Russia – a national holiday revived by Putin in 2005. At the time, many Ukrainians felt that the action was a deliberate attempt to challenge the idea of Ukrainian sovereignty and cultural independence. This was being done by weaponising the saint in the cause of Russian nationalist claims regarding the Ukrainian state, which Russian nationalists traditionally describe as 'Little Russia'.

The deep division between these two Orthodox nations was further revealed in 2019 when the Ukrainian Orthodox Church became independent from the Russian Orthodox Church, much to the anger of both the religious and political authorities in Moscow. Until as late as 1448, the Russian Orthodox Church was headed by the 'Metropolitans of Kiev' (since 1328 these church leaders had been based in Moscow). However, in 1448 the Russian bishops first elected their own metropolitan without reference to the authority of Constantinople and from this point, the Russian church was autocephalous (effectively independent). In 1589, the Metropolitan of Moscow was elevated to the position of patriarch. This elevation occurred with the approval of Constantinople. Moscow then stood fifth in line of honour after the patriarchs of Constantinople, Alexandria, Antioch and Jerusalem. And within the domain of the Russian patriarch lay the Ukrainian lands, from which Russian Orthodoxy had first emerged in the tenth century. In 2019, that Moscow-based dominance, which had been in place since 1328, was broken. For the Ukrainians, it must have seemed a logical step given that Kyiv had been the original seat of the Russian Orthodox

Church and the extent to which (by 2019) the Orthodox patriarch in Moscow – Kirill – had bought into the whole Putinist nationalist outlook. This had meant that the official head of Orthodoxy in Ukraine was part of a movement bent on subjugating Ukraine. Hence the Ukrainian move towards church independence from Moscow in 2019. But for the Russians, what the Ukrainians had done was a spiritual red rag. And it was interwoven with the same deep history of which Vladmir the Great (he of the 17.5-metre monument) was an integral part. But there was more to come on the subject of ancient history and its use by Putin.

In July 2021, Putin published a lengthy article entitled 'On the Historical Unity of Russians and Ukrainians', which made it clear that reunification was on his agenda, whatever the Ukrainians felt about it. Finally, in 2022, the full extent of that Putinist weaponising of history was seen in the Russian military columns, bombers and missiles descending on Ukraine in an attempt to abolish its independence.

Which raises the question of who was St Vladimir/Volodymyr and how did he come to occupy such a contested place in the hearts and minds of two nations that became locked in bitter warfare in 2022? The answer involves Vikings far from home, a reluctant Byzantine princess, the creation of a hybrid national identity and conversion to Christianity. In short: the creation of the original hybrid Norse–Slavic state of 'Holy Rus'. And that – and its echoes down the centuries – is what this book will be exploring. It is a very contested legacy; a millennium-old deep story that led to conflict using 21st-century weapons.

It is a story that begins with Vikings. And that takes us back to Haraldr, Ingvarr's brother, the one whose body had fed the eagles a very long way from Sweden, far away in Serkland…

SOME UNUSUAL SWEDISH RUNESTONES AND A VERY LONG JOURNEY…

The evidence for Viking actions on what we might call the 'Eastern Front' comes in many forms. One of these is in the field (literally, in terms of their original location) of runestones.

At this point, it may be helpful to briefly explain what these objects are. Viking Age Norse communities left written records on a range of different objects using the runic alphabet. This was originally derived from the Latin alphabet of the Late Roman Empire. In the runic alphabet, the angular letters, known as runes, were designed for easy carving on objects made from metal, bone or stone. They appear on objects from as early as the year AD 200 and continued in use well into the Middle Ages. As a result, they were still being used centuries after the Scandinavian communities – both in the northern homelands and in the wider Norse diaspora – converted to Christianity. This runic alphabet is often referred to as the *Futhark*. There is, what is termed, an 'Elder' and a 'Younger' version of it.

Many runic inscriptions were simple statements denoting ownership, such as: 'Nithijo made this' (on a shield found near Skanderborg in Denmark).[12] Some were thought to have magical powers, such as 'I give good luck' (on a gold disc found in Denmark).[13] Many were grave markers and some of these (especially in Sweden) could be quite extensive in their information. It is these that are most revealing when it comes to noting eastward Viking exploration.

A very important runestone is located beside the driveway of Gripsholm Castle, in Sweden. The object in question is an eleventh-century runestone. It was discovered in the early 1820s, built into the floor of a cellar and covered in tar, and had clearly once been used as part of the fabric in an earlier building. This was before being reused yet again to make a threshold in the cellar. Originally, it would have been a free-standing monument, placed in the open air in a prominent position. However, its fame lies not in its mixed history as a building component but in the inscription discovered on it when it was finally removed from the cellar and cleaned, about a century after its discovery. When translated, it bears witness to an adventure that went terribly wrong, a very long way from home. The runes in question were carved within the body of a snake that follows the edge of the stone and then curls into the centre. This runic inscription, as we saw earlier, reads: 'Tóla had this stone raised in memory of her son Haraldr, Ingvarr's brother. They travelled valiantly far for gold, and in the east gave (food) to the eagle. (They) died in the south in Serkland.'[14]

This runestone is known today as Sö 179 and is one of about twenty-six so-called 'Ingvar runestones'. Most of these are found in the Lake Mälaren region of southern Sweden; specifically in the provinces of Södermanland, Uppland and Östergötland. They are named after a Swedish Viking named Ingvar the Far-Travelled, who led an expedition to the Caspian Sea.

This single expedition is mentioned on more runestones than

any another event in Swedish Viking history, which points to its importance to contemporary society in the eleventh century. Other evidence indicates that Ingvar and most of his companions died in 1041. Some of them died in a fierce battle fought at Sasireti in Georgia, to the west of the Caspian Sea. This battle involved Byzantines (from the Eastern Roman Empire, with its capital in Constantinople), Georgians and Scandinavian mercenaries. The battle was fought in a Georgian civil war. Those who did not die in the battle itself later succumbed to disease far from Scandinavia. These included Ingvar himself.

The Georgian chronicler who compiled an account of the expedition, in a fourteenth-century addition to the chronicle known as the *Life of Kartli* (*Kartlis Tskhovreba*), Kartli being a core area of Georgia, added that Ingvar and his men were given slave women in Georgia. A twelfth-century Icelandic saga called *Saga of Ingvar the Far-Travelled* (*Yngvars saga víðförla*) claims they died from disease contracted through sex with these slaves. While this may have been true, with the Norse in question encountering sexually transmitted diseases that they had not previously gained immunity from, it is more likely that this followed the age-old trope of blaming women for problems. Whether we should read this as part of the history of epidemiology or (more likely) the predictable history of misogyny, it was a disaster for most of those who embarked on this expedition to the distant East.

According to that later Icelandic saga (which claimed to tell the story of the expedition in detail, including the sexual health information), some survivors made it back to Russia. Others travelled on to *Miklagarth* (Old Norse: *Miklagarðr*), the Scandinavian name for Constantinople. This was the capital of the Eastern Roman – or Byzantine – Empire. Of these survivors, some it seems eventually got back to Sweden and, as news spread of what had occurred, the runestones were carved by remaining family members to commemorate the dead who had not made it home. For our exploration, the most striking point is the geography of the expedition.

The 'Serkland' that is referred to on this and on four other runestones was the name used by Scandinavians for the Islamic Abbasid Caliphate and other Muslim areas of the East. The term was either derived from the word 'Saracen' (so meaning 'Saracen-land) or from '*serkr*' (gown), referring to the distinctive robes worn by the Muslims living in the East. Either way, it was a long way from home, back in Scandinavia.

Despite the emphasis on battle, there is evidence that the expedition that was led by Ingvar the Far-Travelled was as much about trade and diplomacy as it was about fearless and testosterone-driven adventure and battle. Regarding one of those who died in far-off Serkland and who was also commemorated back in Sweden on a runestone, his sons wrote of him: '*knari stur*' ('He could steer a cargo ship well').[15] The reference on this stone is to a *knarr*, a spacious sea-going cargo ship, not the dragon-prowed longships of Hollywood films, TV and popular expectations. In addition, the blessing on the dead found on this runestone – 'May God help their spirits'[16] – is a formula associated with Christians, so it seems the men in question were not pagans. To underscore this, another of the Ingvar runestones (U 1143, from Tierp, in Uppsala County) specifically prays that '*Guð drottinn hialpi and [ald]ra kristinna*' ('May Lord God help the spirits of all Christians').¹⁷ So that makes the point very clearly, at least regarding some of those who died in the East.

The Icelandic saga version of the Ingvar expedition claims that the Viking fleet was attacked by enemy ships armed with flame-throwers. This is a very real possibility and suggests that these were probably Muslim vessels equipped with a version of the flammable 'Greek fire' employed by the Byzantine navy and copied by its enemies.¹⁸

Taken together, these are thought-provoking clues which remind us of a very different 'Viking Age' to the one we usually envisage. In Western Europe, we associate Vikings with the storm-tossed waters of the North Sea and the North Atlantic, the deep Scandinavian fjords, the cold of Iceland and Greenland and the attacks on the monasteries and settlements of north-western Europe. This popular image rarely includes the river systems of Russia and Ukraine, the wide sweep of the Eurasian steppe, the far shores of the Caspian Sea, eastern slave markets and Arab traders, flamethrowing ships, the incense and rituals of the Eastern Orthodox Church and the high walls and towers of the city of Constantinople. Yet for many Swedish Viking raiders, traders and settlers, it was the road to the East that beckoned. And the society that they helped forge there was the one referred to by Vladimir Putin in his musings on the 'sacred soil' of Crimea and the foundational activities of St Vladimir the Great, which gave rise to the provocative statue in Moscow's Borovitskaya Square. This is because St Vladimir was directly descended from the kinds of Norse explorers whose exploits were recorded on the Ingvar runestones.

VIKING: WHAT'S IN A NAME?

Before we go further in this exploration of the Eastern Vikings and their legacy, it would help to briefly explain who and what Vikings were.

From the eighth century of the Christian era, raiders exploded out of Scandinavia. They did so in a way that both shocked and astonished their contemporaries in Western Europe.

Those at the receiving end of attacks from the north used various names for those responsible for them. In Anglo-Saxon (Old English) written sources the terms 'Danes', 'Northmen' and 'pagans' or 'heathens' were the ones most often used. Confusingly, the term 'Danes' did not carry much geographical accuracy in these records. As a result, when we find 'Danes' appearing in the accounts, we cannot be sure that those responsible actually came from Denmark. For example, after reporting a raid on Portland, Dorset, in 789, the same entry in the *Anglo-Saxon Chronicle* says that those responsible were Danes and that they came from Norway! Clearly, the label was sometimes detached from the geography,[19] which is rather confusing.

Other 'labels' were also used to describe these feared northern raiders. The Franks (in what is now France and western Germany) called them the '*Nordmanni*' (Northmen).[20] As a result, an area ceded to them in the tenth century would become Normandy (land of the Northmen). Within a century – while they kept up connections with communities in Scandinavia – they so assimilated to the local culture that Anglo-Saxon sources frequently referred to them as 'French'. This chameleon-like ability to blend into local cultures will feature in our eastern exploration too.

In the East, it has been suggested that the Slavic term for them was derived from their ruddy complexions, hence '*Rus*' (red).[21] Or the name may have been derived from an Old Norse word for 'rowers' (i.e. seamen). Or it may have been connected to a coastal area of Sweden called Roslagen.[22] The Rus had a huge impact on the culture and later history of Russia and Ukraine, and it is this group of Vikings who will feature most in this examination of Eastern Vikings. The reference to Old Norse is a reminder that it is an umbrella term to describe languages spoken in Scandinavia in the early medieval period.

A related word to *Rus* – *Rhos* – was used in the Byzantine Empire (ruled from Constantinople).[23] There the rulers came to employ them as mercenaries and also met Scandinavians who had travelled down the rivers leading from the Baltic. From these river systems, they eventually sailed into the Black Sea and from there travelled into the eastern Mediterranean and the Byzantine Empire. Others reached the Caspian Sea. The word (in the form *Rus*) would eventually give rise to the national name of Russia (and Belarus). This is due to the fact that the roots of the historical Russian nation started as a mixed Viking–Slav state centred on Kyiv/Kiev, in Ukraine.[24] It is these tangled and contested roots of nationhood that lie behind Russian nationalist claims about Ukraine not being a truly independent nation. It is not the only time the Viking legacy has been seized on by modern nationalists and those seeking to carve out cultural identities. The same has occurred in the US, based on saga and archaeological evidence for Norse explorers reaching the North American continent in the early eleventh century.[25]

The Byzantines also called them '*Varangians*' (those who swear loyalty) and the mercenaries of the Varangian Guard served the Byzantine emperor in Constantinople. They have left some surprising pieces of evidence behind. In the church of Hagia Sophia, in Constantinople (now Istanbul, Turkey), one of them carved a runic inscription into the white marble parapet surrounding the balcony of the upper gallery of the church. It reads 'Halfdan carved these runes' or 'Halfdan was here'.[26]

In Ireland, they were the 'Northmen' again (or '*Lochlannach*' in Irish).[27] It was a designation similar to the one used by the Franks. The Irish went on to differentiate the Norwegians as '*Finn-gaill*' (white foreigners) and the Danes as '*Dubb-gaill*' (black foreigners). The reasoning behind this is not clear and subject to some debate.[28]

Far from Scandinavia, Islamic writers called them '*al-madjus*' (heathens).[29] It was a religiously derived label, similar to that used by Anglo-Saxons. One Islamic source added: 'May Allah curse them.'[30] It is a reminder that they reached the Islamic lands stretching from the Iberian Peninsula to the Middle East and beyond to the Caspian Sea.[31] This contact will play a major part in our exploration.

SHOULD WE CALL THESE SCANDINAVIANS 'VIKINGS' OR 'NORSE'?

The term 'Norse' is used to describe the various peoples of Scandinavia who spoke the Old Norse language between the eighth and thirteenth centuries AD. While Old Norse had eastern and western dialects, it would have been mutually understood across the range of areas within which it was spoken. A third branch of the language was spoken on the island of Gotland in the Baltic. Old Norse was, essentially, the language of the Vikings.

This Old Norse language later developed into modern Danish, Faroese, Icelandic, Norwegian and Swedish. In addition to these modern languages, there once existed the so-called Norn languages of Orkney and Shetland. However, these are now extinct.[32]

Some modern experts prefer the term 'Norse' to that of 'Vikings' as a group term. This is because (as we will see below), strictly speaking, to be a Viking was to have a particular role within Scandinavian society. It was not a term which described an ethnicity or a general culture. Nevertheless, the word has now entered popular usage so that it has become the label of choice when describing Scandinavians generally during the 'Viking Age'. As a result, it will be the term that is frequently used in this book. So, 'Norse' will generally be used when describing the language or culture of the people involved (as in 'Norse mythology', which was basically the beliefs of Vikings), but 'Viking' will frequently be used for the people and the period (as in the 'Viking Age' and 'Viking explorers'). However, we must remember that many Scandinavian 'Norse' people at the time would not have described themselves as 'Vikings'. This is because they were not warriors and/or raiders.

It should also be remembered that some who were part of a 'Viking' community were not ethnically Scandinavian or descended from Scandinavians. Many locals (from Ireland to Russia) threw in their lot with the new powerful social group, adopted their way of dress and language and merged with them. Not all Vikings had Scandinavian DNA. And in time, many who were once recognisable as 'Vikings' eventually assimilated to local culture since the Vikings were quite chameleon-like in this respect. In the East, for example, the influential Norse minority become Slavic in language, naming practice, dress and culture within two or three generations. Life is complex.

VIKING AS A JOB DESCRIPTION OR CAREER CHOICE

It is surprising that we hardly ever hear them called Vikings outside of Scandinavia at the time. So, from where does the familiar term Viking come?[33] There is no clear answer. It has a number of possible origins.

In Old Icelandic (a variant of the Old Norse language), the word *vik* (bay, creek) may have been used to describe seamen hiding in, or sailing from, coastal inlets. This might have been understood as 'sailor' or 'pirate'. So, a geographical term may have become a group name. As well as this, an area of southern Norway was called Vik and may have become attached to those sailing from this area. This would also be a label rooted in geography. However, the Old Icelandic verb *vikja* (moving, turning aside) may have played a part and been used to describe seafarers who were always 'on the move'.[34]

Whatever the exact origins, the term described a career choice. Later Old Norse written sources called a raider a '*vikingr*' and a raiding expedition of such people a '*viking*'. Consequently, 'the word "Viking" described something you *did* rather than what you *were*'.[35]

For many of those who were described in this way, this would have been a part-time occupation. At other times of the year or during other phases of their lives, they would not have gone out 'viking' or been considered as 'Vikings'. Then, they would most probably have been farming and trading.

In Old Norse sources, going out 'viking' was regarded as adventurous; it was taking part in muscular free enterprise. In contrast, those on the receiving end of one of these muscular free enterprise activities viewed things very differently. The victims of the Vikings coined their own terms, which were often not positive or complimentary in their meaning. Even the (apparently neutral) references to red-faced foreigners – that we find in the Slavic and Byzantine accounts – convey the sense of an alien 'other'. It is these Rus (whatever the roots of their name) that we will follow as they sailed eastward...

CHAPTER 2

EVIDENCE FOR VIKINGS IN THE EASTERN BALTIC: TRADE AND SETTLEMENT

In the Viking Age (*c.* AD 750–1100), the modern Scandinavian states of Denmark, Norway and Sweden did not exist. Nor, for that matter, did any of the nation states that we currently associate with continental Europe. The exception to this was England, which was precociously unified within broadly recognisable boundaries and under one ruling royal house, by the mid-tenth century.

Elsewhere, things were more complex. In some areas, the situation was fragmented and would remain so for many more centuries. Scandinavia is an example, and we shall return to it shortly.

In other areas, communities were theoretically more unified under dynasties of varying degrees of power, although always less unified and controlled than implied by the labels applied to them. The most obvious example was the (revived) western 'Empire', later termed the 'Holy Roman Empire',[1] which (in theory at least) brought under one ruler much of Western and Central Europe. When Charlemagne was crowned emperor in Rome on Christmas

Day 800, Western and Central Europe were brought under one ruler for the first time since the collapse of the Western Roman Empire in the fifth century. And this included lands that no Roman emperor had ever ruled. It was an empire that stretched west–east from the English Channel to Bavaria, Carinthia (now southern Austria and parts of northern Slovenia) and Pannonia (present-day western Hungary and parts of eastern Austria). South–north, it stretched from Italy to Frisia, Saxony and the border with Denmark. Under the mid-tenth-century Saxon ruler Otto I, this empire extended its authority further eastward into Bohemia and Moravia and became more stable. Later that century, it seized land along the southern Baltic, so that its eastern border there was close to the river Oder and faced Pomerania. To the east of this empire, in the north, were the lands of the various West Slavic communities (Pomeranians, Silesians and Poles) and beyond them the lands of the Baltic people, the Prussians. To its east, in the south, were the Magyars of what would one day be Hungary.

Which brings us to Scandinavia.

SCANDINAVIA IN THE VIKING AGE

Denmark was a patchwork of lordships until the middle of the tenth century, when a more unified Danish state emerged. This occurred under King Gorm, who ruled from about 936 until his death in about 958. His queen was Thyra, whom he described in a runic inscription on her burial mound as *'tanmarkar but'* ('Denmark's ornament'). We do not know exactly when she died, but this inscription is the first recorded use of the name for the country as a whole. The use of the word at this time was surely significant: a united Danish kingdom was being built. In the 960s, this trend towards unification increased when Gorm's son, Harald Bluetooth (ruled Denmark: *c*.958–*c*.986), extended Danish rule into Norway. His reputation as a strong unifying king has left a curious legacy which is still remembered in the twenty-first century in 'Bluetooth' technology, an open wireless technology, which connects several electronic devices. Ericsson, the Swedish data communication systems company, took as its logo the combined runic alphabet initials of Harald Bluetooth: H or ✶ and B or ᛒ. It recalls the unifying rule of this Danish king.

According to the later saga evidence (often from thirteenth-century Iceland), it was King Harald Fairhair who united the separate mini-kingdoms of Norway into a single country in 872. He died in about 930[2] and was succeeded by his son, the dramatically nicknamed Erik 'Bloodaxe', who had already been ruling before his father's death. However, Erik was killed in northern England in 954 and he was quickly replaced by his half-brother Haakon, later to be known as Haakon the Good. Although these were the first kings of a (seemingly) united Norway, they did not have complete control over all areas of the country and there were many powerful nobles who still had significant influence over their various regions. The most important of these magnates were the *jarls* – or earls – of Lade, whose power was based in the north of Norway. Later, these *jarls* of Lade were to become rulers of the whole of Norway as agents of Denmark, but during the reigns of Harald and Haakon, they seem to have been content to have accepted the Norwegian kings as their overlords.

The situation in Sweden was even more complex, since Denmark ruled much of the south of what we now call Sweden (as part of Greater Denmark) and the rest of the country lacked political unity until after 1100. Even Norwegian kings (who were themselves used to Danish interference in their lands) sometimes intervened in Sweden. From the ninth century, petty kings are mentioned in the scant written sources. However, it should be noted that all of these sources were compiled outside of Sweden itself. From this fragmentary written evidence, it appears that there were two main political units in what we would now call 'Sweden'. One was the dynasty known as the *Svear*. It is from *Svear* that the national name Sweden is derived. They had a royal and religious centre at Uppsala. Today, the early centre at Uppsala is known as Gamla (Old) Uppsala to differentiate it from the modern town of Uppsala. The former site was a hugely important political, religious and trading centre. Here the kings of *Svealand* – the legendary *Yngling* dynasty – held power. The other main political focus was provided by the *Götar*. Their power was centred on the plains of Östergötland and Västergötland, near Lake Vättern.[3] The *Götar* dominated much of what is now southern Sweden. The two dynasties of the *Svear* and the *Götar* were closely related and there is some evidence that some kings of the *Svear* were actually from the royal family of the *Götar*. What we can say more confidently is that the first king who ruled both peoples was Olof Skötkonung, who reigned from about 995 until 1022. However, it was not until the twelfth century that a single Swedish kingdom emerged.[4] And increasing Swedish unity did not prevent kings of Denmark from overshadowing the emerging kingdom for some time.

What all this means is that when we talk of Scandinavian explorers, traders and conquerors moving south-eastward into the lands of the Balts and Slavs, we should not imagine this as part of a unified project. Scandinavia was far too fragmented at this time to launch centrally organised ventures. It was not until after the 980s that one state (Denmark) could launch unified attacks on another state (England). The activities that we shall be exploring were, in contrast, the freewheeling projects of individual petty lords and their followers. This modus operandi was true of much of the Viking Age before the late tenth century. Small-scale activities by Scandinavian lords and their supporters sometimes coalesced into larger groups, divided and reformed, depending on the target(s) of opportunity. This was particularly the case regarding those who moved to the East, because most came from Sweden where state-building was far less advanced when compared with Denmark and even Norway. Whereas Vikings from Denmark and Norway tended to operate to the West, it was to the East that many Swedes turned their attention for most of the period in question. In the West, Vikings from Sweden played no significant part until some sailed with Cnut to England in the early eleventh century.

THE SWEDISH CONNECTION

The Norse expansion into the eastern Baltic was a characteristic example of Viking muscular free enterprise. It was primarily (though not exclusively) Viking adventurers from Sweden who sailed there. As we have seen, these Eastern Vikings are variously described in ancient sources as *Rus* and (in their interactions with the Byzantine

Empire) *Varangians*. Those designations lay in the future but would never have occurred if it had not been for the first steps into the south-eastern Baltic. What occurred next was dependent on that.

We have come across the Rus in Chapter 1 as a *physical description* of those who travelled among the Slavic communities of the East; although, as we saw there, the name may have been derived from other origins. An additional possibility – and with a connection with the eastern Baltic – is that it was derived from the Finnish word *Ruotsi*, used to describe Swedes, which itself may have been from an Old Norse term meaning a 'crew of oarsmen'. The other name – *Varangians* – was derived from the Old Norse word *várar*, meaning 'men who have pledged allegiance'.[5] This final name first appears in the mid-tenth century.

It should be noted that the word *Rus* was only ever used of Scandinavians living in what we now call Russia. The word *Varangian*, on the other hand, was used to describe Scandinavian mercenaries generally, who travelled as far as Constantinople to be employed as soldiers (known as the Varangian Guard) of the Byzantine emperor or who arrived there as traders. Whether they came from the communities of the Rus in what is now Russia, Belarus and Ukraine or originated in Scandinavia proper, these newcomers in the Byzantine Empire got there via communities in Russia which were increasingly assimilating to Slavic culture.

From as early as the late fifth and sixth centuries AD, there is tentative evidence of Scandinavian influence in the eastern Baltic. Artefacts from a cremation cemetery at Proosa, near Tallinn, in Estonia, suggest Scandinavian influences at work. Similarly, a seventh-century picture stone from Grobiņa, in Latvia, is like examples from southern Scandinavia. The cultural connection appears to have continued into the ninth and tenth centuries. Artefacts found in an excavated cemetery at Mokhovoe, in Kaliningrad region of the Russian Federation, have their closest parallels on the Baltic island of Gotland and in eastern Sweden and Denmark.[6]

Whether these artefacts represent the movement of trade goods or people is open to debate. However, this accelerated in the eighth century, when it clearly points to the movement of significant numbers of people as well as of artefacts.

The largest movement of Swedish Vikings eastward began in the century leading up to when the first Viking raiding started in north-western Europe. In England, we first hear of Viking raids on Portland (Dorset) in 789 and – more famously – Lindisfarne, in Northumbria, in 793. This was almost certainly not their first appearance, but these are the ones which attracted chroniclers' interest because the shock of the violence caught the attention of contemporaries and because, with the benefit of hindsight, these raids were seen as the beginning of a new phase in British history (the Viking Wars).

The movement eastward was not recorded because those who first experienced the arrival of Scandinavians there were not literate. As a result, the first contact has not left any written record. To chart its impact, we must rely on archaeological evidence for the appearance of characteristic Scandinavian material culture in areas where it differed from that of the material culture of the local indigenous Balts and Slavs. This eastward movement – already noticed in the sixth century – increased from about AD 650 and led to noticeable settlement, since archaeology reveals the graves of Scandinavians (almost certainly merchants) in eastern Baltic settlements of the Slavs and Balts. During the seventh century, a Gotlandic settlement at Grobiņa, in Latvia, was established. It lay a little inland from the point on the coast closest to Gotland.[7] More significant in size and influence was the settlement known to German-speakers as *Elbing* and called in Polish *Elbląg*.[8] It lay beside Lake Drużno, now in northern Poland. This process of eastward movement accelerated during the eighth century and was much more than simply the movement of objects. People were also on the move, as seen in a number of settlements in the region.

That at *Elbing/Elbląg* had the earlier name of *Truso* in the Old Prussian language. The settlement was first mentioned in a ninth-century English source, which says it lay on a lake called the 'Estmere', near a river called the 'Ilfing'. This source is known as *The Voyages of Ohthere and Wulfstan*, which was added to an Old English (i.e. Anglo-Saxon) version of Paulus Orosius's Latin work *Seven Books of History Against the Pagans* (*Historiarum adversum Paganos Libri Septem*). The original Latin work dated from the early fifth century AD. The Old English version was written in the period 870–930.[9] Ohthere (Old Norse: *Óttarr*) was a Norwegian hunter, whaler and trader. Travelling to the court of Alfred the Great, he recounted stories of his voyages north and east of Scandinavia and round the Kola Peninsula to the White Sea. We do not know the origins of Wulfstan, but his name suggests he was English and he sailed from the Danish trading settlement of Hedeby east into the Baltic Sea. There he visited the port of Truso and went further into the region beyond the mouth of the River Vistula.

The Scandinavians who settled at Truso were attracted by the trade goods of the area. The Old English source just mentions 'a great quantity of honey and fish',[10] but we might add other forest resources and slaves taken in battle, since the same source says: 'There is a vast deal of war and contention amongst the different tribes of this nation [the local Balts].'[11] The Norse were experienced slave traders and sold on their human cargo both westward to the slave markets of northern Denmark and as far as Viking Dublin; and they also sold slaves to Islamic slave traders who travelled up the river systems from the Caspian Sea.

Since the 1980s, an excavated settlement at Janów Pomorski, on the eastern shore of Lake Drużno and near the mouth of the River Vistula, has been identified as a trading emporium of the ninth and tenth century. It may well have been the location of Truso itself. Most of the buildings excavated were typical wooden longhouses built in the Scandinavian manner and the place had clear evidence of being a planned settlement. Ditches separated the building plots and clearly demarcated property boundaries. Although the site lacked a harbour, it is likely that its proximity to the Baltic coast meant that boats could simply be hauled onto the shore and beached there. The long-distance trading nature of the site is clear from the finds. Pieces of over 1,000 dirham coins have been found there. The dirham takes its name from the Greek word *drachma* and these coins became familiar in the Middle East through trade with the Byzantine Empire. Towards the end of the seventh century, coins based on this Byzantine currency became used in the Islamic world and carried the name of the issuing authority (usually a ruler) and an Islamic religious verse. They were accepted as currency across large areas of Europe between the tenth and twelfth centuries. This was particularly the case in trading settlements with Viking connections, and these stretch from Viking Age York and Dublin to the Norse settlements of the southern Baltic.

As well as the dirhams, thirteen other European coins were discovered at Truso, along with weights of different types and scales for weighing bullion. All of this indicates 'the importance of international trade for the existence of the emporium'.[12]

As well as trading items (and slaves?) brought to the site, there is a lot of evidence for production there. Archaeologists found evidence of the working of amber and of bone for combs. Blacksmithing and glass making was also taking place, as was the weaving of textiles.[13] The Viking nature of the place was evident in the moulds, crucibles and tools used for making jewellery of Scandinavian types. This was clear from wasters and finished ornaments unearthed.

From the 950s, the Scandinavian character of the settlement became even more pronounced. From this period, the finds of swords, characteristic 'tortoise brooches', amulets and even pieces from the Scandinavian board game called *hnefatafl* have been found, and these underscore the Norse character of the place. What may have started as a seasonal settlement a century or so earlier had clearly developed into a year-round home for Norse men and women (as evidenced in the tortoise brooches).

The settlement at Truso is typical of a number which were neither agricultural villages nor fortified elite settlements. They were clearly trading places. In the late eighth century, Viking interest in the south-eastern Baltic (already seen in earlier finds) accelerated. From about 800 onwards, this became very noticeable in the scale of the finds from these trading sites.

In a number of cases, they appear to have been sited on frontier zones between different ethnic groups. Consequently, they benefitted from being in more neutral locations and, also, ones which could act as meeting places for different peoples. Such commercial centres were ideal locations within which long-distance trade could take place. Another such settlement has been identified at Wolin, on the lower Oder and now in Poland. While the earliest settlement can be dated to the late eighth century, the place grew into a significant production centre between about 800 and 950. As part of this, its harbour developed from the late ninth century to the late tenth century. The remains of a number of boats were excavated there. While it may have been more of an indigenous settlement than that at Truso, it clearly benefitted from long-distance trade. Frisian combs and pottery from the Rhineland testify to that, as does wood and bone carved in a Scandinavian manner and – more revealingly – a stick inscribed with runic letters. Clearly, someone in the settlement could read runes, and this points to a Norse presence.[14] While some of the whetstones found there come from the modern border between Poland and the Czech Republic, at least one was made from stone found in Norway.[15]

By 750, other Scandinavians were settled in the Finnish trading settlement of Staraya Ladoga, on the River Volkhov, near Lake Ladoga, close to the modern town of Volkhov, in the Leningrad Region of modern Russia.[16] This was a centre of the fur trade and the Swedes living there would have been involved in the purchasing and westward transportation of this luxury commodity. Viking traders were initially drawn to the area to obtain furs from local Finns, particularly miniver, the highly desirable white winter coat of the stoat. This fur was then traded in Western Europe.[17] Some of this access to furs was achieved by peaceful trade; but some clearly involved tribute-taking from groups who had been brought under a loose Viking overlordship. It is now difficult to differentiate the two, as we cannot always disentangle the power relationships at work in the interactions. However, we may assume that a fair bit was mutually advantageous trade, with the application of Viking 'muscle' when the occasion demanded it (to ensure a good deal, from a Swedish perspective).

At first, it seems that Staraya Ladoga was a seasonal trading site, only inhabited at certain times of the year. However, by the middle of the ninth century, it had become a permanent settlement and there is evidence that craft production was taking place there. The inhabitants then were probably a mixture of Scandinavians and indigenous Finns and Slavs. As with the ethnically mixed smaller trading settlements that eventually sprang up along the Volga routeway, Scandinavians probably constituting a small – but wealthy and influential – minority who benefitted from trade.[18] This situation of enhanced commercial opportunities developed because of Arab traders travelling from the south-east. By the 790s, merchants from the Islamic Abbasid Caliphate (centred on Baghdad in modern Iraq) were expanding their trading journeys up the River Volga and bringing with them good-quality silver. They used this to purchase the furs, amber and slaves of the northern world. The dirhams found on the Baltic coast at Truso, and at many other Viking trading settlements, are vivid testimony regarding the scale and geographical reach of this trade. The Abbasids had replaced the previous ruling dynasty in the Muslim empire, called the Umayyads, in 750. At first, this political change had disrupted the northward flow of silver and would do so again in the next century. As we have touched on (in Chapter 1), this was one of the triggers which caused the raiding of Western European monasteries and settlements which occurred in the late eighth century and which signalled the start of the Viking Age.

However, the period 775–861 brought relative stability in the Islamic world under the new caliphs. While it was not a period of unbroken success for them, the return of relative stability was sufficient to act as a platform for expanding trading ventures. We can see this in the strengthening of the connection with the Viking north. These events in the Middle East directly affected the Swedish Vikings of the south-eastern Baltic. They had been active in the area since the middle of the seventh century, but the re-appearance of this coveted high-grade silver encouraged the Swedish merchants and explorers to expand their areas of operation in order to exploit this source of wealth and dominate the trade at its northern end. From the year 800, 'an enormous amount of silver in the form of dirhams struck in Islamic mints (especially in Central Asia) began to enter Russia and the Baltic region in the direction of Scandinavia'.[19] Hoards in Poland from this century are concentrated along the coast. While this flow of silver appears to have slowed dramatically in the 830s (due to renewed turbulence in the caliphate), it picked up again between about 850 and 900 (with a temporary slowing down once more in the 880s). It slowed again in the 970s, before picking up again in the 990s and finally ended in about 1030.[20] Viking communities on Gotland appear to have been particularly astute at spotting debased Arabic coins (in the periods when the flow of good-quality silver declined), even when these coins continued to circulate in other Scandinavian communities. Stockholm University numismatist Kenneth Jonsson has noted that, beginning around 955, the Arab coins were increasingly cut with copper (due to silver shortages) so that they dropped from their previous standard of around 95 per cent pure silver. Gotlanders simply stopped importing them.[21] However, for most of the period, it was the availability of silver from the Islamic world which fuelled the expansion of trade.

What had started as a mainly coastal trading opportunity for Scandinavians – trading raw materials (for example furs and salt), enslaved people and finished goods for local produce and Islamic silver – with a very limited impact on the societies of the interior, became in the ninth century much more expansive, with its reach extending far into the hinterland of Eastern Europe, into what is now Russia, Belarus and Ukraine. And when it expanded, Scandinavians would travel far beyond this too, in the directions of both Constantinople and the Caspian Sea. Viking engagement with the East was about to step up a gear, and it would have huge consequences for their contemporary world and for future societies.

In this expansion, they were assisted by the network of rivers which gave access to the hinterland of Staraya Ladoga and beyond, into the heart of what is now Russia and down into Ukraine. The clear aim of the Norse was to establish direct contact with the silver-rich Islamic world to the south-east. This would allow them the opportunity to eliminate trading middlemen, so that Swedish Vikings directly benefitted from access to the Muslim traders, which promised to hugely improve their bottom line in terms of profits made. It would also mean that they were not dependent on Islamic traders coming all the way to the Baltic settlements to carry out the commercial transactions. The Vikings were about to come to them. But whereas in the western Mediterranean where the Norse came as hated raiders of the Islamic communities, in this eastern area, they came as well-known traders. Violence was always available as an option, but it seems that trade was the higher priority. The Viking Age was far from being one-dimensional.

As early as 830 – just as the western raids of Danish Vikings were ramping up in Western Europe and Norwegian Vikings were raiding and settling in the northern and western Isles of Scotland and down into Ireland – the Viking explorers from Sweden finally established direct contact with Islamic traders on the River Volga itself. And they also made direct contact with the Christian Byzantine Empire, ruled from Constantinople. The Rus were about to appear as a recognisable cultural phenomenon and would soon emerge as a force to be reckoned with in the trade and power politics of the south-western Eurasian steppe and the river systems flowing into the Black Sea and the Caspian.

They were soon to create an integrated trade network which stretched from the Caspian Sea to Iceland. It would be an extraordinary achievement. They did not know it, but they were laying foundations that would have a huge legacy and continues to reverberate in the twenty-first century. The Rus – in what is today Russia, Belarus and Ukraine – were about to arrive.

Tangible evidence for the vast – but connected – diaspora that they were pushing further eastward was unearthed in England, in Dorset, in road widening during the run-up to the 2012 Olympics. A mass execution cemetery was discovered on the Ridgeway between Dorchester and Weymouth containing fifty decapitated skeletons. All the evidence indicates they had been Vikings. Identified (where gender could be ascertained) as men, and mostly aged younger than thirty-five, radiocarbon dating placed the mass killing at between 970 and 1025. Analysis of stable isotopes in the bones and teeth indicated that almost all of the bodies came from outside the British Isles. Several people probably grew up north of the Arctic Circle. Overall, 'the spread of information was consistent with Scandinavia, Iceland, the Baltic and Russia'.[22] The extent of the Viking world was revealed. From the scientific data, it is possible that some of these young men (executed in Dorset around the year 1000) may have grown up among the Rus.

CHAPTER 3

VIKINGS OF THE RIVERS

The river systems of what are today Russia, Belarus and Ukraine allowed Norse explorers, warriors and settlers into the hinterland of the continent. This remarkable achievement was assisted by the particularly striking riverine geography of Russia.

Just south of Novgorod (soon to loom large in this story) are the headwaters of rivers which, between them, flow to the Gulf of Finland, the Gulf of Riga (both giving access to the Baltic), the Black Sea and the Caspian Sea. With their strong construction and shallow draughts, Viking Age vessels were ideally suited to exploit these river routeways. And where waterfalls or rapids interrupted river travel, these ships could be moved overland (portaged), which allowed travellers to leap-frog these obstacles. In the same way, they could be transported from one river system to another to hugely enlarge the transport opportunities open to them as they reached further south and south-east from the southern Baltic.

As a result of this activity, the Swedes were soon in a position from which they could dominate trade from the Baltic to the Caspian and the Black Sea. At the Swedish trading site of Birka, hundreds of merchants with links to the East 'were buried with accessories, clothing, and weapons that reflect their connections to the steppe-nomad, Byzantine, and Arab worlds'.[1] In addition to this artefact evidence, DNA analysis of skeletons from Gotland has revealed that 'the inhabitants of this "island of merchants" were significantly more multicultural than the rest of Scandinavia at the time'.[2] This explosion of interactions with the East influenced communities in other areas too. At a recent exhibition at the Moesgaard Museum in Denmark, the burial ground of Salaspils Laukskola, near the Bay of Riga, was shown to contain two wealthy women who were buried with lavish grave goods from all across the then-known world in a striking display of cultural interactivity.[3]

While people with bases in eastern Sweden and Gotland appear to have predominated in this movement, Scandinavians from other regions were also making journeys to Eastern Europe and Russia. Many artefacts with strong Danish influences are also found across the East.[4]

And it was not just peaceful Scandinavian merchants who travelled these rivers, as Viking raiders and conquerors soon followed and attacked settlements on the Caspian Sea and even launched raids against the great Byzantine capital of Constantinople itself, even if the latter aggressions achieved only very limited results.

THE RIVERS OF RUSSIA

Perhaps the most important of the river routes lay along the Volga and its tributaries.[5] The Volga is the longest river on the European continent. It has historically been the main waterway of western

Russia and its catchment area is the birthplace of the Russian nation. The drainage basin of the Volga covers about 40 per cent of European Russia. Today, it contains almost half of the entire population of the Russian Federation. In the Russian Civil War, 1918–21, the Bolsheviks won largely because they dominated this area with its population concentration (as well as industrial resources). Their enemies – the Whites – might have held much larger areas of land, but the war was not won on the basis of the numbers of trees and squirrels under military control. It was population concentration that supported vast armies. That is getting well ahead of the story, but it is a reminder of the huge importance of this historic area into which Viking explorers began to extend their reach from the late ninth century onwards.

The Volga rises in the Valdai Hills north-west of Moscow. It is a small watercourse in these upper reaches but expands into a sizeable river after several of its tributaries flow into it. As it flows towards the Caspian Sea, the Volga is enlarged by the input of 200 tributaries, most flowing into it from the east. Overall, the vast river system of the Volga contains 151,000 rivers and permanent and intermittent streams. The system has a total length of about 357,000 miles (574,535 kilometres). In total, the river basin drains about 533,000 square miles (1,380,463 square kilometres). The west–east extent of this can be judged from the fact that it extends from the Central Russian Upland, in the vicinity of Moscow, to the Ural Mountains. North–south, it flows for about 2,193 miles (3,530 kilometres) until it empties into the Caspian Sea. Along its length, it flows through four distinct geographical zones. These areas are (settlements identified being the modern ones with their current names): thick and damp forest lands from its source to Nizhny Novgorod and Kazan; then an area of forest steppe until Samara and Saratov; this gives way to the steppe along its route to Volgograd; and, finally, there is a region of semidesert on the final leg of its course until it reaches the Caspian Sea.[6]

The wide variety of landscapes means that many types of natural resources and uses of the land are found along its course, while the large numbers of tributaries allow for travel west and east of the river, as well as simply following it to the south.

To the west of this great waterway, other major rivers are also hugely important and, over the centuries, have been 'the principal channels of trade, migrations, and war'.[7] Not surprisingly, 'the political unity of the early Russian empire [in whose earliest phase the Rus played a key role] rested to a greater extent on rivers than on any other single factor'.[8]

The primary waterways west of the Volga consist of the rivers Dnieper (Dnipro in Ukrainian), Desna, Pripet, Western Dvina, Lovat and Volkhov. The ancient settlements at Novgorod and Kyiv/Kiev – which, as we shall see, played a crucial part in the formation of the hybrid Norse–Slav state of the Rus – were respectively located at the most northern and southern ends of this great river network. The power of the later Rus principality at Kyiv rested on its control of the River Dnieper as it flowed towards the Black Sea. This was the main commercial routeway, from the inner regions, of what became Russia, to Constantinople. To the north, the principality of Novgorod (also a Rus stronghold) grew rich on the trade which was carried on the River Volkhov and which brought goods and people from Central Europe and Scandinavia (via the south-eastern Baltic region) into the Russian interior.

From the Byzantine Empire, supplies flowed north of wine, fine fabrics, spices, jewellery, glassware and, in time, icons and books. The Islamic world provided copious amounts of high-quality silver, silk, embroidered textiles and spices. Southward moved amber, furs, timber, honey, wax, pitch, tar and slaves. To meet the demand for labour in the south, Viking merchants plugged into a network of slave-taking across northern and Eastern Europe which captured huge numbers of people from the local populations (both in large-scale wars and on raids). Traded on by Norse slave merchants, many ended up being eventually transported to the slave markets of the Arab world, North Africa and Spain and also to Scandinavia and beyond. This trade in human misery flowed both south and north. A striking example of its wide-ranging character can be found in the thirteenth-century Icelandic *Saga of the People of Laxárdalur* (*Laxdæla saga*). In this, an Irish princess, captured as a teenager, is sold to an Icelandic chieftain by a Rus merchant operating on the Swedish island of Brännö. It is an example of slave trading which united the west and east of the Viking world.

There is an argument that – while violence and subjugation occurred during Viking activities in the lands south-east of the Baltic – it seems 'the Vikings came to Russian not to loot, as they did in England (Russia was too poor for that), but to use its many waterways for long-distance trade between Europe and Asia'.[9] In other words: Russia was a conduit, a means to an end, rather than an end in itself. There was not enough indigenous wealth of the kind the Norse particularly valued (particularly in terms of artefacts made from, or decorated with, precious metals) to be seized and shipped home. There were no wealthy monasteries from which precious objects could be taken to be melted down for other uses or ransomed back in the case of valuable illuminated Christian scriptures. Nor was there an indigenous precious-metal coin economy (whether used in commercial transactions or as transferrable means to convey tribute, tax and gifts) as there was in Francia or England, to the West. There such coinage could be conveniently 'lifted' by raids on commercial centres, which were often also key nodes in royal tax-collecting systems. Valuables (in terms of silver and gold) were there for the taking. Not so in the Russian lands. There may be something in this analysis, although we might want to counter it somewhat.

Firstly, there were objects with high value in terms of commercial transactions such as animal pelts. Access to these may not have been in the form of raids, but we can postulate that arrangements were not always between equals with comparable levels of agency. If we compare the situation with Viking interactions with the *finnar* or Sámi of the northern regions of Norway, Sweden, Finland and the Kola Peninsula in Russia, we might expect tribute-taking to have occurred and an arrangement of equals should not always be assumed.

There is, it must be said, some debate over this. The Norwegian traveller Ohthere (Old Norse: *Óttarr*), who we met in Chapter 2, mentions that he received (in the Old English version of his account) *gafole* from the Sámi. This was in the form of the skins of otters, martens, bears and reindeers. He stated that these were very valuable commodities. How we view this rather rests on what we understand by *gafole*. It can be understood as a tax or the levying of tribute. In other words, the arrangement could lie somewhere between 'protection money' and 'lordly right' – in which the lord decided the rightness of the arrangement. It has often been read in this way. From this perspective, 'Ohthere's primary source of income shows also that even in the ninth century, outsiders had already begun taxing the Sámi'.[10]

On the other hand, the Norse word *gofga* (which lay behind the Old English term) can be understood to mean 'a personal tie, with strong, mutual loyalty and dependence at its core and embedded with many rules of conduct and respect'.[11] In this interpretation, the Sámi were an important component of the Scandinavian economic order. They made up a crucial part of the overall resource base of the Viking chieftains in a redistributive system. The relationship involved trade relations, alliances and friendship ties and these included marriages.[12] It has been suggested that Norse–Sámi relations were 'not as grim and colonial as previously assumed'.[13]

We might expect a similarly complex relationship with the Slavic peoples, which mixed fairly equal trading arrangements with times of enforced tribute-taking. Around Novgorod, there is striking evidence that the arrival of the Viking settlers was more than just an addition to the local Slavic population. The Viking incomers appear to have had a profound effect on the local culture. Slash and burn farming, which had been practised in the area since the Neolithic period, 'was suddenly replaced by intensive agriculture'. These and other sites are best interpreted as 'centres for the collection of tribute from the surrounding countryside'.[14] The tribute would have come in from Slavic communities. We might guess that this was not an arrangement between equals.

But much more fundamental an issue is the matter of slavery, and here there are direct parallels with the violent exploitation that was also applied to western communities. The trafficked slave (Old Norse: *thræll*) played a major role in society in the Viking Age. Neil Price, distinguished professor and chair of archaeology at Uppsala University, Sweden, has argued:

> Over time, slaving became arguably the main element of the trade that developed during the Viking Age along the eastern rivers of European Russia and what is now Ukraine. No solid infrastructure of purpose-built slave markets, with auction blocks and the like, existed. Instead, transactions were small-scale but frequent, with one or two individuals sold at a time in any circumstances that seemed viable.[15]

There is strong evidence that this was, indeed, a major component of the Scandinavian interaction with Slavic society as they pushed ever further south and east of the Baltic.

The massive amounts of Islamic silver discovered through modern archaeological excavation and metal detecting vividly illustrates the extent of the highly profitable slave trafficking that was taking place. Clearly, thousands were sold out of Eastern Europe every year. It is widely claimed that so many Slavic people were seized during the Viking Age that their ethnic name gave rise to the later term 'slave' to describe a human chattel.[16] This etymology, it must be said, is disputed.

Later, as supplies of silver from the Islamic world dried up in the late tenth century (the Samanid silver mines having been exhausted), new sources of silver in the Harz region of Germany dominated the trade. As a result, the slave markets also moved westwards, from the Volga to the vicinity of Prague.[17] But by that time, the Rus state was firmly established in the East.

VIKINGS OF THE RIVERS

Vikings who sailed down the River Volga connected with the great trade routes of Central Asia – stretching as far as India, China and Japan – as well as journeying south. As we shall see, some of them crossed the Caspian Sea and travelled on to Baghdad (in what is today Iraq). At the same time, other Norse explorers travelled down the Dnieper to reach what is today Ukraine and the northern coast of the Black Sea; and then used this as a routeway by which they could reach Constantinople. It is impossible to understand the remarkable history and progress of these Norse adventurers – and the formation of the Rus state in the tenth century – without taking into account the presence of these great river systems and the ways in which Viking travellers and settlers exploited them.

Trade routes which started in Scandinavian trading centres such as Birka (Sweden), Hedeby (Denmark, now Germany) and Gotland (Sweden's largest island) could extend far into western Eurasia along the river systems of the modern nations of western Russia, Belarus and Ukraine. From the Baltic, Scandinavian travellers entered the Gulf of Finland and followed the course of the River Neva into Lake Ladoga. From the lake, they followed the course of the River Volkhov upstream to Staraya Ladoga, where Viking burial mounds could clearly be seen on the bank of the Volkhov.

From the (originally Finnish) trading settlement of Staraya Ladoga (which, as we saw in Chapter 2, had attracted Norse traders and settlers by 750), it was possible to move goods southwards, down the River Volkhov to Novgorod and, beyond Novgorod, to Lake Ilmen.

A recent study of Old Norse Icelandic literature – sagas, chronicles and law codes – along with references in Russian chronicles and archaeological evidence has argued that Staraya Ladoga acted as an intermediate station on the way from Scandinavia to Novgorod and back. According to this interpretation, Scandinavian travellers were forced to halt there in order to send messengers to the central authorities that were based in Novgorod. The aim of this was to arrange a temporary truce and gain some guarantee of safety as they travelled to Novgorod and back.[18]

Continuing south on the rivers from Lake Ilmen, goods were then transferred some distance overland to the tributaries of the River Dnieper. This involved a considerable amount of effort in order to connect these two river systems (and at least two overland portages between rivers south of Lake Ilmen) and it is possible that some boats were shifted along with the goods being transported. But the effort was worth it because, having finally reached the Dnieper, this river could then be followed to the northern shore of the Black Sea, with the Byzantine Empire beyond.

From the middle of the ninth century, sites showing signs of both Norse trade and settlement were established along this route south and have been found by modern archaeologists. The most striking of these are those discovered at Rurikovo Gorodische, on the shores of Lake Ilmen, and Gnezdovo on the River Dnieper itself. At Gnezdovo, large cemeteries have been excavated. At least ninety graves contained Scandinavian artefacts. At the very least, this demonstrates Norse influence and may well reveal the burial places of actual Scandinavians. This suggests that Gnezdovo was an important trading site and one 'that dwarfed its equivalents in Scandinavia, such as Birka and Hedeby'.[19]

The Dnieper also provided challenges because travellers had to portage their ships around a series of rapids (also known as the 'cataracts of the Dnieper') which obstructed the use of the river. While doing this, they were vulnerable to attacks from Pecheneg nomads who recognised the value of the cargoes being transported.

BY SHIP OR BY SLEDGE?

At times, portrayals of these journeys and portages give the impression of Viking dragon-prowed longships being portaged from river system to river system. This is the stuff of Hollywood films, TV and streaming services and comic book culture. In reality, it was clearly not the case as it is difficult to imagine such large vessels being carried overland in this way. What were in use were reduced versions of these ships and, at times, much smaller locally produced river vessels.

Relevant to this last point is the fact that the Byzantine Emperor Constantine VII (ruled 913–59) referred to the Slavic peoples of the Krivichs, along with other Slav communities dependent on the Rus rulers (at Kyiv), making hollowed-out sailing boats, which they brought to the rivers and sold to the Norse. These locally produced boats were known as *monoxyla* in Greek, which means 'single tree', and we should envisage them as being dugout canoes or logboats. The Byzantine source states that they could accommodate between thirty and forty people, so they were clearly made from very large trees. Once in the ownership of the Norse, they were refurbished to the standard required and loaded with merchandise for use on the rivers. This revealing record is found in *On the Governance of the Empire* (*De Administrando Imperio*), which is the Latin title of a Greek work originally written by Constantine VII.

At Staraya Ladoga, it seems that travellers swapped the larger ships that had carried them across the Baltic Sea for smaller vessels that were more suitable for navigating the narrower and often challenging waterways of Eastern Europe.

Research publicised by the National Museum of Denmark makes it clear that sailing Viking Age ships on Russian rivers could only have been carried out by experienced sailors. Swedish researchers tested this by making a modern summer voyage from the Mälaren Valley in Sweden to Novgorod in Russia. In order to do this, they used a reconstruction of a Viking Age 9-metre-long clinker-built vessel. Despite the researchers' considerable experience in sailing the vessel, this experimental journey took forty-two days to reach Novgorod. From there, they travelled south to the mouth of the River Dnieper on the Black Sea. This section of the voyage took eighty-nine days – or three months. To add to the demands of the journey, they were forced to move the ship over land for more than 155 miles (250 kilometres) of the trip. Dragging it took considerable effort, as one can imagine. From this, the conclusion was drawn that 'a boat trip from Central Sweden to the Black Sea and back could not have been completed before the Russian rivers began to freeze over again'.[20] From this, it is clear that each journey by ship beyond Staraya Ladoga must have involved staying for at least one winter in Russia.

This raises the possibility of the use of horse-drawn sledges as an alternative to summer sailing. The use of sledges on the frozen rivers would 'reduce the journey time from months to a few weeks', which challenges the image we have of how these journeys occurred.[21] Recent comparable Russian research indicates that as much as 93 miles (150 kilometres) a day can be covered in winter using a horse-drawn sledge. This experiment suggests that a journey by sledge from Novgorod to the tenth-century Rus–Slavic settlement at Gnezdovo (in Smolensk Oblast) could have been made in seven to ten days, compared with a boat journey of about thirty days. While a sledge carried less than a boat, deploying them would have saved a considerable amount of time. Given the fact that many sledges have been found by archaeologists in the Novgorod area dating from the Viking period, this form of transport must be considered as a very real option. Furthermore, the finds of sledges from Staraya Ladoga have been dated to as early as the eighth century. Since this date ties in neatly with finds of dateable Scandinavian objects, it is highly likely that sledges were used as part of the long-distance transport network. While the Vikings were highly skilled sailors, they were also very familiar with transport over the winter landscape of their Scandinavian homelands.

Further evidence for winter travel comes in the form of iron crampons that could be fitted to both shoes and horseshoes in order to improve grip on snow and ice. Such crampons were present in a burial from Staraya Ladoga that contained two horse skeletons. Both of these horses had been shod with horseshoes which had crampons attached to them.[22] So, winter sledge travel may have been as (or more) important than ship-based transport into the Russian interior.

A DANGEROUS JOURNEY

Whatever kind of transport was used, the journey could be perilous when it involved the flowing rivers, as written sources from the Scandinavian homeland demonstrate.

Far away, on the Swedish island of Gotland, it was recorded how a Viking traveller died at the cataracts of the Dnieper. On a runestone, known as the Pilgårds stone, or G280, the memorial states: 'Brightly painted, this stone was raised by Hegbjarn and his brothers Rodvisl, Austain and Emund. They have raised stones in memory of Ravn [Hrafn] south of Rufstain. They penetrated far into the Aifur. Vivil was in command.'[23]

'*Aifur*' (or *Aeifor*) refers to the rapids of Aifur on the River Dnieper.[24] The name means the 'unnavigable' or 'ever-noisy' and aptly described this very dangerous stretch of the river. The original location of this runestone is not known, but it was probably originally erected not far from a Viking Age harbour in Boge Bay on Gotland. The stone dates from the second half of the tenth century or perhaps as late as the year 1000. The runes are also translated as: 'They came far and wide in Eifor' – '*Eifor*' (or *Aifur/Aeifor*) being the most dangerous of the rapids, also known as the 'Nenasytec'.[25]

The scale of the journey that gave rise to these runic inscriptions was immense and a testimony to the far-flung nature of the Viking diaspora. In total, from Staraya Ladoga, it was 1,200 miles (1,931 kilometres) to the Black Sea and 1,600 miles (2,574 kilometres) to Constantinople.

The Western Dvina River, flowing through present-day Latvia and Belarus, was also an important gateway, with connections to the Dnieper River system outlined above.

An alternative route to the Byzantine world lay along the River Dniester and then along the western shore of the Black Sea. The latter part of the route was probably shared with the way down the Dnieper once it had reached the sea. Evidence for a Viking presence on this coastal route down the coastline of the Black Sea can be found in the Murfatlar Cave Complex near Constantia (Constanța, Romania). Here, several runic inscriptions have survived, along with a graffito illustrating a Viking navy. These can still be seen on the walls of the rock church from Murfatlar. In addition, a runestone from the Sjonhem cemetery (again in Gotland) and dating from the eleventh century commemorates a merchant named Rodfos who was on his way to Constantinople and was killed north of the Danube. The stone records: 'This stone is in memory of Rodfos. He was betrayed by the Wallachians on an outward journey. God help Rodfos' soul. May God betray those who betrayed him.'[26]

The 'Wallachians' lived north of where the River Danube flows into the Back Sea. This runestone – as with those commemorating death on the Dnieper – is a reminder that danger accompanied the wealth that could be gained from these distant voyages. It was danger that had both natural (e.g. the rapids) and human (e.g. the Pechenegs and Wallachians) causes.

The Volga trade route also had its northern terminus in the vicinity of Novgorod, south of Staraya Ladoga. As a result, Novgorod became a major node in the Rus trade system to both the Black Sea and the Caspian Sea. These were rivers of wealth.

The huge number of silver hoards buried along the River Volga reflects how much of this precious metal was flowing from the Islamic caliphate towards Scandinavia by the tenth century. Gotland alone has produced 700 buried silver hoards, with a total weight of 1,000 kilograms. That is a lot of silver![27] The silver in these Gotland hoards includes about 180,000 coins. The significance of this in the trade moving to and through this island is illustrated by the fact that only 80,000 such coins have been found in hoards on all of mainland Sweden. Sweden is over 100 times bigger than Gotland and had ten times the population in the Viking Age.[28] This is testimony to the vast wealth generated by Gotland's trade with the East.

In addition, silver gained from trade with the Islamic world was not just hoarded and buried. In 922, the Arab diplomat ibn Fadlan reported that 'for every 10,000 dirhams a Viking man accumulates, he has a silver neck ring produced that he gives to his wife to wear; it becomes a visual symbol of the wealth and prestige of those who obtain it'.[29]

While this and most other medieval documentary sources are male-orientated, it should be noted that one modern study found that about 50 per cent of female Norse graves in Russia contained weighing equipment of the type used in market transactions.[30] Consequently, we should imagine women being actively engaged in trade there and not just being passive recipients of wealth generated by men. Some may have been involved in fighting too. John

Skylitzes, an eleventh-century Byzantine historian, recorded that, after a battle fought between Rus and Byzantines in 971 at Dorostopol (modern Silistra, Bulgaria), some of the dead Rus were discovered to be women wearing armour.[31] So, women too may have fought in order to gain access to the riches of the East.

This is what drew Vikings East. Alongside the danger, there was adventure and the possibility of gaining huge wealth. It is little wonder, then, that the East came to have both a mythical and an economic and a political significance to those who knew about it. As our next chapter reveals, this can be seen in a very surprising area of Viking Age mythology. For while the Vikings influenced the cultures of the East, the East in turn fed into the mental and mythological world of Scandinavia. It was an intimate and dynamic connection.

CHAPTER 4

EAST MEETS WEST IN THE WORLD OF THE GODS AND GODDESSES

The central theme of this book is how the story of the Viking exploration and settlement in what is today Russia and Ukraine – which is over a millennium old – has resonated down the centuries and still affects the turbulent events of the twenty-first century. However, the story flows both ways, and events in the East affected the Viking outlook as much as the Viking outlook affected the East. We have seen this in the area of wealth accumulation (all those silver dirhams on Gotland, for example) and the way in which this influenced Scandinavian society in the northern homelands. But it had another curious side to it, and this was the way in which ideas about the mysterious East shaped the outlook and mindset of the Norse. For the East loomed large in Viking Age mythology, as it did in Viking Age economics and politics. In this area of life, East met West in the world of the gods and goddesses of Norse mythology.

A QUICK OVERVIEW OF THE VIKING DEITIES

Before their conversion to Christianity, the Vikings believed in a pantheon (a collection) of northern gods, goddesses and mythical semi-divine heroes and supernatural beings. In this group of deities, most were clearly gendered in some way. However, fluidity in how this was expressed meant that exceptions existed alongside the apparent gendered norms.

The male Norse divinities included Odin, Thor, Freyr, Loki, Baldr, Hod, Njord and many others. The female divinities included Freyja, Frigg, Sif and Hel.

Of the male divinities, Odin was often described as 'All Father'. In Norse mythology, he was regarded as the chief of the Norse gods and the leader of warriors. In this mythology, he ruled from his hall, which was called Valhalla.

Norse mythology envisaged two families or races of gods. These were known as the *Aesir* (Old Norse: *Æsir*) and the *Vanir*. According to the sources that have survived into modern times, it was thought that these two divine families/races had once been at war with each other. However, they had made peace and intermarried. It is very likely that this account (as it was recorded from the thirteenth century onwards) was originally developed in order to explain how different beliefs, from different periods of time, had been combined to make a unified set of ideas. It is possible that the *Vanir* represented an earlier strata of fertility-related deities, whose cult was later subsumed into the – more warrior – culture of the beliefs associated with the *Aesir*.

This seems clear in the mythology, where a *Vanir* goddess named

Freyja taught the *Aesir* a kind of magic known as *seithr*, which enabled her (and then them) to connect with the spirit world. The mythology states that this was common practice among the *Vanir*. Other differences that may hint at an older fertility cult are that the *Vanir* deities Freyr and Freyja were Niord's children by his own sister. However, we are told that among the *Aesir* it was forbidden to have sexual relations with close family members.

If this is so, the surviving narrative hid this and attempted to make all the divinities part of the same story, as if their relationships had always been interconnected. In reality, there was probably a period (unrecorded) in which two different sets of beliefs coexisted – even collided – and one set of beliefs was older than the other. Whatever originally occurred is now lost to us. What we are left with is a set of mythological stories in which two races of divinities interact.

In this account, the gods and goddesses lived in a place known as Asgard. This was connected to other worlds of being by the bridge called *Bifröst*. In a complicated and not always consistent cosmology, Norse mythology envisaged that different worlds of being were united by a cosmic ash tree called *Yggdrasil*. These different worlds included *Midgard*, or 'Middle Earth', which was the realm of people. This is now very well-known through its appearance in J. R. R. Tolkien's *The Lord of the Rings*. 'In the original construct, the idea of a tree – with its roots, trunk, and branches – provided a vivid image of how different levels of time, being, and awareness could be connected, while still having individual identities and features. It also emphasised the connectedness of these different worlds.'[1]

As well as the gods and goddesses, other major players in Norse mythology were the *jötnar* (singular: *jötunn*). This word is often translated into English as 'giants'. Usually portrayed as the enemies of the gods and goddesses, Thor is frequently described in the mythology as the crusher of giants' skulls using his great hammer, called *Mjölnir*.

Giants were regarded as creatures of chaos, the archetypal 'other', who would eventually destroy the world of the gods and goddesses on a day of destruction at the end of the world. On the other hand, there is clear interaction in the myths, and female giants are presented as intermarrying with the Norse divinities and male giants are described as scheming to get possession of a Norse goddess. As an aside, there was a gendered aspect to this, since the mythology insists that *Aesir* gods could marry giants' womenfolk, but a giant could not have an *Aesir* goddess as a wife. As a result, the relationship between the *Aesir* and the *jötunn* in the mythology is complicated. And 'giants' were not necessarily larger in stature that the Norse gods and goddesses.

What is relevant to the East and Norse mythology is the way in which distant lands and communities beyond the borders of mainline Norse culture could be drawn into the myth mindset. In the north:

> Sami are comparable to giants in Scandinavian mythology, since similar characteristics are associated with them: they live outside the 'centre', on the edge of the world and often in the north; snow is their element (as it is for the northern giants) and they know how to ski, shoot with a bow, predict the future and perform magic.[2]

In the same way, the East came to have a similar exotic and otherworldly quality. Although, in the case of the East, it was envisaged as the original home of the Norse gods and goddesses, rather than the home of the threatening giants.

Most of what we know about the Norse myths, which dominated the Viking mindset, comes from two medieval sources. These are the thirteenth-century *Prose Edda* and the *Poetic Edda*.[3] Together, these two sources tell us most of what we now know about Norse mythology. However, clues also exist in other medieval sources, almost all written in Iceland. These clues survive in *skaldic* poetry (a form of Norse poetry),[4] in the works of literature called sagas and in place names.

THE HOME OF THE GODS AND GODDESSES IN THE EAST

The evidence for the impact of the East on the Norse mindset is dramatically revealed in an Old Norse work of literature entitled *Ynglinga Saga*. This is the first part of the Icelandic historian Snorri Sturluson's history of the ancient Norwegian kings, which is titled *Circle of the World* (*Heimskringla*). This is one of the genres of Old Norse writings that is often described as a 'legendary saga'.

A very rich source of Old Norse literature can be found in the sagas.[5] As with so much of the written evidence which survives from the Viking Age, most of these were written in Iceland. These Old Norse sagas are generally classified using titles which indicate their general content. They include kings' sagas, sagas of Icelanders, contemporary sagas, legendary sagas, chivalric sagas, saints' sagas and bishops' sagas. Works of literature, some of these draw on real-life people and events (even if the events are adapted and embellished to fit the story), while others tap into a much older (and originally oral) tradition of mythology and legendary characters and events. The sagas were written mainly in Old Norse prose, although some of them contain poetry embedded in the text. The one that concerns us is the legendary one titled *Saga of the Yngling Family*, usually simply referred to as *Ynglinga Saga*.

It is thought that *Ynglinga Saga* was originally written in Old Norse in about 1225. It covers a period from the mythical origins of Norwegian kingship, through legendary rulers and then into the historical period. Its account ends in 1177, in historical times.

The earliest part of this saga claims to deal with the 'arrival' of the Norse deities in Scandinavia. In this section, it is explained that they originated in a part of Asia to the east of the *Tana-kvísl* River. From Snorri's explanation, this river is what we now call the River Don. The Don flows from south of Moscow to eventually reach the Sea of Azov, which is linked to the Black Sea. Now in southern Russia and eastern Ukraine, this region borders the Caucasus to the south. Snorri knew the river in question as the *Tanais* (*Tanais* being a settlement in the delta of the Don River).

The region east of the *Tanais* River was, according to Snorri, the location of the original city of the gods which was called *Asagarth* (Asgard in other myths). It was the capital of an area known as *Asaland* (literally 'land of the *Aesir*' or 'Asia-land'). In Old Norse, this was *Asaheimr* or the World of the *Aesir*. A great range of high mountains ran from the north-east to the south-west in the vicinity of *Asaland*. We are told that south of the mountains lay 'Turkland'.

The 'geography' of this account in *Ynglinga Saga* was clearly inspired by knowledge of strange lands to the east that had actually been explored by the Viking Age traders who are central to our story. However, it had later been reinvented in twelfth- and thirteenth-century Norway and Iceland as a fabulous 'never-never land' that was situated far, far away. This is revealed by the fact that, in Snorri's account, Odin's eventual journey to Scandinavia is described as being via the Don and Volga rivers and through *Garthariki* (Old Norse: *Garðaríki*), which was the Old Norse name for the lands of the Rus. Odin's route in the mythological story was, in reverse, the historic Viking routeway to the Byzantine Empire and *Serkland*, the Norse name for the Islamic Abbasid Caliphate. In other words, the Viking Age divinities were described as traversing the very same river routes as the real-life traders of the ninth and tenth centuries.

Ynglinga Saga explains that the ruler of this area beyond the *Tanais* River was Odin. 'He is described in what is known as a *euhemerised* way. This means that a mythological figure is presented as if he/she was once a *real* heroic person, who was later regarded as divine.'[6]

The confused nature of this is revealed in the fact that Odin is presented in this account *both* as a magical figure and *at the same time* as a mortal who dies and is cremated.

In this way Snorri – writing in Christian thirteenth-century Iceland – presented the traditional stories of the Norse deities as if they had been human ancestors whose real identity was obscured and distorted by later writers. As a result, the mythological account (centuries old) of a conflict between the divine *Aesir* and the *Vanir* was presented as if it had been a real war between those led by Odin out of *Asaland* and the rulers of a place called *Vanaland* (Land of the *Vanir*), which suffered invasion.

In Snorri's account, Odin was a famous warrior who travelled widely, conquering other nations. He won every battle he fought. Consequently, his people came to believe that it was him who decided who would win and lose in war (hinting at the origins of later beliefs concerning Odin's association with war). Whenever his own people went to war, we are told that Odin blessed them and so they believed that this would assure them of victory. In addition, whenever his people were in trouble, they called out his name and believed that he would help them and protect them.

The mythology explains that Odin took an army of the *Aesir* and invaded the land of the *Vanir*, but they defended their land so determinedly that neither side could gain the victory. Eventually, they arranged a meeting, agreed a peace and gave each other hostages in order to ensure that each side kept to the agreement. As part of this arrangement, the *Vanir* offered up their noblest members. This was the god Njord, who was very rich, along with his son Freyr. The *Aesir* did likewise and gave as hostages Haenir, who was strong and good-looking, and Mimir, who was very wise. The *Vanir* also offered one of their wisest members, who was called Kvasir.

In Norse mythology, this explains the presence of *Vanir* living among the *Aesir* in later stories, such as the god Njord with his children Freyr and Freyia, and *Aesir* among the *Vanir*, such as the deities Haenir and Mimir. It is written as if it was a mythological reflection of the kinds of political compromises that were actually found in the real Viking Age.

In the next stage of the story (which is rather complex), the combined gods and goddesses (envisaged as superhuman people) ruled first in 'Saxland' (Germany) and then Odin took his people to Denmark and eventually to Sweden. There Odin established his royal hall, supported by his followers (who lived in other Scandinavian centres). Along the way, there were encounters with giants, along with supernatural activities which explain the geography of areas of Scandinavia.

Ynglinga Saga goes on to describe how the deity Freyr founded the Swedish Yngling royal dynasty at Uppsala. After this, the storyline follows the line of Swedish kings up until Ingjald, whose descendants settled in Norway and were the ancestors of the Norwegian kings. Snorri is particularly careful to identify this as the line of the famous Norwegian king, Harald Fairhair (died *c.*933). In this way, the world of the East, the tangled roots of Norse mythology and the genealogies of real Viking rulers became combined.

The key point is the way in which the East became incorporated into the Viking mythological mindset. East met West in the world of gods and goddesses. In Snorri's account, when Odin was on the point of death, he had himself marked with the point of a spear. And from this, he claimed for himself all men who died in battle. Odin told his followers that he was going to a place called *Gothheimr* (Home of the Gods), although Snorri claims that the people of the *Svear* (that is in Sweden) believed that Odin had returned to the East – to *Asagarth* – from where he had journeyed long before. There, they believed, he lived for ever.

So, the story ends where it began, in the East. And it is to the East – but in historical times – that we turn again to continue the exploration.

CHAPTER 5

THE CREATION OF THE RUS STATE

It was a Viking–Slav dynasty that created the first 'Russian' state. The new kingdom soon became deeply enmeshed in the wide-ranging trading network that linked the Baltic to the Black Sea, the Caspian Sea – and beyond. The East – as we saw in the last chapter – even made its way into the mindset of the mythmakers of Scandinavia. The East had potency; it had imaginative influence. But it was a potency that was rooted in real events and people, albeit ones who had travelled far from the northern homelands. Mystery was rooted in reality.

The medieval state that emerged has been traditionally known as *Kiev Rus* or *Kievan Rus*, using the Russian form of the name of the city that is now (especially since the Russian invasion of Ukraine in 2022) more commonly referred to by its Ukrainian form *Kyiv*.

It is that state which lies at the heart of the deep stories of both Russia and of Ukraine. Its legacy is quite extraordinary, and it is at the centre of what, today, is considered to be the core identity of both countries' origins.

So far, we have heard more about artefacts and sites than named people. The exceptions have been those commemorated on the Swedish runestones as 'far-travellers' to the East. That is about to change in our story because history is beginning to accompany the archaeology, as we explore the key period in which the Rus state itself (as opposed to a number of influential trading posts) emerged.

However, a slight note of caution does need to be sounded. While the story will now enter a more historic phase – with named people and events featuring in the account – there are aspects of it that have a legendary feel to them. Nevertheless, it is reasonable to conclude that the people and events which appear in the sources are broadly rooted in reality – even if later national and religious spin played an important part in how their significance was expressed.

THE SWEDISH 'VIKINGS' BECOME THE 'RUS'...

For the first time, written sources from Russia itself will start to play a part in untangling events. In the twelfth century, a source of information known as the *Tale of Bygone Years* (*Povĕstĭ Vremęnĭnyhŭ Lĕtŭ*) was compiled in what is now Ukraine. Today, it is generally known as the *Russian Primary Chronicle* as well as the *Tale of Bygone Years*. We will call it the *Russian Primary Chronicle*. The original compilation is sometimes also referred to as *Nestor's Chronicle*, after a monk (died *c.*1114) who, tradition claimed, had begun the work in about 1113. Drawing on lost Slavonic chronicles, legends, Byzantine annals, Slavic oral poetry and some Norse sources, the *Russian Primary Chronicle* claims to tell the story of how Viking adventurers became rulers of the first Russian state. It covers a period of time from *c.*850 to 1110.

While details may be open to question, the general outline represents the foundation story of the rulers of Kyiv and, almost certainly, communicates the gist of what occurred in the early Middle Ages.

According to this account, Viking adventurers (the Varangian Rus) used force to subjugate the Slavic and Finnish tribes living south-east of the Baltic. This clearly refers to some of the northerners who settled in the trading posts and early towns (such as Grobiņa, Truso, Staraya Ladoga, Rurikovo Gorodische and Gnezdovo) that we have referred to so far. But, the chronicler tells us, they were then driven out. However, once free of the Rus, warfare broke out between the indigenous tribes and they decided that perhaps the rule of the Rus was not so bad after all. Consequently, they invited them back to bring order: 'They said to themselves, "Let us seek a prince who may rule over us, and judge us according to the Law." They accordingly went overseas to the Varangian Russes.'[1]

This is clearly later spin designed to enhance the prestige and legitimacy of those 'invited back'. It has a rather modern – colonialist – feel to it: the outsiders brought order and firm rule to replace the division and conflict that was the previous experience of the natives. It was this attitude which led Adolf Hitler, in the twentieth century, to caustically comment: 'Unless other peoples, beginning with the Vikings, had imported some rudiments of organisation into Russian humanity, the Russians would still be living like rabbits.'[2]

Such condescending and racist stereotypes have made it difficult to objectively assess the impact of the Norse in the East. As we shall see, this has dogged reflections on the matter since the eighteenth century.

The curious thing is that the original 'colonial perspective' was penned by one of those colonised, not by one of the outside colonisers.

This, though, is readily explained. Whoever wrote this interpretation of the foundation of the Rus state was one who was heavily invested in it. Therefore, although the spin was sharply patronising in tone regarding the capabilities of the indigenous Slavic and Finnish peoples, its purpose was to trace the arc of history in a providential way. As a result, it was narrated in a fashion that revealed the good order brought by the newcomers, who would eventually be founders of the state and – crucially – converts to the Orthodox Christian faith. Their commitment to order was a signpost to more to come in the creation of 'Holy Rus'. As a result, the possibility that the foundations of the proto-Rus state were actually laid by an indigenous tribe, the Polianians,[3] has been written out of history.

It was then, the chronicler explains, that three Viking brothers came to rule in three communities. This is a common trope found in the origin stories of many nations in the early medieval period. It follows a familiar pattern that goes something like: 'There were two/three noble kinsmen [they are always male] who crossed the sea and founded the kingdom of…'

Similar stories are found in Anglo-Saxon England, where Hengist and Horsa were described as founding the kingdom of Kent and Cerdic and Cynric as founding the kingdom of Wessex, and similar origin myths are found among the Franks and across Scandinavia. This does not preclude the historicity of some of those named, but it does mean that such incomers fulfil a well-known role in many origin myths.

The three brothers referred to in the *Russian Primary Chronicle* were: Rurik (or Riurik) in Novgorod, Sineus in Beloozero and Truvor in Izborsk.[4] The last two may be Slavic versions of original

Old Norse names: Signjotr and Thorvar. Rurik (or Riurik), who was to give his name to the Rus dynasty itself (the *Rurikid*), represents a name that was originally something like Hroerekr (Old Norse: *Hrøríkʀ*) or *Rorik*. The name later developed in the West as Roderick or Rodrick. We will refer to him as Rurik.

All of these settlements were in north-western Russia, in the area of Norse settlement that we have already mentioned. A later source, known now as the *Hypatian Codex* (a fifteenth-century compendium of the *Russian Primary Chronicle* and two other chronicles), claims that Rurik originally settled at Staraya Ladoga but later relocated to Novgorod.[5] This is a site known today as 'Rurik's Stronghold' and its situation is just over 1 mile south of modern Novgorod, on a defensive hillock. The site was fortified from the beginning of its history, unlike the settlement at Staraya Ladoga. By the middle of the tenth century, it also included what has been interpreted as a pagan temple. However, whether this was a focus for Norse pagan worship or that associated with a Slav pagan deity cannot be ascertained. While it is common to describe Rurik as ruling from Novgorod, that settlement – though close to 'Rurik's Stronghold' – did not really develop as a recognisable site until the 930s, well after Rurik's lifetime. And the prince's residence did not move there until the early eleventh century. Novgorod means the 'new stronghold' and it is testimony to the fact that it replaced an earlier defended settlement (i.e. 'Rurik's Stronghold'). Around the same time (but unremarked in the literature), archaeology attests the presence of Norse settlers at Gnezdovo, about 8 miles (13 kilometres) west of Smolensk, located on a tributary of the River Dnieper. This settlement's origins can be dated to around the year

900 but may be earlier. It later developed a central fortified site and industrial quarters within its boundary.

According to the *Russian Primary Chronicle*, the Viking brothers were of the Varangian tribe of the Rus. This is a designation designed to clearly signal that they were the people who eventually gave rise to the state of the Kyivan Rus, using the ethnic name known to both Slavs and Byzantines for the Norse in, what is now, Russia and Ukraine. Their return as rulers, the chronicler suggests, occurred sometime around 860/862. When Sineus and Truvor died, Rurik amalgamated their lands under his rule and so formed the nucleus of what would become the princedom of the Rus. The source now called the *Novgorod First Chronicle* (*Novgoródskaya pérvaya létopis'*), describing events from 1016 to 1471 and drawing, in part, on eleventh-century sources, also records this story of an invitation to foreign rulers to come and bring order and law.

THE CREATION OF THE KYIVAN RUS STATE

The *Russian Primary Chronicle* also claims that, while Rurik was establishing himself at Novgorod, two other Rus leaders – Askold and Dir – travelled southward down the River Dnieper and established their rule in the settlement later known in Russian as Kiev (Ukrainian: Kyiv). It is likely that they took control of a trading post of the Khazars, who were already exploiting a favourable position on the Dnieper River route to the Black Sea.[6] We will hear more of the Khazars in the next chapter.

The *Russian Primary Chronicle* specifically says that Askold and Dir 'did not belong to his [i.e. Rurik's] kin'.[7] They achieved this settlement by encouraging other Vikings to join them. The earliest archaeological evidence for Norse presence in Kyiv dates from the tenth century, so there is no artefactual back-up for such an early establishment of the Viking community there. However, it may be that this awaits discovery, so we cannot totally dismiss Askold and Dir (or other, unnamed, Norse) as being there in the second half of the ninth century.

If the *Russian Primary Chronicle*'s dating is correct, this set up two rival Rus mini-states: Novgorod in the north and Kyiv in the south. Rurik ruled until *c*.879. His successor, named Oleg or Oleh (a Slavic form of the Old Norse personal name Helgi), then struck south and seized Kyiv in *c*.882 and relocated his capital there. The *Russian Primary Chronicle* says that, in so doing, he killed Askold and Dir, the Viking chieftains who had established their rule there a little earlier.[8]

In this way, the new state of the Kyivan Rus – which would last until 1240, when it fell to the Mongols – was traditionally established. The last *Rurikid* (the dynasty claiming descent from the Viking Rurik) to rule Russia, Tsar Fyodor I, died as late as 1598. This was a truly remarkable achievement for the family of a ninth-century Swedish adventurer who had gone East in search of fame and fortune. In time, the Novgorod princes would be appointed by the Grand Prince of Kyiv; this Novgorod prince was usually one of the elder sons of the grand prince. In this way, Kyiv's primacy over Novgorod was made clear, echoing the ancient events which tied the two communities together and which dated from Viking settlement. Things had developed a long way since those early journeys from Gotland and Sweden to the East:

What started out as a commercial venture turned – like the Hudson's Bay and East India Companies in centuries to come – into a political one. Trading posts turned into forts, forts into tribute-collecting points, and tribute-collecting points, by the end of the tenth century, into the largest kingdom in Europe, stretching from the Baltic to the Carpathians.[9]

The *Russian Primary Chronicle* – written in Kyiv – makes the event of Oleg moving south as the way by which the focus of the narrative switches from Novgorod to Kyiv. It is difficult now to know whether this dramatic shift (as described) really constituted a sudden relocation of power or whether the semi-legendary figure of Oleg was introduced in order to switch the focus from the north to Kyiv in the south. The significance of the move is underscored in the account by the words being put in Oleg's mouth that Kyiv was now 'the mother of Russian cities'.[10] It is a claim that sits well within the later Kyivan view of itself as the heartland of Russia. That is a heritage that has become something of a poisoned chalice in the conflicted world of the twenty-first century and the Putinist claim that the 'special military operation' launched in 2022 was to return Kiev (Kyiv in Ukrainian) to its rightful place within the Russian homeland.

The same medieval account also claims that, while Oleg came to rule in Kyiv, he continued to maintain control over Novgorod and also of Gnezdovo/Smolensk. These three centres were the core political units of the early Kyivan Rus state. The chronicler additionally states that Oleg consolidated his power by gaining the submission of three Slavic tribes. These are named as the Derevlians, Severians and the Radimichians. They were made to pay him tribute, which is consistent with what we earlier concluded regarding the relationship between the Rus and the indigenous peoples. A Byzantine account, written by Emperor Constantine VII, *On the Governance of the Empire* (*De Administrando Imperio*), describes how the rulers of Kyiv left the settlement in November and did the rounds of local tribes, literally eating their way round these tributary communities,[11] until they returned in Kyiv in April. This clearly opens a window on how the medieval Kyivan Rus state operated. It is consistent with the way most early medieval rulers exploited resources under their overall control.

By piecing together the clues found in these various ancient traditions, we can see the general shape of events that led to the foundation of the Kyivan Rus state. It clearly occurred in several recognisable stages:

- Stage 1: Swedish Vikings trading and settling in north-western Russia.
- Stage 2: Trade gave way to political domination and tribute-taking.
- Stage 3: The now-dominant Scandinavian rulers subjugated the local Slavic and Finnish tribes and set up their Rus mini-states.
- Stage 4: The ruler of Novgorod gained pre-eminence among the northern Rus.
- Stage 5: Dissident adventurers broke away and founded a rival centre at Kyiv.
- Stage 6: The ruler of Novgorod conquered Kyiv and made it the capital of an amalgamated state, which was that of the Kyivan Rus.[12]

Corroborative evidence for the early activities of the Rus comes from some surprising ancient sources. In 839, the Byzantine Emperor Theophilus sent a diplomatic mission to Louis the Pious, who was ruler of the Franks in Western Europe. With the embassy from Constantinople travelled some members of a group who called themselves the *Rhos*. They had themselves been sent on a diplomatic mission by their own ruler – *khagan* – to Constantinople and then joined the Byzantines as they travelled westward.

Louis was curious about those who accompanied the imperial party and, on enquiry, discovered that these *Rhos* were Swedes. This intriguing episode is recorded in the *Annals of St Bertin* (*Annales Bertiniani*), which is a contemporary source documenting events of the period 830–82. This is the very earliest written reference to the Rus.[13] Incidentally, *khagan* was not a personal name, although it appeared that way in this source. In fact, it is a royal title. It was, for example, the title used to describe the ruler of the Khazars, whose centre of power lay north-east of the Black Sea. It seems that the Rus were picking up some of the political power vocabulary of their new home.

A little later, the Arab writer Al-Ya'qūbī (died 897) explained that the people he knew as the Rus were of the same race as the pirates who had attacked the Islamic Spanish city of Seville in 843. Al-Ya'qūbī lived variously in Armenia, Khorasan (a region encompassing north-eastern Iran, southern Turkmenistan and northern Afghanistan), India, North Africa and eventually Egypt. A Shi'ite, he was well informed about peoples from the Caspian Sea to the Mediterranean, so the Rus came into his orbit of interest.[14] It is more evidence that they were a Viking people.

Another Arab geographer, Abu'l-Qasim Ubaydallah ibn Abdallah ibn Khordadbeh wrote in 846 that the *al-Rus* lived among the *as-Saqalibi*, who are usually identified as the Slavs. They travelled to the northern shore of the Black Sea (termed the 'Roman Sea' in this account) to trade beaver and black fox pelts as well as weapons (he specifies swords). He also refers to Rus visits to Baghdad. When they did so, he writes, 'they used Slavic eunuchs from Muslim households as translators' to assist their transactions.[15] The implication from this is that the Viking Rus had learned to speak the Slavic language.

Yet another Muslim writer, Ahmad ibn Rusta (died in 903), described how the *al-Rus* attacked the *as-Saqalibi* in order to seize slaves to sell to the Khazars and the Volga Bulgars.[16] The account specifically refers to these attacks being from Rus ships, which connects with the riverine nature of their penetration of the Russian heartlands that we examined in Chapter 3. Another Arab writer, Ahmad ibn Fadlan (alive in the 920s), also refers to the Rus selling young female Slavs as slaves (along with furs) to the Bulgars in exchange for glass beads and silver dirham coins. The appalling nature of human beings lumped together, by the sellers, with animal pelts – in return for beads and silver – is easy to quickly pass over when discussing the economic underpinning of the early Rus state, but it demands recognition. As with so much in the past (and so often in the present too), the wealth of some is gained through the misery of others. The specific reference to 'young Slavic female slaves'[17] shockingly reminds one of the sexual slavery that, no doubt, was a core part of this terrible trade in people.

If the story of the rise of the *Rurikid* dynasty is remarkable, even more astonishing is what came next; for within a century, they had morphed into rulers of an Orthodox Christian state, whose pagan Viking past was rapidly subsumed by a new Christian and Slavic character. That is the subject of Chapter 7 and the basis of the claim by Vladimir Putin, in 2015, that Crimea constitutes a spiritual Russian heartland, comparable to the Temple Mount in Jerusalem for Jewish people.

THE RUS AND THEIR ASSIMILATION TO SLAVIC CULTURE

Under the Rus rulers, the mixed Norse/Slavic settlements of Russia soon developed into significant urban trading centres. Not for nothing did the Swedes know the region as *Garthariki* (Old Norse: *Garðaríki*), meaning the kingdom of the towns, or just *Garthar* (Old Norse: *Garðar*), meaning the towns. When Novgorod (the 'new fortress') was founded in the tenth century, it relocated the settlement from what had once been a much smaller Slavic trading post on the island of Gorodisce. The fame of the later settlement eclipsed memory of the former site to the extent that, when the *Russian Primary Chronicle* named the seat of Rurik's original power, it was Novgorod that was identified, although that settlement had been little more than a staging post on the trade route south in the 860s. Back in Sweden, it was called *Holmgarthr* (Old Norse: *Hólmgarðr*). Almost all the events occurring in Russia in the Norse sagas are associated with it and the so-called 'Eastern Quarter' (Old Norse: *Austrhálfa*) of Viking settlement.

In a similar way, the settlement of Kyiv (centre of the Rus state) became an important trade hub connecting the Baltic to the Black Sea and further afield. This was built on the previous century of exploring and trading down the river systems of Russia and Ukraine that we examined in Chapter 3. And it soon eclipsed Novgorod/ *Holmgarthr* in its power, wealth and influence.

While the Scandinavians bequeathed a far-flung trading network to the state that eventually emerged, we must not credit this entirely to the Swedish adventurers. This is because the Slavic peoples that they came to (apparently) dominate were skilled craftworkers and traders and their settlements were already on an upward trajectory of development. In addition, the Scandinavians rapidly assimilated to the culture of their neighbours. In the twenty-first century, there are no more than seven loanwords from Old Norse in the modern Russian language. This vividly illustrates the significance and confidence of the Slavic component in the state of Kyivan Rus. It also indicates something of the population imbalance as well. As later in Normandy, we should imagine the Rus as an immigrant elite minority and not a mass folk movement. There is nothing like the archaeological evidence for an influx of lower-class Viking settlers that we see in parts of Lincolnshire or on Orkney or Iceland. And even if there had been a large input of northern settlers, such numbers would rapidly have been diluted in the huge areas of the new state which linked the Baltic to the Black Sea. The East absorbed the West and North. Where there is archaeological evidence for Swedish Viking immigrants (such as characteristic Viking-style oval 'tortoise' brooches), these incomers were town-based and their presence did not extend far into rural settlements, which were almost undiluted in Slavic ethnicity (or

Finnish in the north). Even in the developing towns of the Kyivan Rus, the Swedes were a warrior and merchant minority. They were highly influential but low in numbers. In short, the Slavic peoples were always going to make up the majority of the new state.[18] Just as in Anglo-Saxon England and in Normandy, this accelerated the transformation of the newcomers. The Vikings were a chameleon people, who soon resembled those among whom they settled.

The first three rulers of the emerging Rus state carried Norse names and this can be seen through the later lens of Slavonic written accounts. So, Rurik was *Rorik* in Old East Norse, Oleg was *Helgi* in Old Norse and Igor was *Ingvar* in Old Norse. While such names do not prove ethnicity, the pattern is surely significant. These men had Norse names that, while adapted by the writers of chronicles who spoke Old East Slavic and who drew on traditions written in Old Church Slavonic, are still clearly visible in the written record. However, in 945, Igor's son came to power and he was named Svyatoslav. His name was clearly Slavic and the decision to name him in this way reveals both an assimilation of the Rus mindset to Slavic culture and an appeal to a subject population by the gesture of naming a ruler of the state in the language of the indigenous people. Culture was in flux. Even then, the Norse influence in personal naming was not over. When he, in turn, named his son Vladimir (Ukrainian: Volodymyr), it was derived from the Germanic *Waldemar*.[19]

While it took until 945 for the ruling dynasty to adopt fully Slavic personal names, there is other evidence which suggests that indigenous people were becoming incorporated into the Rus state before this. When the Rus made a treaty with the Byzantine authorities in 944, the *Russian Primary Chronicle* states that there were seventy-six people named as Rus envoys to Constantinople. Of these, many carried Slavic and Finnish names. This was especially so among members of the princely family of the Kyivan Rus.[20] Clearly, those at the top of the social hierarchy included members of the indigenous elites, even if lower down the social scale, the relationship between the Rus and local people was more exploitative.

That the Rus were energetic in squeezing the most out of the surrounding population is made clear by the actions of Olga, widow of the Rus ruler Igor (who died in 945 in a conflict with a Slavic tribe). Following his death, she established several tribute centres (termed *pogosty* in the *Russian Primary Chronicle*) in northern Russia. These were clearly designed to maximise the collection of tribute which could then be moved south to trade with the Byzantine Empire.

In the 940s and 950s, this expansion of tribute-taking power was at the expense of the Slavic Derevlians to the north and north-west. In the middle of the 960s, under the Rus ruler Svyatoslav I (son of Igor and Olga), it was at the expense of the Khazars to the east. The Rus victory over them meant that their tribute-collecting system now came under Rus control.[21]

Until the middle of the tenth century, there was still a distinction between the language of the ruling dynasty and the rest of the population. The rulers spoke the eastern form of Old Norse, while Old East Slavic was the language of the majority; but the name-giving indicates the way that things were developing.

But this was not the only Slavic feature in the ruling dynasty of Kyivan Rus in the middle of the tenth century; for Svyatoslav I and his son, Vladimir, were both worshippers of the Slavic pagan god

Perun. It is clear that Rus Norse paganism had adapted to the local paganism of their subjects.

When Vladimir finally succeeded his father Svyatoslav I (after the latter was ambushed and killed by the Pechenegs on his return from campaigning in the Balkans), it was only after a civil war between the sons of Svyatoslav that lasted until 980. During that civil war, Vladimir had eliminated a rival Rus community (not one of the *Rurikids*) whose power was based on Polatsk on the Western Dvina River and he had also defeated his brother. This made him ruler of Kyiv but needing to politically and culturally unify the land over which he had gained control. He knew the power of symbols and established the trident badge that is still a Ukrainian symbol today. He also tried to mobilise support by his encouragement of Slavic pagan religion and making disparate local cults dependent on Kyiv. He set up idols of a number of Slavic gods in Kyiv and used silver and gold to adorn the statue of the pagan god Perun. He was trying to establish a unified religious cult, based on Kyiv, which drew on local cults but made them dependent on the state religious centre. Given that he later converted to Orthodox Christianity, this earlier promotion of indigenous Slavic religion is striking. Clearly, Vladimir was looking for a unifying religious settlement which would reflect his unifying political settlement. To begin with, he rooted this in Slavic pagan religious beliefs.

At the same time, Slavic speakers fought alongside the Rus both as soldiers and as commanders of armies. But a more dramatic change was soon to occur; a change which would signal a massive shift in policy; a change which would influence the cultural future of the people of the Rus for over a millennium. In 988, Vladimir converted to Christianity.

Before we examine that momentous historic moment, we need to examine something of the complex backstory of the relationship of the Rus with the Byzantine Empire and the great city of Constantinople.

CHAPTER 6

TO THE 'GREAT CITY': THE LURE OF CONSTANTINOPLE

Under the Rus rulers, the mixed Norse–Slavic settlements of Russia–Ukraine soon developed into significant urban trading centres. As we have seen, the Swedes knew the region as *Garthariki* (Old Norse: *Garðaríki*), the 'kingdom of the towns', or just *Garthar* (Old Norse: *Garðar*), meaning 'the towns'. However, to the south, there lay an urban settlement which dwarfed the trading towns of the Rus. And it captured their imagination with the stories of its splendour and riches. That city was the capital of the Eastern Roman Empire (the Byzantine Empire) at Constantinople (modern-day Istanbul). It became an object of raiding and then of diplomacy and, at times, extremely violent behaviour which was mixed with the diplomatic aim of gaining trading advantages.

MIKLAGARÐR: 'THE GREAT CITY'

One of the reasons the Vikings travelled eastwards was their desire to establish trading connections with the Byzantine Empire. The other was the establishment of direct trade with the Islamic caliphate; but it was the lure of the 'Eastern Rome' which, arguably, had the greatest pull on their imagination. Its capital, Constantinople, was the trading centre for goods from the whole of the Mediterranean region, North Africa and the Near East.

What became the 'great city' to the Vikings was first established in the seventh century before Christ on the site of an earlier settlement named *Lygos*. From these beginnings, its prime geographical location between Europe and Asia, and its natural harbour, assisted its growth into a major port in the eastern Mediterranean. Named in ancient Greek *Byzántion*, it is now more usually known by the Latin version of the name: *Byzantium*. In AD 330, the Roman Emperor Constantine (the first emperor to convert to Christianity) re-founded it as *Nova Roma* (New Rome), in the Greek-speaking East. But it soon became known, by association with the name of the emperor who re-founded it, as Constantinople. For this reason, the two names Byzantium and Constantinople are both used at times for the one city. It has also become traditional to differentiate the city from its empire by referring to the city as 'Constantinople' and the area ruled as the 'Byzantine Empire'. These are the terms used in this book.

Constantinople was the heir of the Roman Empire in the East and was fabulously wealthy. When Rome fell to barbarian invaders in the early fifth century (the last Western Roman Emperor was finally deposed in 476), the empire in the East survived the calamity which fragmented the West and led to a plethora of successor states emerging there. Since the fourth century, the Roman Empire – though still officially viewed as one unit – had been effectively divided into a western and eastern sphere of influence, usually having two rulers, one in the Latin-speaking West and one in the Greek-speaking East. Life was more complex than this at times – but this was the basic framework of the Late Roman state.

When the last Western emperor (Romulus Augustus, nicknamed 'Augustulus' or 'little Augustus') was removed from power by his barbarian military commander, Odoacer, the Western imperial regalia was sent to Emperor Zeno in the East, and Odoacer swore allegiance to him, ruling without further imperial successors in the West. In effect, there was still one Roman Empire, but its Western regions rapidly fell out of the control of the Eastern emperor in Constantinople. Various attempts were made to regain control of the West, but from the mid-sixth century onwards, its future increasingly lay beyond the control of the Eastern imperial authorities.

This fragmented situation in the West continued until Charlemagne, King of the Franks, was proclaimed 'Emperor of the Romans', in Rome, on Christmas Day in the year 800. This reinstated a version of the empire in the West, as distinct from that in the East, which had increasingly become separated from its Western co-religionists by theological disputes dividing what we would term the 'Catholic' and the 'Orthodox' churches (in the Latin West and the Greek East respectively). In contrast to this division, both still made universalist claims and the elevation of Charlemagne 'gave him equal status with his tainted [from a Catholic perspective] rivals in Constantinople'.[1] It should be noted that those Eastern rulers still regarded themselves as the full and true inheritors of Rome and guardians of the true – hence 'orthodox' – formulation and expression of the beliefs of Christianity.

Reflecting these claims made by the empire in the East, Islamic sources frequently referred to this Greek-speaking political unit as '*Ar-Rūm*' (the Romans) and they are known by this title in the Qur'an (*surah* 30). This was very much how Scandinavians saw things too. As far as they were concerned, the fabulously wealthy Roman Empire still lay to the south and it was always tinged with the lure of *Romanitas* (Roman-ness), which so often drew the attention of the northern peoples. This also fed, as we shall see, into the deep story of those in Russia/Ukraine who claimed (and claim) to be the inheritors of its distinctive and unique holiness in its Orthodox form. When Constantinople fell to Islamic forces in 1453, those to the north – in the Orthodox Russian lands – saw themselves as inheritors of its sanctity. As the monk Philotheus (of the Yelizarov Monastery, near Pskov in north-western Russia) expressed it so memorably in the early sixteenth century: 'Two Romes have fallen, the third [Moscow] stands, and there will be no fourth.' It is a theme strongly worked into the concept of 'Holy Rus' and the idea of the God-sanctioned *Russkiy Mir* (Russian World), which has echoed down the centuries and continues to reverberate in Putin's Russia in the twenty-first century. Its roots go deep into the Viking Age fascination with Constantinople and the tenth-century conversion to Orthodox Christianity which grew out of this. History matters. It is engrained within our story.

A CITY OF FABLED WEALTH AND POWER

Constantinople attracted Vikings because it was a place where northern goods and slaves could be exchanged for 'exotic products such as silk, embroidered cloth, wine, fruit, spices, as well as semi-precious stones like carnelian and quartz'.[2] There was a very high demand for these goods in the markets of Scandinavia and the long and difficult transport routes made them even more valuable when they finally reached the trading towns of Birka, Kaupang and Hedeby back home. With its huge urban population, its large markets and its access to trade routes across the Mediterranean, North Africa and the Middle East, the city was a source of considerable interest to the Norse communities who had established themselves between the Baltic and the Black Sea.

The Vikings knew Constantinople as *Miklagarth* (Old Norse: *Miklagarðr*), which means the 'great city'. This translated the Greek term for it of *Megalopolis*. It had an elaborate system of defences and large and highly decorated churches and stone buildings, which took a northern visitor's breath away. In comparison to Constantinople, the wood and thatch settlements of Scandinavia, such as Hedeby and the other trading towns, must have seemed unimpressive, to put it mildly.[3] Constantinople was protected by about 12 miles (19 kilometres) of high walls and imposing towers. In addition, a great aqueduct supplied the city's half a million inhabitants with clean water, in a display of classic Roman engineering and water management. While Constantinople's fine Christian churches and civic buildings were extraordinary in their numbers and scale, what attracted the Viking traders most were the city's markets and its exotic goods. For a people experienced in long-distance trade, it was the ultimate goal.

A key advantage of the location of the Rus settlement at Kyiv was that it allowed its rulers to control the trade to Constantinople across the Black Sea. This made it 'the southern terminus of much Rus trade' heading for Constantinople.[4] At first, in the ninth century, this was a staging point for raids (rather than trade) to the south. After all, Viking raiders were seizing booty and slaves across Western Europe at this time. And Constantinople offered a greater source of riches than the lands of the West. There is evidence that, after first visiting the city in about 839/40, the Vikings mounted a series of raids.

In the year 860 – in the words of Photios I, the Patriarch of Constantinople – a Viking fleet of 200 ships emerged from the Bosphorus 'like a swarm of wasps' to assault Constantinople. Photios wrote of the 'wholesale massacres' which were perpetrated by the Vikings as they looted the suburbs. The islands in the Sea of Marmara were similarly devastated.

According to Photios, it was 'like a thunderbolt from heaven' and 'irresistible lightning'.[5] The *Russian Primary Chronicle* dates it to between 863 and 866 and attributes the raid to Askold and Dir from Kyiv.[6] This is not possible because the Viking community at Kyiv was not established as early as this and the chronicler was reading back later realities in order to explain earlier events.[7] The chronicler explains that the raid was eventually foiled by a great storm sent by God.

The apparent cause of the attack was the construction of the fortress of Sarkel by Byzantine engineers, which had restricted the Rus's trade route along the River Don in favour of the Khazars. This Volga–Don portage had been used to cross from the Black Sea to the Volga, and from there to the Caspian and north to the Baltic.

After this raid, Byzantine sources claim that the Norse made contact with imperial authorities negotiating the possibility of baptism. In 867, Photios – he of the description involving 'wasps' – wrote a letter stating that some had already received baptism and that a bishop had been sent to them. This is over a century before the famous baptism of the ruler of the Rus on Crimea in the late tenth century and it is difficult to ascertain which of the Rus were referred to in this baptism request.

The Viking Rus laid siege to the great city three times: in 860, in 907 and in the 940s. As well as targeting the city, they also raided Greek settlements on the coast of the Black Sea. However, they lacked the military capabilities to break the walls of Constantinople, and the Byzantine military resources far outweighed those of the Rus. Furthermore, it became clear that a more constructive relationship might benefit both parties. Furs, slaves, wax and honey (traded by the Rus) were in demand in Constantinople.[8] And the great city itself was a trading hub of goods desired by the Rus. Added to this, for the Byzantines, was the fact that a military ally north of the Black Sea would provide a counterbalance to those steppe tribes who sometimes threatened imperial trading interests, and this would also offer protection for the trade routes heading north into the hinterland of Eurasia. An accommodation was necessary, and the conversion of the Rus – when it finally occurred – was a key event in this improvement in relations. But first there was a mixture of diplomacy, violence and treachery.

NEGOTIATION BY VIOLENCE

During the tenth century, several of the Kyivan rulers attempted to attack Constantinople, with varying degrees of success. What is particularly notable is the way that treaties evolved through this relationship of sporadic violence. These treaties, which were negotiated following each of these violent episodes, open a window into the complex and convoluted relationship that was developing between the Rus and the Byzantine Empire. As a result of them, the Rus were allowed to run their own slave market in the city and received permission to serve as members of the emperor's elite imperial bodyguard. The numbers doing so caused this unit to eventually be known as the Varangian (i.e. Norse Rus) Guard. On the other hand, the imperial authorities were wary and there were also restrictions placed on the number of Rus merchants allowed inside the city and the goods they were able to purchase. So, clearly, they were still viewed as a potential danger. However, despite these sporadic outbursts of (what one might term) 'negotiation through extreme violence', trading relations between the two states were established even if they could still be highly volatile. It was during this time that the early trading settlements – such as those at Novgorod and Kyiv – became permanent urban residences. At the same time, the Rus culture began to reflect aspects of imperial culture. Still, violence continued.

The Rus ruler Oleg carried out an attack on Constantinople, between 907 and 912, which forced the Byzantines to agree to giving the Rus traders preferential treatment in the city. This was ratified by a treaty in 907. However, in order to monitor their activities, the Rus were restricted to the area of St Mamas until the imperial authorities had taken down their names and checked that all was in order. Then the Rus were allowed into the city to trade without paying taxes but were limited in how many could enter. All these details are given in the *Russian Primary Chronicle*. A few years later, in 911 or 912, another treaty was created, which established a tariff of payments to cover any injuries or other offences that the Rus might commit while in the city. All the Rus signatories to this treaty have Scandinavian names. The treaty also refers to the Rus acting as soldiers within the imperial army in Greece, which indicates that there were mercenaries acting in this capacity even before Kyiv became a major economic player.[9] The final treaty is also noteworthy for naming the 'great princes' who were subject to Oleg's overlordship. From this, we can conclude that 'local Rus rulers could be found in key towns located along the major water routes'.[10] These were all now benefitting from the Kyivan-led trade with the Byzantine Empire.

This appears to have been something of a watershed moment which accelerated diplomatic correspondence between the two powers. Evidence of this has been found in the form of official Byzantine seals, dating from the tenth century, discovered at Kyiv.[11] They originally identified official correspondence and merchandise. This accompanied increased trading interaction, such that by 950, great flotillas of Rus merchant ships were sailing from Kyiv to Constantinople each year.[12] By this decade, the merchants of Kyiv dominated the Black Sea trade to the imperial capital.

Despite this, attacks by the Rus on Byzantine towns around the Black Sea continued. A large number occurred between 941 and 945 and culminated in another large-scale attack on Constantinople. The raiders attacking the Black Sea towns were destroyed by the

Byzantine navy.[13] The attacks in the 940s are recorded in several imperial sources. They occurred when a ruler named Igor had come to the throne of Kyiv. Unlike the earlier raid, in 860, there is no reference to the Rus seizing large quantities of treasure in this later raid that targeted Constantinople in the 940s. However, there are vivid reports of atrocities carried out by the Rus. This raises the question of whether this was, indeed, a terror attack and one designed to force imperial authorities to grant even more advantageous trading terms to the Rus. If so, it was a political strategy in order to achieve an economic goal.[14] And it was a shocking insight into the way in which the lives of defenceless Byzantine non-combatants were destroyed as a means by which this could be extorted. The attack was beaten off by the Byzantine use of 'Greek fire' against the assembled Viking fleet, which may have been five times larger than the fleet engaged in the raid that occurred in 860.

If the intention of the attack was to use atrocities and terror to force concessions from the Byzantine authorities, then the strategy appears to have failed. While it did lead to a new treaty, it was one with some significant clauses which did not favour the Rus. Only fifty of their ships were allowed into the harbour of Constantinople at a time; limits were placed on the amount of silk that the Rus could purchase; and military requirements to provide recruits to the imperial army were placed on the Rus. They were also banned from spending the winter sheltering at the mouth of the Dnieper where it flowed into the Black Sea. The only way to interpret this is that the Byzantines clearly felt that the Rus posed a threat to their colonies on Crimea and wanted to keep the Norse some distance away from these.

In support of this interpretation is a hint in the Byzantine source *On the Governance* [or *Administration*] *of the Empire*, by Emperor Constantine VII Porphyrogenitus, that the Rus's ability to reach Constantinople was severely reduced if they were at war with the Pechenegs, who attacked them when they portaged their boats on the way south.[15] The ongoing threat posed by the Pechenegs continued to be a problem for the Rus. As late as 972, the Pecheneg Khan Kurya killed the Rus ruler Svyatoslav. Svyatoslav was returning from an invasion of the Balkans which he had conducted at the behest of the Byzantines (who had paid him 1,500 pounds of gold to ally with them) and who wished him to attack the Bulgarians. In the end, the Byzantines had fallen out with him (possibly concerned at over-reach on his part) and forced him to withdraw. After being killed by the Pechenegs, the *Russian Primary Chronicle* states that they cut off his head, made a cup from his skull, overlaid it with gold and used it as a drinking cup.[16]

The earlier document, written by Constantine VII, does not specifically say that Byzantine diplomacy was aimed at encouraging the earlier Pecheneg attacks, but the coincidence of the effects of these attacks and the increased security for Constantinople makes one wonder if diplomatic efforts were being made to keep the Rus on the back foot while they were still a long way from the great city. Later, in the 970s, it seems that the Byzantines did orchestrate the Pecheneg campaign against Svyatoslav which led to his death.[17]

As we have seen, the treaty in the mid-940s reduced the amount of silk that the Rus could buy during their visits to the city. The limit was set at the value of fifty gold coins. It seems that the imperial authorities knew the value of ensuring that the market was not flooded with the silk that was so desired in north-western Europe. It appears to have been a policy designed to manage supply in order to maintain demand and to ensure that the Rus did not grow too wealthy on the trade. A hierarchy in the power relationship was being maintained. Finds of silk at Birka and at York indicate that this importation of Byzantine silk relied on a Viking conduit to northern Europe. The treaty also insisted on letters of recommendation from the ruler in Kyiv for each merchant, which stipulated the number of ships involved. Finally, the Rus were to supply as many fighting men to the imperial army as the Byzantines demanded. Clearly, the interaction with the Rus was now a fixed part of imperial policy, but the treaty indicates that large parts of it were dictated by the Byzantines.

Other treaties followed, in which Byzantine officials attempted to strictly control the conduct of Rus trade within Constantinople itself. This included banning the carrying of weapons by the incoming Rus traders and their companions.

Relations improved somewhat towards the end of the century. As we shall see in the next chapter, Olga – who was the wife of the Rus ruler Igor – visited Constantinople in 957 and appears to have converted to Christianity there. Despite this dramatic move, she could not persuade her son Svyatoslav to do the same. Although the Christianisation did not spread further into the royal family at this point, Svyatoslav continued to enjoy good relations with the Byzantines. This smoothed the way for a later Rus ruler, Vladimir, to also enjoy positive connections with the empire. And it was this Rus ruler who would make the most decisive step of all. It was a decision which would reverberate down the centuries and its significance would be both recognised and amplified by Vladimir Putin, President of the Russian Federation. It is to that decisive step, in the developing deep story, that we will now turn.

CHAPTER 7

THE MAKING OF 'HOLY RUS'

The Orthodox Christian conversion of the state of Kyivan Rus was a game-changer in its diplomatic and military relationship with the Byzantine world. The *Russian Primary Chronicle* recounts the dramatic story of how Prince Vladimir (Ukrainian: Volodymyr) of Kyiv (consequently remembered as Vladimir the Great) decided to abandon the traditional paganism of the Norse and the Slavs.

According to early tradition, the crucial baptism in question took place on Crimea. This was why in 2015 – as we heard at the start of this exploration – Vladimir Putin justified his 2014 annexation of Crimea, from Ukraine, by asserting that Crimea has 'sacred meaning for Russia, like the Temple Mount for Jews and Muslims', and is 'the spiritual source of the formation of the multifaceted but monolithic Russian nation'. As if that was not sufficient mining of ancient history, the President of the Russian Federation then figuratively dug even deeper into the buried layers of historical events: 'It was on this spiritual soil that our ancestors first and forever recognized their nationhood.'[1] He was thinking of – and weaponising – the baptism of Vladimir in the tenth century. It is a deep story indeed.

THE REORIENTATION OF THE KYIVAN RUS

The conversion of Vladimir points us towards the source of the greatest cultural influence on the Kyivan Rus in the second half of the tenth century. This was from Constantinople and the Byzantine Empire. Scandinavia was losing its place in the shifting cultural and political character of Eastern Europe between the Baltic and the Black Sea. This shift in the cultural centre of gravity would almost certainly have occurred anyway, given the power and prestige of the Byzantine Empire, as we explored in the last chapter. But the decisive shift was accelerated by other factors too.

While the Varangian Rus would continue to travel the well-known paths (or rather rivers) that led from Scandinavia to Constantinople until the eleventh century, the flow of Scandinavian cultural influence was dwindling, and the Viking character of the Rus was not being replenished from the homelands to the extent that it once had been. After the 960s, the silver mines of the Islamic world (situated at Ilak and the Pamir in Central Asia) ceased production. This was hugely important, as they had been a key factor driving the trade which linked the Caspian Sea to the Baltic, by way of the River Volga trade route. By the first decade of the eleventh century, they and the trade they fuelled were both things of the past. In short, the 'inter-continental monetary-commercial system [based on Islamic silver coinage] had during the tenth century disintegrated'.[2] As a direct result of this, there was what has been called a 'silver famine' which affected societies from China, in the east, to the Atlantic coast, in the west. Due to this, by the end of the eleventh century, not a single Islamic ruler was minting coins in silver in a great arc of territory which stretched from the Atlantic to the border of Ghaznavid India. But the impact of the collapse in silver coin production had been shaking previous trading certainties for over a century before this. Its effects were profound.

Until this 'silver famine' occurred, the flow of trade around the Baltic and down through the Russian river systems to the Caspian Sea had been dominated by Swedish Vikings, from Sweden proper and those based on the island of Gotland. Overall, Sweden accounts for about 800 coin hoards – that add up to more than 200,000 coins – from this period. And, of this total, about 50 per cent were minted before 970 in Islamic states. This huge total was already draining silver out of the Islamic lands even before the so-called 'silver famine' took hold.

There is some debate among historians of the period over whether the silver mines in question ceased production completely in the 960s. Some experts argue, instead, that it was the destruction of the Khazar and the Bulgar empires in western Asia, along with the decline of the Samanid Empire (which at its height stretched from modern-day Iran to Afghanistan), which caused problems in *access* to silver, rather than actual *supply* of the precious metal ceasing. And that this decline in access accompanied a growing emphasis on gold (rather than silver) as a medium of exchange in the Islamic world.[3] Whatever the final verdict on its cause – and the evidence for actual exhaustion of the silver mines seems strong – the key point is that the (once plentiful) supply of silver into Scandinavia collapsed. As a result, the trade routes to the East faltered and then collapsed as well. Incidentally, it was then that Swedish Vikings turned elsewhere for the means of getting their hands on supplies of silver and began to appear among the large Viking armies raiding England and using it as a cash cow from which silver could be extorted. This was the infamous 'Danegeld', although it was not actually termed this at the time. It was an example of the law of unintended consequences. And that 'law' affected the East as well as the West.

At first, not everyone in Scandinavia gave up on the hopes of rich rewards that might be discovered in the East. It was as late as the 1030s that Ingvar the Far-Travelled and his ill-fated companions set out on their eastern exploits, which led to catastrophe. These Swedish Vikings were clearly still hoping that prosperity could be rung out of the old routes which led down the Volga. This last hurrah of the Viking–Volga venture ended in failure.

More significant than the doomed enterprise of these Swedish Vikings (as exemplified by Ingvar the Far-Travelled) to keep the old trade route going was the – ultimately more successful – re-orientation of the Rus onto the Christian world of the Byzantine Empire. For if trade with the Islamic world of the Caspian Sea region could no longer turn a reliable penny, or rather dirham, then that with the Byzantine Empire was still highly lucrative. There was a distinct pivot from the Islamic world to the Byzantine world in the second half of the tenth century. This shift was not new, but the 'silver famine' accelerated it.

When conversion to Christianity finally occurred, it is noteworthy that the language of the Kyivan church became Old Church Slavonic. It is indicative of the culture that was rapidly absorbing the once-Scandinavian Rus. Old Norse was in terminal decline among the elites of Kyiv. The 'Rus' were becoming 'Slavs'. It was Byzantine stonemasons who built the 'Church of the Tithes' in Kyiv, between 989 and 996, for the newly converted Vladimir, as the premier church for the newly Christian state of the Kyivan Rus. The central tower and dome of this great church proclaimed the Byzantine influence in Kyiv. The source of cultural influence was obvious. The Rus transitioned away from both the Norse north and the Islamic east to the Byzantine south. It was a hugely important geo-cultural shift. Its reverberations are with us still. The trading pivot, which was accelerated by the late tenth-century 'silver famine', found its cultural reflection – and its most significant characteristic – in the decision to embrace the faith of the Byzantine Empire.

THE CHRISTIAN CONVERSION OF THE KYIVAN RUS

The story of how the conversion occurred has the hallmarks of legend about it but is based on historical events. The *Russian Primary Chronicle* tells how Grand Prince Vladimir of Kyiv (ruler there: 980–1015) decided to abandon the traditional paganism of both the Norse and the Slavs. In this decision, he was encouraged by the example of Olga, his grandmother, who had already converted to Greek Orthodox Christianity.

Probably as early as 957 (there is some debate concerning the date), she had personally visited Constantinople. It seems that prior to this, Olga had begun issuing coins which included the Christian symbol of the cross. A badge – often described as the 'Christian falcon' symbol – had already been associated with her and now these coins had the cross added above the head of the bird. In this way, these imitations of Islamic dirham coins were made specifically Christian in their declaration.[4] During her visit to the great city, she was baptised and took the baptismal Christian name of Helena. This was highly symbolic, for Helena (St Helena) had been the mother to the first Christian Roman emperor, Constantine the Great. Furthermore, he had been closely associated with Constantinople, the city that he elevated to increased imperial status and which bore his name. It seems clear that there were high hopes that the royal Rus line of Olga/Helena would achieve great things for the Christian Orthodox faith. If so, there was to be initial disappointment.

On returning to Kyiv, Olga called for assistance from the Eastern Franks, but this does not appear to have led to any significant Christian missionary activity among the Rus. It is curious that she did not turn to Byzantine clergy at this time. Perhaps she wanted to control Byzantine imperial influence by mixing it with that of the Catholic West. Whatever lay behind this, she was later revered as the one who took a decisive step towards Christianity in the process of converting the Rus. The *Russian Primary Chronicle* later described her as 'radiant among infidels like a pearl in the dung'.[5] It has been suggested that part of her motivation for conversion was to gain favour with the Byzantines at a time when trade with the caliphate via the Caspian Sea was faltering (as evidenced by the reduction in silver dirhams appearing in sites along the Middle Dnieper by the middle of the tenth century).[6] By the 960s, as we saw earlier, that eastern trade route to the caliphate had largely collapsed, to be replaced by silk flowing north on the trade route from Constantinople.

In the period of this royal event, in *c*.957, significant adoptions of

Christian faith were occurring among other 'barbarian' peoples too. A number of Baltic Slav tribes had converted by 968 and the rulers of both the Danes and the Poles had officially adopted Christianity in the 960s. While this would take time to percolate down through society, it meant that the new religion had the backing of influential elites in these societies. Clearly, religious change was on a number of contemporary agendas.

The question was: which faith should Vladimir adopt? It seems that he was undecided. According to one traditional (and famous) account, he dispatched Rus emissaries to different locations, in order to explore the religions that they found there. Other versions of the story say he summoned representatives to Kyiv itself. These included representatives of Western Roman Catholicism; Jews from among the Khazars who had adopted Judaism in around 865; Muslims from among the Volga Bulgars who had converted to Islam in 922; and, finally, the Byzantine Orthodox Christians of Constantinople. According to the traditional account, he rejected the faiths one after another. He is said to have decided not to adopt Islam principally due to its prohibition of alcohol and pork. This was despite Vladimir's initial attraction to the idea of seventy-two virgins that he was told would be awaiting him in paradise. He rejected Judaism because the God of the Jews had allowed the chosen people to lose their homeland. Catholicism was set to one side because he found its rites to be dull and he also disliked its emphasis on fasting.[7] That left Byzantine Eastern Orthodox Christianity. The tradition which states that Vladimir sent out emissaries claims that when the Rus visited the great cathedral of Hagia Sophia in Constantinople, they were amazed at its beauty and also at the grandeur of its formal liturgy. It seemed to them to open a doorway into heaven. So, Vladimir weighed it all up and decided that the faith of the Byzantines was the best one for himself and the Rus. We should note that it was also the faith of the most significant of the Rus's trading partners by the late tenth century and an empire which – even though diminished in size and power compared to its heyday – was still something of a superpower. These factors, we may assume, also played a part in the final momentous decision.

The way that the Rus converted suited the Byzantines very well, as it gave them a co-religionist ally north of the Black Sea. This was particularly important as, at the time, Emperor Basil II was facing the loss of Byzantine Crimea to rebels. So, it was in this context (by tradition in 988) that he proposed an alliance with Vladimir and offered him his sister's hand in marriage on condition that Vladimir accepted baptism. Vladimir accepted Christian baptism into the Orthodox faith and married Byzantine Princess Anna Porphyrogenita. She was not happy but accepted her diplomatic and royal conjugal fate. Writing in about 1015, the German Bishop Thietmar of Merseburg accused Vladimir of being 'an immense fornicator', which only stopped after his marriage to a 'decent wife from Greece' (i.e. Princess Anna Porphyrogenita of Byzantium) and his adoption 'of the holy faith of Christianity at her instigation'.[8] This highly personalised version of the events leading to Vladimir's conversion obscures the fact that the diplomatic marriage almost certainly accompanied a previous commitment, on the part of Vladimir, to accept Orthodox baptism. It is highly unlikely that a Byzantine emperor would have married off his sister to an out-and-out pagan in the hope that she *might* eventually persuade him to abandon his previous pagan beliefs and – if Thietmar of Merseburg was correct – his rampant sexuality. Clearly, this diplomatic marriage accompanied a commitment to ideological change. Regarding the sex – it is anyone's guess.

It was a highly symbolic moment in the history of the Vikings in the East and in the history of the Russian lands. To confuse matters a little, two later Western European chroniclers (Adémar de Chabannes, died 1034, and Pietro Damiani, died 1072) claim that Vladimir's half-brother had earlier converted to the Catholic version of Christianity but was murdered on the orders of his half-sibling – who then converted to the Orthodox form of the faith. If true – and it is impossible to definitively decide on the matter – one can readily understand why later Orthodox chroniclers in Russia would have supressed this fact. Given the intense rivalry between the followers of the Catholic and Orthodox churches, it would not have fitted the later narrative to record that the decisive movement towards Christian faith had seen Catholicism take the pole position from Orthodoxy. Either way, it was the Orthodox faith that Vladimir accepted and he is now remembered as 'St Vladimir the Great, the Apostle of the Rus'.

Once converted, Vladimir was very energetic in applying the new faith. The statue of the pagan Slav god Perun was dragged down and beaten. Following this, it was pulled through the River Dnieper to cleanse it from former pagan rites and to signal the purification of the state. After this, a mass baptism was arranged in the river and Vladimir let it be known that any who refused this rite would be regarded as his personal enemy. It was conversion with attitude and the threat had the desired effect. The event later became known as 'the baptism of the Rus'. In this manner, the Kyivan Rus converted to the Orthodox Christian faith of the Byzantine Empire.⁹ To commemorate the historic event, Vladimir built the first stone church of the Kyivan Rus, known as the 'Church of the Tithes'. It was designated as the place where his body and the body of his new wife would eventually be buried. Another Christian church was built on top of the hill where pagan statues had once stood. It was a striking statement of the victory of the new faith over paganism.

While some sources state that the historic baptism of Vladimir took place in Kyiv, the seat of his power, the *Russian Primary Chronicle* asserts that it occurred at Chersonesus, which was an ancient Greek colony in the south-western region of the Crimean Peninsula. So it was that Crimea passed into the deep story of 'Holy Rus'. Remember the words of a later Vladimir in 2015? As the President of the Russian Federation then stated: Crimea has 'sacred meaning for Russia, like the Temple Mount for Jews and Muslims'. It is an event that is still capable of stirring intense emotions.

The change that the baptism of Vladimir symbolised was profound. Significantly, it included the Christianising of the area around the Sea of Azov, which was where the later Icelandic historian Snorri Sturluson claimed that the original home of the Viking gods and goddesses had been located. A new myth of Rus national ethnic identity was replacing an older one – and would long outlive the previous myth.

On Volodymyrska or Saint Volodymyr Hill, in modern-day Kyiv, stands the 'Monument to Prince [Vladimir] Volodymyr'. Erected in 1853, the statue of the prince of the Rus stands 4.4 metres (14.4 feet) tall, on a pedestal of 16 metres (52.4 feet). He holds a great cross in his right hand. According to the *Russian Primary Chronicle*, it was on Volodymyr Hill that Svyatopolk II of the Kyivan Rus built the 'St Michael's Golden-Domed Cathedral and Monastery' in 1108. The cathedral was demolished by the Soviet government of the USSR between 1935 and 1937. However, the religious complex was rebuilt after Ukrainian independence in 1991. The cathedral itself reopened in 1999, with the ceremony to sanctify the completed cathedral taking place in May 2000.

In Moscow's Borovitskaya Square, a similar monument, to 'St Vladimir the Great', was erected in 2016. This statue stands 17.5 metres (57.4 feet) tall. Taking into account its plinth, the whole monument stands over 25 metres (82 feet) tall. As in present-day Kyiv, he stands with a great cross in his right hand.

Overall, the monument in Moscow is about 4.6 metres (15 feet) taller than the comparative monument in Kyiv. In the competition of sanctity-by-size, that in Moscow was clearly designed to out-compete that in the Ukrainian capital.

The statue in Kyiv had to be shrouded with protective layers to shield it from the blast and fragments from incoming Russian missiles, bombs and drones following the Russian invasion of Ukraine in 2022. A war of words over competing origin myths became a war fought with military weapons in the twenty-first century.

THE CHRISTIAN STATE OF THE RUS

Vladimir the Great (as he became known) founded his own church for his realm and established an ecclesiastical network to Christianise his people. Unlike the earlier rulers of the Rus, he also produced coins that resembled those of his Byzantine contemporaries.[10] The cultural identification was clear.

The new faith had huge implications for the future development of culture in Kyivan Rus. The church liturgy was written in the Cyrillic alphabet, which became the form of writing used in the new state and in Russia and Ukraine to the present day. Greek literature that had been translated for the Slavic peoples was read in Kyivan Rus, providing access to Greek science, philosophy and styles of writing history. Written in the vernacular, this greatly expanded its accessibility.

Following the 'Great Schism' of 1054, between the Roman Catholic and the Eastern Orthodox churches, the church in Kyiv kept up communion with both Rome and Constantinople for some time. Eventually, though, it shifted decisively into the Eastern Orthodox camp. Despite this – and in contrast to other Orthodox groups in the Greek-speaking world – the church of the Kyivan Rus maintained a generally more positive attitude towards the West.[11]

During the reign of Yaroslav the Wise (1019–54), this outlook was a hallmark of his diplomacy. Yaroslav arranged for his sister and three daughters to marry the rulers of Poland, France, Hungary and Norway. In addition, he worked to improve relations with the Byzantine Empire, which had become strained. His granddaughter Eupraxia (daughter of his son Vsevolod I) was later married to the Western emperor, Henry IV. Due to this, Kyivan Rus stood at the centre of a web of key diplomatic alliances.

Yaroslav was also active in furthering Christian government and culture, issuing the *Russkaya Pravda* – the first East Slavic law code. Furthermore, he had St Sophia Cathedral in Kyiv and St Sophia

Cathedral in Novgorod built, with both named from the great cathedral in Constantinople (Hagia Sophia or Holy Wisdom). But the historic roots in the north were not forgotten, as there was also a Swedish church in Novgorod dedicated to St Olaf of Norway (who died in battle in Norway in 1030). As evidence of this, a runestone from Sjusta in Sweden states that the man commemorated on that stone met his death '*i olafs kriki*' (in Olaf's church), in *Hólmgarðr* (Novgorod)'.[12]

Yaroslav also supported local clergy and the development of monasticism in his realm. He even gave up his mistresses, which must have pleased his wife. Tradition says that he founded a school system in Kyiv, which shows a commitment to expanding education. This approach to learning outlasted his rule, since his sons developed the great monastery of Kyiv, known as Pechersk Lavra, which fulfilled the function of a central educational centre for the church of Kyiv.

The new Christian state of the Kyivan Rus further developed its trading relations with the West; the route to the East being much reduced as we have seen. In the north, the continued steady debasement of the Arabic dirham coinage (from 90 per cent silver in 1000 to just 5 per cent silver by 1050) led the merchants of Novgorod to look westward for markets for their furs and amber. This shift of focus was assisted by the fact that these Rus traders were now Christian, and this clearly facilitated increased trade to Christian Anglo-Saxon England and the Christian communities of northern Germany.[13] To the advantage of the Rus, these latter communities still had abundant silver coinage to exchange for the products of Eastern Europe and the Byzantine world, due to the discovery of new sources of silver in the Hartz Mountains of Germany in the 960s. So, the silver was flowing again, but this time the current flowed from the West instead of from the East.

At the same time as these westward trading developments occurred, the eleventh century also saw the Novgorod Rus carve out more developed tributary arrangements with their northern pagan neighbours: the Finns, the Ugrians and the Sámi. They fought off competition from Norway, Sweden and, from the south-east, the Bulgars, who also traded for furs in the north.[14] According to the later Norse sagas, Yaroslav the Wise's wife, Ingegerd, appointed the Christian *Jarl* Rognvald of Sweden as her governor in the area around Lake Ladoga. Clearly, the Viking connection was still real and active, despite the increasingly Slavic nature of the Rus dynasty. The thirteenth-century document the *Catalogue of Norwegian Kings* (*Nóregs konunga tal*) records how he and his successor, *Jarl* Eilif, were employed to 'defend the kingdom against pagans'. This was how far in terms of faith that Kyivan Rus had travelled by the eleventh century.[15] Modern archaeologists have found Christian graves from this period in the cemetery at Ladoga, which had probably belonged to members of this group of influential Norse.

The Viking–Slav kingdom of the Kyivan Rus was now firmly within the Byzantine orbit but still connected to the north. Many of the later runestones from Sweden refer to men who not only travelled to Eastern Europe and Central Asia (to *Garðar* and to *Serkland*) but went further south still. One runestone, at Skepptuna, mentioned Folkmar, who 'died among the Greeks'. Another, at Ed, commemorating a man named Ragnvald, proclaimed that he 'was in Greece as commander of a brigade'. The Old Norse title on the runestone is *'liðs forungi'*, which meant 'chief of a fighting force'. From this title, we can deduce that he commanded a unit of the Byzantine emperor's Varangian Guard. Such adventures in the East could be highly lucrative. Another runestone, from Ulunda, explicitly states that one man 'journeyed boldly, made his money abroad in the land of the Greeks'.[16]

Nevertheless, despite these continuing northern connections, in the long term, the die was cast. The Rus had become irrevocably part of the Byzantine world. A new door had opened in the history of the Vikings in the East. And Eastern Orthodoxy had become a defining feature of the Kyivan Rus. It continues to be so today in modern Kyiv and in Moscow.

CHAPTER 8

VIKINGS ON CAMELS

Viking warriors and traders interacted with the Islamic world from the middle of the ninth century to the middle of the eleventh century. This ranged from battles on the Caspian Sea to trading expeditions to the capital of the caliphate itself in Baghdad.

In the East, the Vikings connected with a highly heterogeneous mix of peoples: 'Orthodox Christians, pagan Slavs, Jewish Khazars and Muslims from the Abbasid Caliphate and the Samanid Empire.'[1] On top of this, other factors also differentiated their experiences from that of fellow Scandinavians who targeted Western Europe or, for that matter, targeted the southern and eastern Baltic:

> The hit-and-run attacks that were carried out in the West were not possible. The journey from the Baltic to the Black Sea or the Caspian [via an alternative river route] was dangerous [for the Norse] as the river systems offered ample opportunities for ambushes and piracy. It was an expensive and risky journey even for military expeditions, let alone traders.[2]

As a result, interactions with indigenous peoples were often more negotiated even if, at times, targets of opportunity might prompt more violent actions by the Viking incomers to the lands on the western end of the 'Silk Roads'.

THE ATTRACTIONS OF THE 'SILK LANDS'

Viking traders called the Islamic caliphate '*Serkland*', which, as well as 'Saracen Land', may have had the meaning of the 'Silk Land'. To reach it, Viking explorers took the eastern of the great river routes south from the Baltic.

The more *western* route was that which led south – from either the Gulf of Riga and the Western Dvina River or the Gulf of Finland and the River Neva – via Staraya Ladoga, Novgorod and Kyiv, until the River Dnieper flowed into the Black Sea (with Constantinople as the goal).

The *eastern* river route was accessed either from Staraya Ladoga and Novgorod, or via Lake Onega, to reach the River Volga and then travel south to Bulgar.[3]

Bulgar/Bolghar (at various times the capital of the Bulgar people of the Volga) was an important international market centre. Indeed, it was the westernmost destination of Chinese silk merchants. Here – situated on a bend of the River Volga – their silk caravans met intermediaries who would take the precious cargo onward to the West. A trans-European route led westward from there to Mainz, Kyiv, Kraków and Prague. To Bulgar also came fur traders from the Perm forests, located to the east.[4]

Bulgar was a place where large amounts of Arab silver could be found (until the tenth-century 'silver famine' disrupted it). This silver reached Bulgar by caravan from Khiva, to the south of the Aral Sea. Large numbers of the silver coins found in Denmark were struck in the modern-day towns of Samarkand and Tashkent. This is not surprising, since important and very productive silver mines were in this area.

Strangely, finds of imported silk products originating from this eastern trade network of the Silk Roads are not as commonly found in Denmark as one might expect.[5] The exception being the Arab silver which testifies to the enormous amount of trade going on. 'This is possibly because certain types of imported products from the Viking period are unlikely to survive until today. Silk and embroidery, for instance, are only very rarely found intact.'[6]

Consequently, we should think of Scandinavia as an important end point of the Silk Roads, but we cannot usually identify the silk itself in modern archaeological deposits there. However, items other than silk (and silver) certainly reached Scandinavia and are evidence for the movement of goods from the East. One of the most striking of these being a copper-alloy Buddha figurine, probably made in the Swat Valley in modern Pakistan and excavated on the Swedish island of Helgö, in an early medieval context.

From Bulgar, the eastern trade route continued south to Itil, the capital of the Khazar people, and then to the Caspian Sea. The communities on the shores of the Caspian were then accessible for trade or raiding. Alternatively, camel trains travelled from Gorgan (in what is now Iran) to Baghdad.[7]

VIKINGS ON THE WESTERN END OF THE SILK ROADS: SLAVES, SILVER, SILK

According to an early tenth-century account by the Persian geographer Ahmad ibn Rusta (died 903), silk was not the only resource sought by the Norse as they pushed towards the Silk Roads. The Rus were 'nomadic raiders who would set upon Slavic people in their boats and take them captive'.[8] For the slavers, these human beings were the raw materials that they would convert into silver, in order to purchase Asian goods. The human cargo was taken to Khazaria or Bulgar, which (as we saw earlier) was a Silk Roads trading hub on the Volga.[9] There, humans and northern fur were turned into hard cash. As ibn Rusta described it: 'They [the Rus] sell them for silver coins, which they set in belts and wear around their waists.'[10] From Itil (the capital of the Khazar Khaganate), situated on the edge of the Caspian Sea, overland access to Baghdad (the capital of the Abbasid Caliphate) was available.[11]

There is some debate over whether the Vikings also transported Slavic slaves back to Gotland. However, slavery was integral to life there and probably included Slavic slaves. A compendium of Gotlandic law – called the *Guta Lag* – and usually thought to have been written down in 1220, includes rules regarding purchasing *thralls* (slaves). The way in which people were considered commodities is revealed in the fact that the law code allowed a purchaser to try out a slave for six days and, if not satisfied, to return them for a refund. In this way, people and livestock were given the same consideration. Poorly furnished burials, located on the edge of graveyards on Gotland, may represent the burials of such slaves.[12]

We are on surer ground at the other end of the Viking stretch of the Silk Roads, for here there is no doubt that Slavic slaves (usually young women) were a staple product used to get silver and silk. The tenth-century Arabic writer Ahmad ibn Fadlan (alive in the 920s) described Rus traders coming ashore on the banks of the Volga with slave girls and sable skins for sale. The Rus would then pray to their gods: 'I would like you to do me the favour of sending me a merchant who has large quantities of dinars and dirhams [Arab coins] and who will buy everything that I want and not argue with me over my price.'[13]

It is to the direct interaction of the Rus with these Islamic traders that we now turn. And this will involve evidence for Vikings in contexts both exotic and horrifically brutal.

VIKINGS WITH CAMELS

Writing in the late 840s,[14] the Director of Posts and Intelligence in the Baghdad caliphate's province of Jibal (in north-western Iran), Abu'l-Qasim Ubaydallah ibn Abdallah ibn Khordadbeh, recorded that a group of newly arrived foreign traders, who he called the '*ar-Rus*', had brought merchandise to Baghdad on camels. The newcomers claimed to be Christians. However, this may have been because this reduced their tax burden (being 'people of the book', rather than pagans). It may not amount to evidence for genuine early conversion, as ibn Khordadbeh specifically linked their religious claim to them paying lower taxes because of their (apparent) beliefs. What is striking is that these Rus traders had got as far as Baghdad in modern Iraq.[15] Vikings with camels!

They had arrived at the extreme end of the River Volga trading system that linked the Islamic world to Scandinavia. More to the point, they had appeared there in person. They were not just acting as middlemen, further up the supply chain. In this interaction with the East, they were actively plugging into the trading network of the so-called 'Silk Roads' that ultimately connected China with the furthest extremities of Western Europe. 'Vikings' and the 'Silk Road' are not concepts which are usually put together. But that is just one of the incongruous aspects of the world of Vikings in the East.

There is evidence they went even further. When ibn Khordadbeh compiled his work – *The Book of Roads and Kingdoms* (*Kitāb al-Masālik wa'l-Mamālik*) – he drew from the archives a range of evidence regarding the trade connections of a number of peoples who were of interest to the caliphate. It was this intelligence-collating activity that drew his attention to the Rus and their movements. If the journey to Baghdad seems extraordinary, there are even greater surprises that emerge from his trawling through the archives. The people he knew as Rus were reported as also travelling to Syria and Egypt. They had been noted further east, in Persia. Sailing through the Persian Gulf, they had reached lands described as 'Sind, India, and *al-Sin*'. There are debates over whether the last place named represented Tang China or the khaganate of the Uyghurs.[16] The Islamic intelligence report specifically refers to Rus travelling through Transoxiana (a Central Asian region that roughly corresponds to modern-day eastern Uzbekistan, western Tajikistan, areas of southern Kazakhstan, areas of Turkmenistan and southern Kyrgyzstan).

If Vikings in Baghdad sounded incongruous, then here we have Vikings in Central Asia, perhaps even Vikings in western China!

However, it is the more westerly edge of that eastern region that is of particular interest to us. In the ninth century, Viking trade ventures took them to Baghdad. In the tenth century, the nexus of that trade shifted, and Islamic and Rus traders then met directly at the large Volga markets of the Bulgars and the Khazars. This latter trade reached its peak in the 940s and 950s. Somewhere in the region of 30 per cent of all the silver dirhams that reached European Russia and the Baltic arrived in these two decades alone. This is testimony to the intensity of the direct trade with the Islamic East at this time.[17] By this point, the Vikings had long been familiar with the Khazars, paying a tithe of their goods to the Khazar *khagan* (ruler), settling disputes in Khazar courts, signing-off raids on Islamic settlements – in what is today Azerbaijan – with the *khagan*.[18]

Later rulers of the Orthodox Rus seem to have played down these earlier connections. By that time, the elites of the Khazars had converted to Judaism and such an intimate (earlier) connection did not play well with the new commitment to the Orthodox faith. But the evidence could not be disguised. In the tenth century, an Islamic writer described the Grand Prince of the Kyivan Rus as a *khagan* (a Khazar title); as late as the middle of the eleventh century, the metropolitan of the church in Kyiv itself also described the grand prince ruling from there as a *khagan*. It is clear that the early Vikings had had a close relationship with this nomadic Turkic people of the steppe.[19] They had earlier had a close relationship with the Islamic traders of Baghdad too. This is rarely mentioned today, when the image of 'Holy Rus' and its origins are discussed in Russian nationalist circles.

We would like to know a lot more about those early camel-leading (maybe even camel-riding) Vikings, who journeyed to Baghdad in the ninth century, but we need to turn to later (tenth-century) sources to get more of a picture of their descendants and of their society as it interacted with the Islamic world. When we do so, the picture we get of the Vikings of the Volga mixes the extremely shocking with the exotic. Perhaps the most famous – one could say infamous – of these accounts is found quoted in a later medieval Arabic source.

VIKINGS OBSERVED ON THE VOLGA

Yakut ibn Abdallah was an Islamic writer working in the early thirteenth century. One of his works was a geographical lexicon (a collection of geographical and ethnographic information), in which he quoted an older account written by the Islamic explorer ibn Fadlan referred to earlier. We will turn to that account in a moment, but first it is worth reflecting on ibn Abdallah's introduction to it. In that introduction, he wrote:

> Rus, written also Rs, is a people whose country borders on that of the Slavs and Turks. They have their own language, a religion, and a divine law, in all which they have nothing in common with any other people. Mukaddesi [another writer] says that they live on a pestilential island, which is surrounded by a lake, and which

serves them as a stronghold against those who seek to molest them. Their number is estimated at a hundred thousand. They have no crops nor herds. The Slavs conduct expeditions against them, and despoil them of their goods.[20]

His description of them as having 'nothing in common with any other people' suggests a community which was maintaining its Norse character and, in this, stood out from other people in the area: Slavs, Khazars, Bulgars. He went on to describe a Rus society that he clearly thought was fundamentally violent. How far this represented reality among these Norse who lived on the furthest eastern frontier, and how far it represented a stereotypical view of the violent and alien 'other', is open to question. But the anecdote is certainly striking:

> When a son is born to one of them, he flings down a sword, saying, 'Only that is yours which you win with your sword.' When their king pronounces judgment between two contestants, and they are not satisfied, he says to them, 'Decide it for yourselves with your swords.' He whose sword proves the sharpest is then the victor.[21]

After that dramatic anecdote, ibn Abdallah went on to quote a piece of writing which has since become extremely famous. The person he quoted was Ahmad ibn Fadlan.

Ahmad ibn Fadlan wrote an earlier *Risala*, a popular genre of travel literature written in the medieval Middle East. It is a first-hand account of his experiences as a member of the Abbasid Caliphate's embassy from Baghdad to the King of the Volga Bulgars, who had recently converted to Islam. The Bulgar ruler had requested assistance from Al-Muktadir, the caliph of Baghdad from 907 to 932. The assistance sought was Islamic missionaries to teach his people the faith of Islam, to erect mosques in Bulgar territory and to construct a fortress for the Bulgar ruler which would defend him against his enemies. Ibn Fadlan left Baghdad in June 921 and eventually arrived at the Bulgar king's residence in May 922. In just under a year of travelling, his journey was a roundabout one which went by way of Bokhara and the region between the Caspian and the Aral Sea, and eventually to south-eastern Russia, north of the Caspian. While travelling, he met Norse Rus traders camped beside the River Volga in the vicinity of the Khazar capital at Itil. This was probably in 922. The Rus made a strong impression on him, as is revealed in the vividness of his account of the meeting. It opens a window on the world of these Viking traders and slavers. It is both extraordinary and shocking:[22]

> I saw how the Rus had arrived with their wares and had pitched their camp beside the Volga River. Never did I see people so gigantic; they are as tall as palm trees, and florid and ruddy of complexion. They wear neither coats nor caftans, but the men among them wear a garment of rough cloth, which is thrown over one side, so that one hand remains free. Every one carries an axe, a dagger, and a sword, and without these weapons they are never seen. From the tip of the fingernails to the neck, each man is tattooed with pictures of trees, living beings, and other things.

The tattoos must have been particularly striking to an observer from a culture which disapproved of pictorial representation.

Their wealth was publicly stated in the ornamentation of their wives in displays of conspicuous consumption, in which silver and gold chains signalled riches: 'If the husband has 10,000 dirhams, he has one chain made for his wife; of 20,000, two; for every 10,000, one chain is added.'

Many of the habits of the Rus deeply shocked ibn Fadlan, and he went into detail in order to communicate this to his readers. Here are a selection of the things that he saw and which he wanted his readers to know regarding these tall, alien strangers:

> They are the filthiest creatures that God ever created. They do not wipe themselves after defecating or urinating, nor do they bathe after sexual relations or after eating.
>
> They are like wild asses.
>
> Each man has a raised platform where he sits with the beautiful women he has for sale.
>
> As likely as not he enjoys one of them while a friend looks on. At times several of them are busy in this way at the same moment, each in full view of the others.
>
> Every morning a woman comes and brings a tub of water and places it before her master. He proceeds to wash his face and hands in this and then his hair, combing it out over the tub. Then he blows his nose and spits into the tub. She continues carrying the tub from one to another, until each of those in the house has blown his nose and spit into the tub, and has washed his face and hair [in the same tub of water!].

Perhaps the most striking aspect of ibn Fadlan's description of the Rus is his account of what occurred at a funeral of a Rus chieftain. The cremation ceremony is reminiscent of what we know from archaeology of the Scandinavian homelands. However, the account by ibn Fadlan provides shocking details that cannot be known from the archaeology alone. Having read the way that the traders treated female slaves, we may have some insight into why some volunteered for a part in the funeral ceremony. They may have seen it as an escape. We would like to know their perspective on what happened. However, like most of the marginalised and abused individuals in human history, they have no voice and have left no record of their feelings. The account is detailed and this is a reduced version which conveys the main features of the event:

> When the man [a Viking chieftain] I mentioned above had died, they asked his slave girls, 'Who will die with him?' One of them answered, 'I.'
>
> When the day had now come that the deceased man and the slave girl were to be committed to the flames, I went to the river where his ship was, but found that it had already been drawn ashore.
>
> Then they carried him [the dead man] into a tent placed in the ship, seated him on the wadded and quilted coverlet, supported him with the cushions, and bringing strong drink, fruit, and basil, placed these all next to him. Then they brought in bread, meat and onions which they set out before him.
>
> The slave girl who had devoted herself to death meanwhile went back and forth, entering one after another of the tents which

they had there. The occupant of each tent had sex with her, saying, 'Tell your master, I did this only for love of you.'

[The slave girl is lifted three times above a door frame and spoke each time before being lowered.] The third time [she said], 'There is my master, who is sitting in Paradise. Paradise is so beautiful, so green. With him are his men and slave boys. He calls me; take me to him.' Then they led her away to the ship.

Then they lifted her into the ship, but did not yet admit her to the tent. Now men came up with shields and staves and handed her a cup of strong drink. This she accepted, sang over it and then drank it. By this time, as it seemed to me, the girl had become dazed.

At this moment, the men began to beat on their shields with their staves, in order to drown out the noise of her cries, which might have terrified the other slave girls and deterred them from seeking death with their masters in the future. Then six men followed her into the tent and had sex with the girl, one after another. Then they laid her down by her master's side, while two of the men took her by the feet and two by the hands. The old woman known as the Angel of Death now knotted a rope around her neck and handed the ends to two of the men to pull tight. Then with a broad-bladed dagger she stabbed her between the ribs, and drew the blade out, while the two men strangled the girl with the rope until she was dead.

The cremation of the dead, the ship and the assembled possessions then occurred. The account is as shocking as it is vivid. One wonders if the reason why the slave girl was 'dazed' was due to a drugging of her drink in order to make it easier to complete the brutal ceremony.

What is striking is that ibn Fadlan seems more shocked by the open way that the Rus had sexual relations with their slave women than with the actual fact of the non-consensual casual sex between Rus masters and their female slaves. It was the impropriety of the activity that shocked him, not the activity itself. But, of course, ibn Fadlan himself came from a society where there were many slaves (including Slavic women traded to Arab masters by the Rus). Though it would have been more discreet, we can assume that the non-consensual nature of sex between masters and female slaves was little different in the society of the caliphate compared with that of the Rus.

SEA BATTLES ON THE CASPIAN

Regarding a man who died in *Serkland* and who was commemorated back in Sweden on a runestone, his sons wrote of him: '*knari stur*' ('He could steer a cargo ship well'). Clearly, trading as well as raiding drew Vikings into the Islamic world. However, warfare too played a key role.

Viking fleets harried the shores of the Caspian as they did the shores of western seas. In 912–13, a huge raid devastated Muslim Caspian communities. As part of an agreement with the Khazars to allow the raiders to sail through the Khazar lands, the Norse had agreed to share half of their plunder with the *khagan* of the Khazars. However, things did not end the way that the marauders had anticipated. When news of the atrocities they had perpetrated against the – almost defenceless – civilians of the towns around the

Caspian percolated back to the Khazars, it so shocked them that they abandoned their alliance with the Viking raiders. They were so outraged at the Vikings' violence that they ambushed and destroyed the fleet as it returned home through Khazar territory.[23]

In addition, as we have seen, twenty-six so-called 'Ingvar runestones' – most of which are found in the Lake Mälaren region of southern Sweden – are named from Ingvar the Far-Travelled, who led an expedition to the Caspian Sea. This single event is mentioned on more runestones that any another event in Swedish Viking history, which testifies to its importance and to its impact on communities back in Sweden. Other evidence suggests that he and most of his companions died in 1041, some in a fierce battle fought at Sasireti in Georgia – to the west of the Caspian Sea – that involved Byzantines, Georgians and Scandinavian mercenaries. It is a reminder of how the Viking warriors and explorers became entangled with the complex politics and conflicts of the lands to which they sailed. And their skills in warfare gave them advantages both as mercenaries and as players in their own right.

The later Icelandic saga version of the Ingvar expedition talks of the Viking fleet on the Caspian being attacked by enemy ships armed with flamethrowers. These were probably Muslim vessels equipped with a version of the flammable 'Greek fire', employed by the navy of the Byzantine Empire and clearly now copied by its enemies. However, just as the exchange of slaves for silver and silk was based on cooperation between the Rus and Islamic traders, so some curious evidence suggests that other interactions could be peaceful as well as violent.

MUSLIM VIKINGS?

The Vikings were highly adaptable. Despite the dramatic northern traditions communicated by the cremation ceremony described earlier, the Norse frequently adapted to the cultures of the peoples among whom they settled.

It is possible that some of the Volga Vikings may have converted to Islam. Ibn Fadlan, in the tenth century, refers to a group of people he called '*al-baringar*', who had converted to Islam. It is very likely that this name represents an Arabic version of '*Varangian*'.

Many centuries later, the writings of Amin Razi (who died in the early seventeenth century) preserve accounts of Rus converts among the Volga Bulgars. He noted that these converts continued to eat pork, despite its prohibition as a Muslim food.[24] Clearly, they had preserved non-Islamic eating habits for centuries after they converted. If they were, indeed, the descendants of the '*al-baringar*', then their old habits had lasted for over 600 years.

CHAPTER 9

A NEW SLAV STATE AND THE LAST HURRAH OF THE VIKINGS

By the time of the baptism of Vladimir the Great, in 988, there is an argument that it 'no longer makes sense to refer to the Rus as Scandinavians, as most of them had been living along the Dnieper and Volga for many generations'.[1] They had become a distinct hybrid people. Even earlier, from the time of Svyatoslav I (died 972), the rulers of the Kyivan Rus had been taking on the Slavic customs of their subjects. To this cultural adaptation can be added the Byzantine characteristics that became very visible during the reign of Vladimir the Great (ruled as grand prince: 980 to 1015). In fact, the coins that were produced during his reign 'differ significantly from those of his Scandinavian contemporaries, instead resembling the coins produced by Byzantine emperors like Basil II and Constantine VIII'.[2]

Consequently, as the state of Kyivan Rus developed, it rapidly lost its distinctive Norse character. With the Rus state established as a serious player in southern Russia, rulers increasingly recruited mercenaries from the nomadic steppe peoples who lived further east. Such steppe cavalry was more mobile and so had the edge over the foot-soldier Varangians, who fought in the traditional Viking way as axe-wielding infantry. In 1024, for example, at the Battle of Listven, such infantry were defeated by these nomadic auxiliaries. The battle was fought in the aftermath of a Kyivan succession crisis (1015–19) which followed the death of Vladimir the Great in 1015. The battle was fought between his sons Mstislav of Chernigov (Ukrainian: Chernihiv) in northern Ukraine and Yaroslav the Wise (who was backed by the resources of Kyiv and had become ruler there in 1019). The battle was something of a stalemate. As a result, the brothers divided control of Kyivan Rus, with the Dnieper River being the frontier between them. Yaroslav ruled the western or 'right bank' and Mstislav ruled the eastern or 'left bank' (from his base at Chernigov). This continued until Mstislav died in 1036. After this, Yaroslav was sole ruler of Kyivan Rus until his death in 1054.

The key thing about the earlier battle was the impact of steppe-nomad allies on the fighting at Listven. This was a signpost to the future. The age of Vikings in Russia, as effective infantry warriors, was drawing to a close.

The growing cultural Slavic orientation of the Rus was clearly seen by the reign of Yaroslav the Wise. His court was thoroughly Slavic in character. It was under his rule that the power and wealth of Kyiv grew considerably. It was then that the Golden Gate was built at Kyiv, with its tiered battlements as a symbol of the grandeur of the distinctive Kyivan Rus state. Times were changing. A new Slavic state was emerging.

THE LAST HURRAH OF THE VIKINGS?

Despite these developments, the Rus did not completely lose their Scandinavian connections, and their Norse origins were not entirely forgotten. And there were still plenty of Norse adventurers and traders to be found in both Kyiv and Constantinople. However, while the first Viking travellers to the East had come as traders, the ones who travelled there from the middle of the tenth century frequently came as mercenaries. These were the famous Varangians, who frequently appear as the bodyguards of the Byzantine emperors and in the retinues of high-ranking Byzantine officials. Such Varangians had assisted Vladimir the Great to take power in 980 and their fighting talent would continue to play an important role in the policies of the Grand Princes of Kyiv.

It would be wrong to just view these warriors as simply hired 'muscle', because many of the Varangians were Scandinavian aristocrats. They appeared in the East as political exiles or in search of prestige and a fortune (often accrued to fund military activities back home).

Many used this as a base from which to return to Scandinavia and pursue their royal claims there. As a result, the connection between the homelands and Kyivan Rus continued even as the latter was becoming increasingly Slavic in its culture. And it could go both ways. When Grand Prince of Kyiv Svyatoslav I died in 972, his son Vladimir (the future Vladimir the Great) was forced to flee to Scandinavia, where he enlisted help from his uncle, before returning to the East and taking the throne of Kyiv in 980.

Back to the northern exiles who went to the East. Both Olaf Tryggvason (King of Norway 995–c.1000) and Olaf Haraldsson (King of Norway 1016–28, when he was expelled, who was then killed in 1030 when he attempted to retake the throne) had earlier spent time as exiles at the court of Vladimir the Great in Kyiv. According to later legend, it was there that Olaf Tryggvason learned military skills. Olaf Haraldsson had ended up in Kyiv because he was offered refuge there with his Swedish wife's relatives.

Another famous Norwegian king, who earlier served as a Varangian, was Harald Hardrada ('hard-ruler' in Old Norse), who served both the Kyivan ruler Yaroslav the Wise and the Byzantine emperor in the years between 1029 and 1046. Only then did he return to Norway, 'with boats laden with gold'[3] that financed his efforts to force a political compromise there which resulted in him becoming co-ruler of Norway alongside a ruler named Magnus the Good. Clearly, Eastern treasure could still fund an elite Viking lifestyle – and a lavish one at that! His is a very dramatic story and, arguably, represented the last great hurrah of the Vikings in the East.

While in the East, Harald Hardrada married Elizabeth, the daughter of Yaroslav the Wise. Her mother, Ingegerd, was a distant relative of Harald and she was also the granddaughter of King Olof Skötkonung of Sweden. Once again, we see the continuing northern connection, at least among the elites.

Harald trod a well-worn path. Earlier, Harald's half-brother Olaf Haraldsson had been in exile among the Rus following his expulsion from Norway in 1028, as a result of the warfare which often divided early Scandinavian kingdoms. Although now thoroughly Orthodox Christian and Slavic in culture, there was clearly still a lingering Rus tradition of connection with the distant homeland in Scandinavia. Harald was eventually to return home, seize the crown of Norway and then die at the Battle of Stamford Bridge in September 1066 (the battle which preceded the more famous Battle of Hastings that October and which led to the Norman Conquest). Before that, the deeds of this future King of Norway took him to a very different kind of world in the eastern Mediterranean. His activities there were later recalled in several thirteenth-century sagas. One of these was the *Catalogue of Norwegian Kings* (*Nóregs konunga tal*), which was written, possibly in Trondheim, Norway, early in the thirteenth century.[4] While the accounts of Harald's time in the East have legendary features, they clearly recall a general picture of the exploits of the man while he was there.

After some time in exile among the Kyivan Rus, Harald travelled south to Constantinople. There he sought employment for himself and his men as mercenaries. It was a well-travelled road. The naming of Empress Zoe and Emperor Michael (Michael IV the Paphlagonian) in this account suggests that Harald's transfer to the Byzantine capital occurred sometime between the years 1034 and 1041. Having entered imperial service, Harald then campaigned in Africa and Sicily, where he indulged in 'the harsh sport' (a typical Norse poetic allusion to warfare).[5] It is a geographical context in which we would not normally expect to find Vikings operating.

After this theatre of conflict, he then travelled to Jerusalem. There, we are told, his military skills resulted in the region coming under his control. How much this represents what a thirteenth-century compiler thought was a suitable achievement for a tough Christian king, and how much it reflects reality, is now hard to say. What we can conclude is that this later tradition opined that, as a result, it could be expected that 'the mighty king's soul [would] live ever with Christ in the Heavens where it is well pleased'. While campaigning in the Holy Land, Harald bathed in the River Jordan, 'as was the pilgrim practice', and made gifts to the Church of the Holy Sepulchre. We are specifically told that he gave gifts to the shrine of Christ's tomb and the relic of the 'True Cross'. He also imposed order on the road from Jerusalem to the Jordan and executed robbers who threatened those travelling along this road.[6] This Viking warrior thus combined Christian piety with energetic rule.

What occurred next is clearly the stuff of legend and designed to catch the attention of readers. On returning to Constantinople, Harald allegedly became caught up in a love triangle. This involved himself, the Empress Zoe and a noblewoman named Maria. As a result of these improprieties, he was imprisoned. But the story then takes on an even more legendary tone. We are told that he was eventually rescued from prison by a widow who had been ordered to save him by St Olaf of Norway. This St Olaf was none other than Harald's half-brother Olaf Haraldsson. Having been killed in battle in 1030, Olaf Haraldsson had rapidly been sanctified in popular Norwegian thought as a Christian ruler fighting pagans among his own people (he was canonised in 1031) and as a defender of Norwegian identity against interfering Danes. That his enemies in 1030 had included rebellious Norwegians rather muddies the waters in this pool of Norwegian national sentiment. Be that as it may, we are told that he (as a saint) intervened from heaven to free his brother. In another aspect of northern connectivity, he became the last Western saint who was accepted as such by the Eastern Orthodox Church.

Back to the prison break. Harald woke up his men – who were still in the emperor's service – and they seized the emperor and blinded him. It was a horrifying act which was frequently used to make a person ineligible for royal office. They then hanged those Varangians who remained loyal to the (now deposed) emperor. The later Norwegian tradition claims that the emperor who was so brutally ill-treated was Constantine IX Monomachos. However, the tradition has become confused because it was, in fact, Emperor Michael V Kalaphates (the predecessor of Constantine IX Monomachos) who was deposed and blinded in 1042. Just what part Harald really played in these events of (quite literally) Byzantine intrigue is hard to decide. The later tradition claimed that he was the one who was responsible for both the deposing and the blinding of the emperor. This, though, may simply give him too much agency in what was a palace coup.

Despite this doubt, we can say with some confidence that Harald was involved in the intrigues and politics of the Byzantine court. We can be fairly sure of this because another source confirms the high military rank that he held at this time. A late eleventh-century source, called in Greek *Word of Wisdom* (*Logos Nouthetetikos*), recounts how Harald served Emperor Michael IV the Paphlagonian and Emperor Michael V Kalaphates and – while in their service – he fought for the imperial cause in Sicily and Bulgaria. He was granted honorific titles within the Byzantine court. These had originally been ranks within the emperor's bodyguard, so they may reflect a memory of real military titles accorded to Harald. Interestingly, the account in *Word of Wisdom* makes no mention of him being part of an insurrection but does say that, when Emperor Constantine IX Monomachos came to the throne, Harald asked permission to return to his homeland but was refused. Despite this imperial blocking of his wishes, we are informed that Harald 'slipped away' and returned to Norway. We are also told that Harald 'did not complain about the titles' he received in Constantinople, which might suggest that they were later thought unfitting for a man who was eventually a king himself. However, this shows the benefit of hindsight, since nobody at the time knew Harald would be successful in his bid for power back in Norway. Furthermore, we are told that Harald continued to show 'good faith and brotherly love towards the Romans [the Byzantines]'. This was clearly written to remind the readers of the bond between Christian rulers who had once fought on the same side in a distant eastern land.[7]

IN THE FOOTSTEPS OF HARALD HARDRADA

The Kyivan, and then Mediterranean, career of Harald Hardrada vividly illustrates the opportunities open to Christian Vikings who were in the pay of both the grand prince in Kyiv and the Byzantine emperor in Constantinople. Many runestones in Sweden refer to men who not only travelled to Eastern Europe and the Islamic East (to *Garðar* and to *Serkland*) but also went into the Byzantine Empire. One traveller was commemorated at Fjuckby who was involved in trade rather than fighting. We know this because he 'captained a merchant ship [to] Greek harbours'.[8] But such Eastern adventures

– whether they were military or mercantile – could be dangerous, as the brothers of Gulli's wife discovered, since both of them 'met their deaths on active service in the east'.[9] The phrase used on this runestone, translated as 'active service', was '*i liði*' in Old Norse. It literally meant: 'in an army' and used the same Viking military term used at Ed to describe the military career of a man named Ragnvald. These runestones underscore the point that Harald Hardrada was not the only Christian Viking who embarked on the long and perilous journey to Kyivan Rus and then onward to the eastern Mediterranean for the military opportunities that beckoned there. These were opportunities which were now more than ever open to Christian Vikings who could take military service with Kyivan Rus rulers and Greeks (Byzantines) who were now co-religionists (albeit Orthodox ones, the Norwegians being Roman Catholics).

Despite this, the relationship of the more northerly state of Kyivan Rus with Scandinavians such as Harald Hardrada was complex and could be ambiguous. On one hand, these northerners were useful swords for hire. It was Viking muscle, after all, which had helped Vladimir the Great seize the throne of Kyiv. On the other hand, Vladimir was a wily operator and he did not want these Viking mercenaries hanging around and causing trouble in Kyiv. So, he kept a few in his service there but sent the rest on to Constantinople. Yaroslav the Wise did the same with Harald Hardrada. The violent northerners were welcome – up to a point. However, there were limits to the welcome. As well as not fully trusting these volatile Varangians, there were (as we saw earlier) now other swords (and lances) for hire. Now that Kyivan Rus was firmly established as a serious player in southern Russia, the grand princes in Kyiv had several options open to them when it came to raising armies. As we saw earlier, increasingly the advantage in military recruitment lay with recruiting mercenaries from the nomadic steppe peoples who lived further east and fought from horseback. The Viking way of war was approaching the end of its shelf life.

THE WAY OF HOLINESS TO THE EAST

Military men were not the only Norse travelling to the East. Others who journeyed to the Byzantine Empire and the neighbouring states included those travelling there due to Christian piety. Their memorials are also found in Sweden. At Staket, a women named Ingurin had engraved that 'she intends to travel eastwards, as far abroad as Jerusalem'. In contrast to the runic memorials, we can assume that this was the vow of a pilgrim to travel to the sacred Christian places of the Holy Land. Some died while on this holy mission. When Æstrid's husband, named Östen, took the same road, we are told on a runestone that 'he went out to Jerusalem and died in Greece'.[10] This memorial, at Brody, was accompanied by a second one that was raised by the man's son and which was built into a bridge.[11] These glimpses of Scandinavians travelling on pilgrimage to the Christian shrines of Jerusalem contrast with the image of Vikings on journeys of plunder in the East, of Volga slave traders or even simply of those selling their swords and axes to foreign rulers. Not everyone who travelled to the East had violence or acquisition of wealth on their minds. Some northerners travelled there prayerfully and for the good of their souls.

OTHER LINGERING CONNECTIONS WITH NORTH-WESTERN EUROPE

The lingering connections with north-western Europe revealed themselves in other – equally surprising – ways. When Cnut of Denmark (he of the legendary wet feet in the rising tide) seized power in England in 1016, his accession led to the children of the last Anglo-Saxon king, Edmund Ironside, being sent out of the country. This 'Viking Conquest' of England in 1016 (which lasted until 1042) has been so overshadowed by the later 'Norman Conquest' of 1066 that it is virtually unknown in popular culture in modern England. Yet the earlier one led to some surprising connections with the world of the East.

The children of Edmund Ironside eventually ended up in Hungary. Only at that kind of distance from England were they judged to be safe from the long arm of Cnut's murderous influence. Edmund Ironside left behind two infant children: who are remembered as Edward Ætheling and Edmund Ætheling. The Old English word ætheling meant 'royal family member' or 'prince'. A later (twelfth-century) English chronicler, named John of Worcester, says that, in order to remove these rivals from the scene:

> [Cnut] sent them after a short passage of time to the king of the Swedes to be killed. He would by no means acquiesce in his requests, although there was a treaty between them, but sent them to the king of the Hungarians, Solomon by name, to be preserved and brought up there.[12]

John of Worcester then goes on to say that, in Hungary, Edmund *Ætheling* died but that Edward *Ætheling* married a woman named Agatha, the daughter of the brother of the Holy Roman Emperor Henry III (reigned as emperor: 1046–56). From this marriage, they had three children: Margaret (who later married the King of Scots), Christina (who became a nun) and Edgar *Ætheling*. It is conventional to call Edward *Ætheling* 'Edward the Exile' after his exile to Hungary and his foreign-born son: Edgar *Ætheling*. What is intriguing is that there seems to have been a Rus connection in the mix.

One of the sources recording this distant movement of the children into exile was written by Geoffrey Gaimar, who was active in the mid-1130s (and so was a contemporary of the chronicler John of Worcester). In his *History of the English* (*L'Estoire des Engleis*) – written *c.*1136–40 – he says that the æthelings travelled from Sweden to Russia. After five days of travel, they reached a settlement that Gaimar called '*Gardimbre*'. There they were met by the Hungarian king. Gaimar records that, having eventually settled in Hungary, the elder ætheling married the King of Hungary's daughter.

There have also been other suggestions that the young æthelings were taken from Sweden to Kyiv, before eventually ending up in Hungary,[13] that concur with the account by Gaimar. This line of argument rests on a number of points. The first is the well-established Viking connection between the Baltic and the Black Sea via Russia and Kyiv. The second is that the King of Sweden was related by marriage to the ruler of Kyiv. As we saw earlier, Olaf Haraldsson of Norway had been in exile among the Rus due to this royal connection. Third, the German chronicler, Adam of Bremen (writing between 1073 and 1076), specifically says that the æthelings were taken to Russia. Fourth, Gaimar's settlement named '*Gardimbre*' clearly was a confused form of the Old Norse name *Garðaríki* ('kingdom of the towns'), used to identify the trading settlements founded by the Rus. Finally, there is also a reference to exile in Russia found in the so-called *Laws of Edward the Confessor* (*Leges Edwardi Confessoris*), an early twelfth-century commentary on English law.[14] If all this is correct – and it seems persuasive – the journey into exile was via Denmark, Sweden, Russia and then, eventually, arriving in Hungary.[15]

While in Kyiv, or in Hungary, Edward the Exile married the woman named Agatha. She is variously described as: (a) a relative of the Holy Roman Emperor (in the *Anglo-Saxon Chronicle*, by the later chroniclers John of Worcester, Simeon of Durham, Ailred of Rievaulx and Matthew Paris); (b) daughter of the King of Hungary (by the chroniclers Orderic Vitalis and Gaimar); (c) sister of the Hungarian queen (by the chronicler William of Malmesbury); and (d) a women of noble or royal family in Kyivan Rus (in the *Laws of Edward the Confessor* and by the chronicler Roger of Howden).[16] 'The range of options is rather striking, to put it mildly.'[17] What is beyond dispute is that Edward the Exile became drawn by marriage into the power politics of Central Europe and this probably included some time spent among the Kyivan Rus.

He and his son eventually returned to England in 1057. However, Edward the Exile swiftly died. His son, Edgar *Ætheling*, was a teenager and so, when King Edward the Confessor died in January 1066, a non-royal strongman, Harold Godwinson (he who died at the Battle of Hastings in October that same year), took the throne.

The rest, as they say, is history. But it was a history route that went via the Rus in the East. And it might have included marriage to a princess of the Rus.

Later, Anglo-Saxon warriors, who saw no future for themselves in England after their defeat at the Battle of Hastings, trod the well-worn path to join the Varangian Guard. Many of them will have travelled by the northern route through Kyivan Rus. In that way, the Vikings of the East and the world of the Battle of Hastings are also intertwined.

ENTERING TROUBLED WATERS

After the death of the Grand Prince of Kyiv, Yaroslav the Wise, in 1054, the golden age of Kyivan Rus became increasingly overshadowed by growing political instability. In the period after his death, the regional elite families among the Rus frequently challenged the power of the grand princes.

As a result of this, a complex succession strategy developed. Rather than passing from father to son ('primogeniture'), the throne of the grand prince passed down the line of remaining brothers. Only once this had been exhausted did it pass to the next generation. A succession caused all on the ladder of the principalities to move up the hierarchy. It was as if, having secured control of the engine, everyone else (well, in the princely hierarchy, anyway) moved up a carriage. This was 'collateral succession' and it tended to make political unrest endemic at a succession, due to the constant pre-existing rivalry within the members of the extended Kyivan royal family, with attendant and predictable political turbulence.

A NEW SLAV STATE AND THE LAST HURRAH OF THE VIKINGS

When the grand prince died, a large group of power-hungry princes were on the prowl. It was not until 1097 that this was regularised so that collateral succession only applied to rule of Kyiv itself (the ultimate prize). The other princely domains became fixed in the possession of particular branches of the ruling family. Nevertheless, these internal rivalries broke up what had once been a unified and very large political unit, whose influence stretched from the Baltic to the Black Sea and beyond.

After the reign of Yaroslav the Wise, there was a particularly prolonged and complex period of infighting with far-reaching repercussions. The political instability accompanied a reduction in the power of Constantinople and a decline in trade with the Byzantine Empire. This added to the weakening of the power of Kyiv, which had acted as the main conduit of the north–south trade route.

During the twelfth century, Kyiv stagnated and suffered continued political fragmentation. This was now a pronounced feature of the Rus state because 'Kyivan Rus was a loose dynastic federation of principalities rather than a kingdom in the European sense'.[18] Earlier movements towards the unification of power had failed to gain sufficient traction and had stalled. Consequently, the grand prince in Kyiv had limited clout elsewhere. By the time the twelfth century dawned, Kyiv had come to have limited (or no) authority over other Rus towns and polities such as Suzdal, Ryazan, Smolensk, Chernigov and others.

However, the original Rus centre of Novgorod grew increasingly more influential and independent. It continued to benefit from the trade route between the Baltic and the Volga and it enjoyed closer access to the trading powerhouses of the German coastal towns of the Hanseatic League. Finally, in 1136, it broke free from the control of Kyiv and became an independent city republic, with the title of 'Lord Novgorod the Great'.

By that time, the Viking roots of Kyivan Rus were far in the past, but their legacy would continue to be debated for centuries. What is beyond dispute is that the disunity outlined above could not have happened at a more dangerous moment in the history of Eastern Europe. A terrible destruction lay just ahead; a time of devastation which would radically change Eastern Europe and which would have huge implications for the cultural and political balance of power in Russia and Ukraine for centuries to come. Bad as things were for the Kyivan Rus in the twelfth century, far worse things lay ahead in the thirteenth. Unbeknown to them at the time, the Mongols were coming and, after their arrival, Kyiv would not be the same again. A great shadow was about to fall across the lands of the Rus.

CHAPTER 10

THE ECLIPSING OF KYIVAN RUS: THE CALAMITOUS THIRTEENTH CENTURY

As we have seen, during the twelfth century, the declining central power of Kyiv continued to accelerate. Nevertheless, the Rus principalities still dominated trade in the region and, ultimately, decline was not inevitable. There were positive ingredients, as well as potentially toxic ones, in the rather mixed cocktail of Kyivan politics at the time. Kyiv was increasingly connected by dynastic marriage to Western Europe. A balance of power between the crown and the nobles (the *boyars*) could have set it on a path of political development of a kind found during the Middle Ages in Western Europe. In towns, the assembly (the *veche*) began to develop embryonic powers of government. In Novgorod, for example, the *veche* elected the city's mayor after 1126. Within ten years, Novgorod was choosing its own prince. City states – similar to Venice – might have developed.[1] *Might* have developed; *could* have occurred. The possibilities of Kyivan development must remain speculative because the trajectory was halted. It was more than halted – it was smashed.

Nomadic Cumans/Polovtsy tribes, who had previously pillaged the eastern frontier settlements of the Rus, suddenly tried to develop peaceful relations with the communities they had previously attacked. It was a puzzling change in tactics, and it had a terrible causation. The attempt at reaching an accommodation with the Rus was a reaction to something more terrifying to the east. They warned the Rus: 'Terrible strangers have taken our country, and tomorrow they will take yours if you do not come and help us.' The 'terrible strangers' were the Mongols, also referred to as Tatars from the name used by some of the nomadic people involved.

STORM FROM THE EAST: THE MONGOL CONQUEST

The Mongol, or Tatar, armies appeared in force on the southern steppe lands in 1223. They swiftly overwhelmed the resistance of the Cumans/Polovtsy. The latter were a nomadic Turkic-speaking confederation, who were called the Polovtsy in Rus sources, the Cumans in Western records and the Kipchaks in other Eastern references. By 1055, the Cumans/Polovtsy occupied lands stretching from what is today Kazakhstan to the River Danube. Rus sources differentiated two distinct Polovtsy, terming them 'wild' (enemies to the Rus) and 'non-wild' (allied with the Rus). The nomadic animal-herding Cumans/Polovtsy clashed with the agriculturalist settlements of the Rus as these latter settlements expanded eastward. They caused problems for Rus farmers, but they were no match for the whirlwind of violence that had descended on them from the east.

In 1223, the same Mongol army next routed the Rus at the battle of the Kalka River, which was a historic defeat still remembered in Russia and Ukraine. It was the start of an escalating disaster which would culminate in the destruction of Kyiv itself in December 1240. But who were these Mongol invaders?

The army that swept into the southern steppe lands in 1223 and then vanished eastward, as fast as they had arrived, were a reconnaissance-in-force, sent into the region by their leader Chingiz Khan (also known as Genghis Khan). Born as Temüjin, in 1162 near Lake Baikal, in Mongolia, he brought the many nomadic tribes of Mongolia under his rule. In so doing, he created a disciplined military state committed to expansion, which targeted the settled communities who resided beyond the borders of his (nomadic) people. This led to a series of Mongol campaigns of plunder and conquest, which reached as far as the Adriatic Sea and Hungary in the west and the Pacific coast of China in the east. Mongol armies also advanced into the Middle East. There were failed attempts to invade Japan, by Kublai Khan of the Yuan dynasty in China, in 1274 and 1281. These attacks are the earliest events for which the Japanese word *kamikaze* (divine wind) was widely used. It described the two typhoons that disrupted the Mongol fleets.

The connectivity of this 'Mongol world', across vast distances, was astonishing. The Flemish Franciscan missionary and explorer Willem van Ruysbroeck (William of Rubruck) reached the vicinity of Qaraqorum (Karakorum) – the capital of the Mongol Empire between 1235 and 1260, located in modern-day north-central

Mongolia – in the mid-1250s. There he met a woman, originally from Metz (Germany), who had been captured in Hungary, c.1241, during a Mongol raid. In Mongolia, she had married a young craftsman from the Russian lands.² The distance between her original home and her final place of residence in Mongolia was immense. The reference to her Russian husband reminds us both of the international nature of the Mongol Empire and of the impact it had on the lands of the Rus, as well as on huge numbers of other peoples.

The effects of their conquests were devastating for all who attempted to resist the 'Mongol blitzkrieg'. Chingiz Khan used terror as a weapon against those resisting him or those who were contemplating it. The tribes he had welded together were known as the *Yeke Monggol Ulus*, in which the word *ulus* signified the lineages of the Mongols. All other peoples were termed the *irgen* or people. It was nomenclature that defined non-Mongols as 'the alien other' and these peoples could be subjected to extermination and deportation without hesitation. It should, though, be added that this same ruthlessness could also be applied to related steppe tribes if they stepped out of line. But the most savage treatment was usually reserved for the settled people of the *irgen*, if this advanced Mongol ends.³ The citizens of cities that refused Mongol calls to surrender were massacred in vast numbers when the cities were successfully stormed. This became standard Mongol practice. The power of horrifying terror – used as a tool of conquest – paralysed enemy forces. At other times, huge numbers who had surrendered might be killed for tactical reasons, as when the city of Balkh, in Afghanistan, surrendered promptly but was not spared mass murder. During the Mongol invasion of Khwārezm, in western Central Asia (1218–23), city after city was stormed and their civilian inhabitants massacred or used as human shields as the Mongol armies attacked further targets. A single act of resistance in conquered territory led to the massacre of all living in the area. Stories spread of single Mongol horsemen entering villages and killing peasants at random, in order to test loyalty and subservience. Of course, had the peasants struck back, more Mongol soldiers would have arrived and killed everyone.

While exact numbers are difficult to establish, it is clear that vast numbers died at the hands of invading Mongol forces. The Persian historian Rashid al-Din (lived 1247–1318) wrote of massive casualties. The Persian sources claimed that the Mongols killed 1.5 million people in the cities of Herat and Nishapur.[4] While these figures are almost certainly too high, it is clear that the numbers killed were huge. The Mongols themselves claimed to have killed 200,000 people when Baghdad fell to them in 1258.[5] The vast majority would have been unarmed civilians, who were systematically butchered. A North Chinese census in 1207 recorded 7.68 million households, while a Mongol census in 1236 recorded only 1.83 million. Even allowing for major undercounting in the later census, it is certain that 'a demographic catastrophe' had occurred.[6] It has been estimated that between the reign of Chingiz Khan in 1206 and that of Timur (Tamerlane) in 1405, 'the death toll from their military expeditions fell between 20 and 57 million people'.[7] The thirteenth-century English chronicler Matthew Paris, in his reports of what he had heard happening in the East, connected the tribal name 'Tatar' with 'Tartarus' (Hell) because of the terrible things he had been told.

The conquests of Chingiz Khan led to the establishment of the largest contiguous land empire in world history. As this occurred, the Mongols proved remarkably adaptable. At first, their armies were almost exclusively made up of fast-moving cavalry, but in time they co-opted the technical skills of the peoples whom they conquered or who entered into alliances with them. As a result, the later Mongol armies came equipped with siege engines, with which cities and fortifications could be stormed.

Despite their well-deserved reputation for appalling atrocities, the Mongols also created a tightly organised empire; established efficient government administration and tribute-taking structures; set up secure and swift postal communications across huge distances; expanded trade, craft and artistic production in areas under their rule; and allowed for cross-fertilisation of cultures and ideas across a vast area of the Eurasian landmass, from the Pacific to Central Europe and the Middle East. When the violence of conquest was over, these were features of the 'Pax Mongolica' ('Mongolian Peace') that followed.[8] This underlines the complex impact and legacy of these steppe nomads and their conquests.

The Mongol Empire did not disintegrate at the death of its first and most famous (infamous) khan. As a result, it would be a force to be reckoned with for centuries (and this included in Ukraine and Russia). In fact, the Mongol Empire was at its largest extent two generations after the death of Chingiz Khan.

It was eventually divided into four main units. These were the Yuan (empire of the great khan), which was its central and most important component; the Chagatai Khanate in Central Asia (c.1227–1363); the Golden Horde in Ukraine and southern Russia, whose influence extended into Central Europe (c.1227–1502); and, finally, the Ilkhanid dynasty in Greater Iran (1256–1353).[9] Of these, the Golden Horde will feature most prominently in the story that we are exploring. But first, there was the terrible violence.

THE END OF THE KYIVAN RUS STATE

What had been founded in the tenth century, by the descendants of Swedish Viking adventurers, disintegrated in the middle of the thirteenth century. The first Mongol incursion in 1223 left the Rus reeling with shock at what had occurred and struggling to comprehend what had happened. One chronicler wrote that 'we know neither from whence they came nor whither they have gone' and concluded: 'Only God knows that, because he brought them upon us for our sins.'[10]

In 1237, the Mongols returned. And this time, their numbers were even larger, including many allied tribes who had thrown in their lot with the Mongols (or had been forced to do this, to survive). An Arab chronicler described the invaders as 'a darkness chased by a cloud'.[11] Another chronicler commented that 'nothing could be heard above the squeaking of his [the Mongol] carts, the bawling of his innumerable camels, and the neighing of his herds of horses, and the land of Rus was full of enemies'.[12]

The new army was under the leadership of Batu Khan, grandson of Chingiz Khan. They swiftly destroyed the towns of the northern Rus. Ryazan, Suzdal and Vladimir fell to them in swift succession. After the siege of Kozelsk, which fell after a seven-week siege, a wholesale massacre was carried out of the inhabitants. The Mongol army then turned south, towards Kyiv itself. Batu promised that he would 'tie Kiev [as a captive] to his horse's tail'.[13]

In December 1240, the great city – seat of Holy Rus and Orthodoxy – fell to the invaders. All that had been built by the successors of Vladimir the Great was in ruins. After this traumatic event, 'Kiev went into a long, near terminal decline'.[14] Subsequent Mongol raids prevented the city from recovering. As a result, it shrank in size and became – in effect – three much reduced settlements. None of these bore comparison with what had existed before the disaster of 1240.

After the destruction of Kyiv, the Mongol army advanced into Hungary. It was then, and there, that they captured the woman who later met Willem van Ruysbroeck at Qaraqorum. How far they might have reached beyond this is a matter of conjecture because, at that point, an event threw their plans into disarray and Western Europe was spared their onslaught. In December 1241, the great khan – Ögedei Khan, the second ruler of the Mongol Empire and the third son of Chingiz Khan – died. When news of his death reached Batu, in the spring, he gathered his army and returned to Mongolia in pursuit of his claim to the great khanship.

The casualty figures resulting from this devastation of the Rus territories are hard to accurately ascertain. A Russian source, known as *The Tale of the Destruction of Ryazan by Batu* (*Povest' o razorenii Riazani Batyem*), described the effects. It was probably written not later than the middle of the fourteenth century[15] and was compiled from earlier texts. While the shaky historicity of key parts of its narrative reveals it is not a fully reliable documentary account, it still provides a vivid and raw insight into the impact of events and how they were remembered. Its compiler claimed that 'not one man remained alive in the city [of Ryazan]' and 'there was not even anyone to mourn the dead'.[16] When the ambassador of Pope

Innocent IV passed through Kyiv in 1246, on his way to a meeting with the Mongol khan, he described how 'we came across countless skulls and bones of dead men lying about on the ground'.[17] Overall, it is estimated that two-thirds of the towns of the Kyivan Rus were destroyed. As this occurred, the civilian population was either killed, enslaved or fled into the forests. Urban life collapsed. In 1470, what remained of the city of Kyiv was described as 'plain and poor' by a Venetian visitor.[18]

Batu did not succeed in his bid to become the great khan. Instead, he returned to the southern steppe lands and established his own state, which stretched from the Urals to Bulgaria and became known as the Golden Horde. The focus of rule in the lands of the Golden Horde lay in the eastern part of the southern steppe. Here they could dominate the silk routes which connected Samarkand, Baghdad and the Black Sea. From the capital of the Golden Horde, at Sarai (near the Lower Volga), the khan, his administrators and his army could exercise direct control over the eastern trade route but could levy tribute from the Russian populations living in what remained of the towns in the western forest lands. In this latter area of indirect rule, they established outposts of Mongol power where officials (*baskaki*), appointed by the khan, oversaw the collection of tribute and soldiers carried out terrible reprisals against any communities who were slow to pay. Between 1275 and 1300, the towns of Vladimir and Suzdal were each sacked five times as a result of this policy. It was a protection racket on a massive scale.[19] But it also illustrates the resilience of the Rus peoples, as the survivors rebuilt their lives and towns after each violent reprisal.

So began the period of time often referred to as the 'Tatar yoke' by Russian historians. All the surviving Russian princes were compelled to swear allegiance to the khan of the Golden Horde. Having done this, they were given a *yarlyk*, the khan's permission to rule. Where a succession to a Russian princedom was contested, the khan would give the *yarlyk* to the one who promised the highest level of tribute. These tributes occurred alongside the regular carrying out of censuses to ascertain the taxable wealth of the communities involved. An administrative procedure, which had been perfected in China (which was now under Mongol rule), was applied to the Russian lands, far to the west. The tithe extracted on this basis included people taken as slaves, as well as possessions given up to the Mongol tax collectors.[20] The Russian princes and nobles collaborated with this system in order to preserve both their positions and their lives. The exercise of indigenous *realpolitik* led to complicated compromises which are not fully represented in the later mythmaking. For example, the Russian Alexander Nevsky, prince of Novgorod and Pskov, is lauded in later Russian culture for his defeat of the Swedes in 1240 and of the Teutonic Knights in 1242. However, he also served the Golden Horde, suppressing rebellions against Mongol taxation and clearly regarded the Catholic West as a greater threat to his Eastern Orthodox lands than the distant Horde with their lack of interest in making interventions into religious matters.[21] As long as he was loyal to the Horde, he could continue to benefit from the trade routes to the Baltic – trade routes which had existed since the Viking Age. He was made a saint of the Orthodox Church in 1547 and continues to be held up, in Russia, as an example of how Russia sacrifices itself in order to save the West but gets little gratitude for it.

The Orthodox Church also benefitted from the period of Mongol rule in surprising ways. It was exempt from taxation and free from persecution, as long as priests prayed for the khan. Protected in this way, it was better able to Christianise rural areas and extend its influence. Peasants on church estates were free from the heavy Mongol taxation system and would not be coerced into military service for the khan, so they had an incentive to gravitate to these estates and come under church control. The 'Tatar yoke' was clearly complex and included ambiguous aspects. After the horrors of the initial conquest – which were very real – the Mongol overlordship does not always fit as easily into the official Russian narrative as that narrative insists.

THE EFFECTS OF THE MONGOL INVASION ON THE TERRITORY OF KYIVAN RUS

We have seen how the conquest of the great city in 1240 was catastrophic for the centre of Rus power. The political unity of the Rus lands, already severely compromised by internal rivalries, was broken. The Mongols recognised two centres of (tribute-paying) princely rule in what had once been Kyivan Rus. These were Vladimir–Suzdal (in what is today Russia) and Galicia–Volhynia (in what is today western and central Ukraine). Both claimed to be inheritors of the old Rus state. Also responding to the undeniable changes on the ground, Constantinople did the same with regard to the Orthodox Church and recognised two parts to what had once been an ecclesiastical whole.[22] Kyivan Rus was broken.

After the destruction of Kyiv, it was the prince of Vladimir who first emerged as the predominant ruler among the surviving Rus. The lands which had once constituted Kyivan Rus became culturally as well as politically divided by the impact of the Mongol invasions.

The lands of Galicia–Volhynia, to the south-west, were increasingly drawn into the political sphere of influence of Lithuania and Poland. Here Mongol rule was less intrusive than elsewhere and was, effectively, over by *c*.1350.[23] We will return to this important development in the next chapter, when we outline something of the history and significance of the Polish–Lithuanian Commonwealth to Ukraine from the sixteenth to the eighteenth centuries. Here the Rus were protected from Mongol attacks and continued to be closely linked to the West and also to Catholicism. This reorientation would have repercussions far beyond the Middle Ages and its impact continues to be felt in Ukraine today.

The north-eastern areas, of what had once been the lands of Kyivan Rus, entered into a significantly different arrangement and were set on a different political and cultural trajectory. In this area, ruled from Vladimir, before Moscow became the dominant force, Mongol rule was felt until *c*.1500. Because the prince of the city of Vladimir was the first of the Rus rulers to pledge allegiance to the Mongol khan, he was elevated by the khan to the rank of 'Grand Prince of Rus' and gained 'the right to install his *voevoda* [governor] in Kiev'.[24] As we have seen, later Russian historians would term this as being under 'the Tatar yoke'.[25] But here, princes – who were accorded a *yarlyk* by the khan – were regarded as the supreme rulers in their realm and owners of all lands and people residing there. It was out of this arrangement that Muscovy arose, with the pre-eminent urban settlement eventually being Moscow. In this state, 'patrimonial autocracy emerged from the Mongol occupation as a ruling principle', which would have huge significance for the kind of political system that developed in Russia under later tsars.[26] This was not entirely due to Mongol influence, but their rule accelerated pre-existing trends, while in the south-west various political and cultural features were encouraged by a different political set-up. 'In Crimea the Mongols facilitated a takeover by the Turkic-speaking Kipchaks that had started long before the Mongol incursions. Despite later claims, the Mongols did not bring the "Crimean Tatars" to the peninsula.'[27]

THE LONG-TERM IMPACT OF THE MONGOL INVASIONS

The Mongol overlordship and the rule of the Golden Horde, which emerged in the thirteenth century, brought huge changes to the region. With Kyiv destroyed, Moscow (first recorded in the Russian chronicles in 1147) became the centre of Russian Orthodox Christianity from 1325 onwards. While it continued to pay tribute to the khan of the Golden Horde until the late fifteenth century, the trajectory of history steadily moved in favour of this newly powerful Russian state and its allies. From a village in the mid-twelfth century, its position on the Moscow River (which linked it to the rivers Volga and Oka) assisted its rise to prominence as an important commercial hub by 1300. Populations fleeing Mongol activities to the east and south found that its forested and marshy surroundings made it a secure place in which to settle.

This rise of Moscow, as the successor state (Muscovy) to the one that had once been centred on Kyiv, ultimately led to the development of imperial tsarist Russia. As a direct consequence, the Russia of Muscovy would become the dominant political force in Eastern Europe. This took time to emerge and develop, but it was a clear break with the past and was made possible by the destruction of the (already weakened) Kyivan state. By 1350, its prosperity was such that its ruler Ivan I Danilovich (ruled 1325–40) – Grand Prince of Moscow (1328–40) and Grand Prince of Vladimir (1331–40) – was nicknamed *Kalita* (moneybag) and succeeded in making Moscow the most powerful, and richest, principality in north-eastern Russian territory. While he failed to secure the khan's support to take control of the major principalities of Tver, Suzdal and Ryazan, his close cooperation with the khan, in support of the Golden Horde, ensured the stability and wealth of his state and allowed him the opportunity to build a strong foundation for its territorial expansion. This he achieved more by the purchase of land than by military campaigns; although in 1327, he accompanied the khan on his military expedition against Moscow's chief rival, Grand Prince Alexander of Tver, whose subjects had risen in revolt against the khan. As with Alexander Nevsky (the earlier prince of Novgorod and Pskov in the thirteenth century), the success of Ivan 'Moneybag' was largely due to his careful management of relations with the Golden Horde and in ensuring the efficient collection of the tribute demanded by the khan.

Ivan's position was also strengthened because the ruler of the Golden Horde feared the rise to prominence of Lithuania, which had expanded into the western territories of the Kyivan Rus. The khan was ready to allow an increase in the territory of Moscow, in order to have it as a buffer vassal state against the Lithuanians and the Poles to the west. We will explore the significance of this in the next chapter.

Ivan also developed a crucial close alliance with the metropolitan (ecclesiastical leader) of the Russian Orthodox Church. The 'Metropolitan of Kiev and all Rus' transferred his seat from Vladimir to Moscow in 1325. It had earlier been moved to Vladimir in 1299 because of the Mongol invasions. This latest move of the head of the Russian Orthodox Church made Moscow the spiritual centre of all the Russian lands. What had once been the spiritually defining position of Kyiv (ever since the baptism of Vladimir the Great in the tenth century) had now shifted to the successor state of Moscow. It was a highly symbolic move and it cemented Moscow's position within Russian Orthodoxy. What followed in the history of Russian Orthodoxy was predicated on this movement.

Until as late as 1448, the Russian Orthodox Church was headed by the 'Metropolitans of Kiev' (despite the fact that, since 1325, they had been based in Moscow). However, in 1448, the Russian bishops first elected their own metropolitan without reference to the authority of the head of the Orthodox Church in Constantinople. From this point onwards, the Russian church was *autocephalous* (ecclesiastically independent). In 1589, the 'Metropolitan of Moscow' was elevated to the position of 'patriarch'. This elevation occurred with the approval of Constantinople. Moscow then stood fifth in line of honour within Orthodoxy after the patriarchs of Constantinople, Alexandria, Antioch and Jerusalem. A new chapter in the sacred history of Russia was being written.

This church primacy of Moscow within the Russian lands would last until January 2019 when – following the Russian annexation of Crimea in 2014 and its fostering of disaffection in the Donbas area of eastern Ukraine – the Orthodox Church of Ukraine declared itself independent of the Moscow patriarch. It was a move sanctioned by the ecumenical patriarchate of Constantinople (the honorary primate of all Eastern Orthodoxy). In anticipation of the formal declaration of Ukrainian church independence, of which the ecumenical patriarch had approved, the Russian Orthodox Church cut its ties with the ecumenical patriarchate of Constantinople in October 2018. Prior to this change, the Ukrainian Orthodox population had made up about 30 per cent of all the Orthodox believers under Moscow's patriarchate; so, its loss was highly significant, practically as well as symbolically. Ecclesiastical structures and roles which were rooted in the reign of the Viking–Slav ruler Vladimir the Great (in the tenth century), and revised (in the fourteenth and fifteenth centuries) in the aftermath of the Mongol destruction of Kyiv in 1240, had come to an end during the regime of Vladimir Putin in the twenty-first century.

THE LEGACY OF KYIVAN RUS IN MUSCOVY

So, how much did Muscovy owe to Kyiv of the Rus? A critical approach could suggest that the answer is: surprisingly little. Kyiv was smashed and the structure of Kyivan society was destroyed. What eventually re-emerged there from the wreckage had to reinvent itself. Continuity had been broken by the Mongols, and Muscovy had a very different political trajectory which, arguably, drew little on the earlier Kyivan foundations. 'Two hundred and fifty years of

Mongol occupation [it can be argued] had created a fundamental break between the two.'[28] In that sense, it might be said that 'it is absurd to claim that Kievan Rus was the birthplace of the modern Russian or Ukrainian state'.[29]

And yet... and yet... Connections are about more than institutional continuity. Inheritance is about more than lineal connectivity in terms of government and rulership. While later Moscow chroniclers and church leaders of the fifteenth century claimed descent from Kyiv, in order to both bolster their own legitimacy and lay claim to the lands that had once constituted Kyivan Rus, there was more to it than just opportunistic pragmatic posturing. Orthodoxy itself – which had been such a defining feature of the Kyivan Rus state – also became the defining cultural characteristic of Muscovy. When Constantinople fell to an Islamic army in 1453, the mantle of Russian Orthodoxy (already burnished by association with the golden age of Kyiv after Vladimir the Great) took on a whole new aura. For, if Kyiv had been closely associated with the 'Second Rome', then Moscow became the 'Third Rome'. And there would – it was asserted – not be a fourth! Continuity of ideology and identity was in the mix as well as Muscovite hubris.[30]

In that mythical deep story of cultural and ethnic continuity and inheritance, central to the enduring idea of Orthodox Holy Rus, what had occurred in the tenth century was of crucial importance. And even if the direct line of connection between that Orthodox Kyivan state and the later polities and communities of Russia and Ukraine was broken, it endured as a theme in the mind. When it comes to deep stories, their potency is as much dependent on *what is perceived* as on *what is*. Consequently, whatever we conclude about the strict details of continuity versus the novel aspects of what emerged from the wreck caused by the Mongol invasions, the myth of the Rus has continued to develop. Our story continues. The game was still in play for ownership of the legacy of the Vikings of the Rus. Then, as now, that inheritance was contested. This will become clear as the story of the Vikings in the East, and their complex legacy, continues.

CHAPTER 11

CONTESTED LANDS, 1300–1654

This chapter explores the contested nature of what is now Ukraine in the shifting alliances and turbulent politics that characterised the period from the fourteenth to the seventeenth century. In the beginning of this period, a Lithuanian army under Grand Duke Algirdas captured Kyiv in 1362; at its end, the Ukrainian lands became a Russian protectorate, by the Treaty of Pereyaslav in 1654.

LAYING FOUNDATIONS FOR LATER MYTHS

Viking characteristics might have faded in Kyiv by the eleventh century – and been long gone by the fall of Kyiv to the Mongols in 1240 – but the legacy of the Rus state that they had established continued to be influential in the development of the deep story of national origins in the successor state of Muscovy (Russia).

This grew alongside another idea that would run and run in the later history of Russia (and continues to reverberate into the twenty-first century) and that is that Russia sacrifices itself to protect the West but is never fully credited with it. The way in which the Russian lands had absorbed the shock of the thirteenth-century Mongol conquests, and the years of subjugation to Asian overlords, was very much part of this mindset. Later, the suffering in the First World War and then the horrors of the Second World War – in which vast numbers of citizens of the USSR died and the Red Army was responsible for the deaths of about eight out of every ten German soldiers who died – would feed into this perspective. This is an outlook that has been actively promoted in the Russian Federation of Putin since 2000. Like much in his view of the *Russkiy Mir* (Russian World), it has deep roots.

The twin myths of 'Holy Rus' and the 'Ungrateful West' are both ancient viewpoints. Both reach back into the period of the eclipse of the Rus state in the thirteenth century and what followed.

AWARENESS OF DIFFERENCE

Despite the catastrophe that overwhelmed the Rus in the thirteenth century and later (Russian) historiography – which claims that from this time onwards, those who subsequently called themselves Russians and Ukrainians in effect merged – things were much more complex. By the fourteenth century, Muscovites increasingly called themselves *Russky* and their political community *Rossiya* (derived from the Greek for *Rus*).[1] In contrast, those living in what is today Ukraine and Belarus in the later Middle Ages tended to self-identify as *Rusyny*. It is a term which frequently appears in English as *Ruthenian*. As with so much in the entangled ethnic and cultural history of Ukraine and Russia, the terms are related but not the same.

Earlier (in 1187 and before the Mongol invasion), the term *okraina* – derived from the Slavic word for 'periphery', 'borderland' – had first appeared.² It is a reminder of a regional identity which was rooted in the self-awareness of the earlier Kyivan Rus – of the great days of Kyivan supremacy, before the destruction of Kyiv at the hands of the invading Mongols. However, it was not originally a distinct *national* awareness, and it fluctuated over time. We should not read the past through the lens of current sensitivities regarding 'difference' – such sensitivities developed from the late nineteenth century, increased in the turmoil of the twentieth century and hugely accelerated in the wake of the violent expansionism of the Putin regime in the twenty-first century. History is more complex – and messy.

ENTER THE LITHUANIANS, THE POLES AND THE 'COSSACKS'

Today, Lithuania is a Baltic state. In the Middle Ages, it became something of an eastern superpower. As Kyivan Rus collapsed, and Mongol armies withdrew from direct occupation of its lands, the rulers of Lithuania moved to fill the vacuum. A warlike and still-pagan people, they had successfully resisted Germanic crusading movements. Now they expanded their territory southwards and, in a century, quadrupled the size of their duchy. It was an extraordinary achievement. In 1362, a Lithuanian army, led by Grand Duke

Algirdas, occupied what was left of Kyiv. In 1363, they defeated a Mongol army on a bend of the River Dnieper in the Battle of Blue Waters. As a consequence, Lithuanian territory stretched from the Baltic to the Black Sea and absorbed about half of what had once constituted the lands of the Rus.

As they did so, they allowed the surviving Rus nobility a surprising degree of autonomy. Many incoming Lithuanians became Orthodox believers. Ruthenian – the language spoken in the area – continued as a common language among the varied ethnic groups. In time, it would develop into the Ukrainian and Belarusian languages. The language – and the term – became increasingly associated with lower-class rural citizens. This continued until after 1918, and radically changed after 1945, when Poles were removed from the area by the Soviet government, as part of post-war forced population movements.

A major impact of these events was to tie the western part of the Rus area closely to that of the Poles. In 1385, the grand duke of Lithuania began negotiations for a dynastic marriage with the young Polish queen. In 1386, he was baptised (as a Catholic) and the marriage took place. This creation of two states with a shared monarchy eventually turned into 'The Most Serene Commonwealth of the Two Nations' in 1569, by the Union of Lublin. As a result of this union, huge areas of what is now Ukraine (including Kyiv) were ruled from the Polish capital of Kraków. Western Ukraine, which Russians would one day call part of 'Little Russia', became, for Poles, 'Eastern Little Poland' and open to a great deal of Polish cultural influence.[3] Although rule of this area by an independent Poland would be reduced in the middle of the seventeenth century, and then Poland itself would cease to exist in the eighteenth century (due to Russian annexation of large parts of it), western Ukraine would be closely associated with Poland for 500 years (first under Polish rulers and then under Russian tsars). It would only be after 1918 that this was radically altered. In this area, different ethnic groups would mingle, cooperate and – at times – conflict, in bewildering complexity. For many peasants, it felt like they lived in 'a sort of colony',[4] whether their landlords were Poles, local Ruthenian elites, Lithuanians or one of the other ethnic and linguistic groups who made up the nobility. From the sixteenth century, Polish identity in the area became increasingly identified with Catholicism and became a source of friction with the Ruthenian (aka 'Ukrainian') Orthodox population. Many in the western areas in question found themselves part of a hybrid 'Greek–Catholic' or 'Ruthenian Uniate Church', which was a form of Orthodoxy that accepted papal authority after 1596.

The Uniate Church considered (and considers) itself a successor to the church that was established in 988, following the Christian conversion of Kyivan Rus by Vladimir the Great. Needless to say, the other Orthodox believers did not see it that way and regarded it as a defection to Catholicism. The Uniate Church remains very influential in modern western Ukraine.

Other developments added to the complexity of these southern lands, which became something of a 'Wild South'. In the early fifteenth century, the grand dukes of Lithuania constructed a series of fortresses to protect their newly acquired territory from incursions by Tatar-ruled Crimea. The first garrisons were composed of Tatar mercenaries. But soon this wild frontier attracted a whole range of runaways. By 1500, communities of militarised settlers had evolved, which were semi-independent of Lithuanian rule. They elected their own leaders – *hetmans* – and met in an open-air assembly, the *Rada*. Perhaps the most famous of their stockaded settlements was the Zaporozhian Sich, located on the Lower Dnieper. It was like a new Sparta, as was observed by a seventeenth-century Venetian envoy. These settlers became known as 'Cossacks'.

The Cossack communities are now sometimes thought of as a forerunner to the later Ukrainian state – a kind of proto-Ukraine. The Ukrainian national anthem (written by Pavlo Chubynskyi in 1862), states: 'Soul and body shall we lay down for our freedom / And we will show, brothers, that we are of the Cossack nation!'[5]

However, the Cossacks, for all their dramatic image, lacked the structures, ideologies, organisation or ethnic makeup that might suggest that this was the case. Occupying the lawless lands of what are today eastern Ukraine and southern Russia, they took their name from a Turkish word meaning 'free man'.[6] The Zaporozhian Cossacks epitomised them. Another famous group were the Don Cossacks, living along the River Don. Fundamentally, as the modern Polish-British historian Adam Zamoyski succinctly put it: 'The Cossacks were not a people, but a way of life.'[7] Something of this definition would also apply to Vikings.

Under the Polish–Lithuanian Commonwealth, the government attempted to divert Cossack aggression against Muscovites, Tatars and other Cossacks. In 1578, more-settled Cossacks were granted payment in return for military service. Between 1600 and 1620, these Cossacks in royal service mounted naval raids against Tatar towns and even burned parts of Constantinople on two occasions.

The problem was that the Cossacks were never fully under control. They were inclined to rebel against Polish overlordship. Between 1591 and 1637, there were five such Cossack rebellions. However, none were as consequential as that which broke out in 1648 under *Hetman* Bohdan Khmelnytsky. Often mythologised in Ukraine as leader of the first Ukrainian war for independence, and in Russia as a fellow Slav who led Ukraine out of Polish control, the reality was that events were far too chaotic to fit into these neat later constructs. The uprising arose out of a personal response to an atrocity by a Polish rival against his family, which soon became a widespread campaign against landlords, royal officials, Jews and Catholics. Appalling massacres were carried out by his rebel forces, including vicious pogroms against Jewish communities. About 60,000 Jews were murdered in 1648 alone.[8] In later tsarist Ukraine, a statue was erected which presented him as a warrior who brought Ukraine back to Russia. The original design had envisaged him trampling a Polish nobleman, a Catholic priest and a Jew.[9]

Things turned against Khmelnytsky when his Tatar allies deserted him in 1651. To survive, he looked to Russia for assistance. This would turn out to be of huge historical significance. In 1654, at Pereyaslav, south of Kyiv, Khmelnytsky met the representative of Tsar Alexey and swore an oath of loyalty. It seems clear that Khmelnytsky thought the arrangement would secure him a continued semi-independent position under Russian overlordship and protection against the Poles. Later Ukrainian writers viewed the whole revolt as the creation of an independent '*hetman* state'. The Russians interpreted the matter very differently. To them, the 'Wild South' was being brought under tsarist authority. It was a 'union'.

That was revealed by the fact that the tsar changed his royal title from 'Autocrat of all Russia' to 'Autocrat of all Great and Little Russia'.

In 2024, when Vladimir Putin was giving a history lecture to an evidently bemused Tucker Carlson, he made clear the lesson that Russian nationalists drew from the events of 1654:

> Here are the letters from Bohdan Khmelnytsky, the man who then controlled the power in this *part of the Russian lands that is now called Ukraine* [author's italics]. He wrote to Warsaw demanding that their rights be upheld, and after being refused, he began to write letters to Moscow asking to take them under the strong hand of the Moscow Tsar.[10]

For Russian nationalists, this was not an alliance between different peoples. Instead, it was a homecoming, a reunification of the Rus. This is a narrative that is well developed in Russia and was not an invention of Putin. And it occurred because – following the Mongol invasions – Muscovy, ruled from Moscow, had become the dominant power in the lands that had once been part of Kyivan Rus.

THE RISE OF MUSCOVY

By the beginning of the fifteenth century, the hold of the khans of the Horde was weakening over the vassal Russian communities. Despite this, there could still be extended periods of great suffering. In 1408, a Mongol army, which was reputed to number 30,000 troops according to the Russian *Trinity Chronicle* (*Troitskaya letopis*), laid siege to Moscow. The invaders also burned the towns of Pereiaslavl, Rostov, Dmitrov, Serpukhov, Nizhnii Novgorod and Gorodets; and they occupied Klin in the Tver principality and Ryazan. When they finally withdrew, it was later claimed that each warrior of the Horde took forty enslaved Christians with him into captivity. It was said that blood ran from icons in Kostroma, where the Grand Prince of Moscow, Vasily Dmitriyevich, was sheltering from the attack.[11]

Yet the Horde's control over the Rus lands was declining. A fifteenth-century Russian source claimed to contain a letter of complaint from the ruler of the Horde to the Grand Prince of Moscow, which outlined how the latter had reneged on his tributary duties since the late 1390s. He had, it was alleged, failed to pay the customary taxes, not presented himself before the khan and had not sent his 'princes, senior or lesser boyars (*ni stareishi boliar ni menshikh*), his son or brothers' to the courts of the khans.[12] While there are debates among historians over exactly when Russian rulers adopted Mongol methods of administration and taxation,[13] what is clear is that they soon deployed them to their own advantage and not that of the khan. The rulers of Moscow had become a force in the land.

This had become apparent as early as 1380, when Grand Prince Dmitry of Moscow had defeated a Mongol army at the Battle of Kulikovo, near the River Don (modern Tula Oblast, Russia). He became known as Dmitry *Donskoy* (of the Don) following the battle. While the battle did not end the Mongol domination of Russia, it has become traditionally viewed as the point at which that domination entered a period of terminal decline. Weakened by bubonic plague in the fourteenth century, overshadowed by the new Turco-Mongol Central Asian empire of Timur (Tamerlane) between 1370 and 1405 and facing increasing resistance from the Russian princes, the lands of the Horde broke up into the three khanates of Astrakhan, Crimea and Kazan during the fifteenth century. Of these, the second one will feature at key points in our developing story and the peninsula became a flashpoint of conflict in 2014.

After 1380, Moscow progressively asserted its pre-eminence among the Russian principalities. This would eventually see it emerge as the central city in an increasingly united (and expansionist) Russian state. From the sixteenth century onwards, the battle became part of an ongoing Russian narrative which presented itself as the protector of Europe. It is a battle and a narrative frequently referred to by Putin in the twenty-first century. While Moscow would continue to be a vassal of the khan until 1502, it was effectively an independent state long before this vassal status ended.

THE EXPANSION OF MUSCOVY

Between 1462 and 1533, Muscovy experienced 'substantial growth in land and population, virtually tripling in size'.[14] In the south-west, it gained land through treaties with Lithuania. Muscovy annexed the principalities and republics of Iaroslavl (1471), Perm (1472), Rostov (1473), Tver (1485), Viatka (1489), Pskov (1510), Smolensk (1514) and Ryazan (1521). Most significant, though, was its annexation of Novgorod in 1478.[15] Later Russian historians would describe this as part of the 'gathering of the Russian lands'.

In the 1550s, Tsar Ivan IV Vasilyevich (known to later history as 'Ivan the Terrible') took control of the khanates of Astrakhan and Kazan (the Crimean Khanate would not be incorporated into Russia until 1783). Russian movement eastward into Siberia continued this expansion and would not be completed for several hundred years.

As this empire grew, changes in the state transformed Muscovy from 'a loosely organised confederation, roughly equivalent in structure to any of the neighbouring steppe khanates', to one 'with a quasi-bureaucratic administrative structure equal to that of any European dynastic state'.[16] It became a force to be reckoned with.

Things did not always go its way, though. During the 'Time of Troubles' in the early seventeenth century (caused by disputed succession), the Poles even occupied Moscow (to be expelled in 1612).[17] But the trajectory was generally upwards.

THE SHADOW OF THE RUS

Kyivan Rus might have fallen, but it continued to cast a very long shadow. When Ivan IV sought to bolster his claim to be the successor to the Grand Princes of the Kyivan Rus and the Byzantine Empire (conquered by Islamic armies in 1453), he turned to Vladimir the Great – the Viking–Slav ruler – as his claimed predecessor in this role. Ivan IV was named the 'Grand Prince of Moscow and all Russia' from 1533 until 1547 and was then called the first 'Tsar and Grand Prince of all Russia', in addition to the earlier royal title, from 1547 until his death in 1584.[18] 'All Russia' evoked memories of the ancient Rus state.

His reign typified the way in which the tsars of the emerging

Russia created an imperial image which was part Byzantine emperor (which took them directly back to Vladimir the Great) and part khan (a reimagined Chingiz Khan). It combined the spiritual authority of the former with the territorial expansionism of the latter. At his coronation in 1547, Ivan IV was crowned with a golden skullcap, trimmed with sable, inlaid with jewels and surmounted with a cross. It was claimed to have been a gift from the Byzantine Emperor Constantine IX Monomachos (reigned 1042–55) to the Grand Prince of Kyiv on his coronation. In reality, it was probably from the early fourteenth century and a gift from a Central Asian Mongol khan.[19] In further support for Ivan's claim to descend from Vladimir the Great (and ultimately from the Byzantine emperor) and so claim the right to rule all the lands of the Kyivan Rus, carvings illustrating this claimed pedigree decorated Ivan's throne in the Kremlin's Dormition Cathedral. The claim to Rus heritage was a politically charged one in Muscovy.[20]

During Ivan's reign, a centrally administered Russian state was created. This became the foundation on which he began the construction of an empire which included non-Slav states. In many ways, expansionist imperial Russia grew out of the reign of this ruler. As tsar, Ivan also fought long and largely unsuccessful wars, against both Sweden and Poland. There would be more of these in future reigns and their course would have profound effects on the relationship between the lands of the Rus, both those centred on Muscovy and those whose identity was centred on Kyiv. His policies, which were geared to imposing both military discipline and a centralised administration on his lands, accompanied a reign of terror against the hereditary nobility (the *boyar* class). Hence, from one perspective (state-building), he is often seen as 'Ivan the Great'. Yet from another (use of terror), he is also recalled as 'Ivan the Terrible'.

It will come as no surprise to discover that Josef Stalin was an admirer of Ivan IV. In a tense conversation with director Sergei Eisenstein, regarding his film *Ivan the Terrible*, in February 1947, Stalin commented:

> Tsar Ivan was a great and a wise ruler ... The wisdom of Ivan the Terrible is reflected by the following: he looked at things from the national point of view and did not allow foreigners into his country, he barricaded the country from the entry of foreign influence ... Peter I [Peter the Great] was also a great ruler, but he was extremely liberal towards foreigners, he opened the gate wide to them and allowed foreign influence into the country and permitted the Germanisation of Russia. Catherine [the Great] allowed it even more. And further. Was the court of Alexander I really a Russian court? Was the Court of Nikolai I [Tsar Nicholas I] a Russian court? No, they were German courts.[21]

We will return to this idea of the Romanovs as 'Germans' later (in Chapter 13) because it is directly relevant to the way in which the Viking Rus were considered from the eighteenth century onwards. But to briefly return to Stalin's praise of Ivan IV. 'One of the mistakes of Ivan the Terrible was that he did not completely finish off the five big feudal families. If he had destroyed these five families, then there would not have been the Time of Troubles.'[22]

Clearly, Stalin knew a thing or two about wiping out enemies, potential enemies and even those who had not yet opposed him. He was no stranger to terror as a political tool and he clearly felt that Ivan IV – the so-called 'Terrible' – should have been much more terrible.

What is also fascinating is the way in which the conversation – which must have been intensely uncomfortable for Eisenstein – then encompassed the Vikings of the Rus. Stalin's Foreign Minister Molotov was also present and chipped in with his own view on interpretations of Russian history. As with everything done by Molotov (for example, he said nothing when his wife was purged and sent into the Gulag system), it was in line with Stalin's view. Molotov never deviated from the line that was approved of by 'the boss'. Molotov added:

> It is necessary to show historical incidents in a comprehensive way. For example, the incident with the drama of Demian Bednyi's *BOGATYR* [a reference to Bednyi's 1936 opera *The Bogatyrs*, which mocked the tenth-century Russian acceptance of Christianity]. Demian Bednyi mocked the baptism of Russia, but in reality, acceptance of Christianity was a progressive event for its historical development.[23]

Stalin then added that, though Bolshevism was atheistic, the baptism of the Rus was 'progressive' because it orientated Russia towards Europe, rather than Asia.[24] It is a fascinating insight into the way that the Rus have been interwoven into the later deep stories of Russia. In this case, into that which became the official narrative of the USSR under Stalin.

Stalin would also have approved of the way in which Ivan IV deployed the Rus in his own use of history. In Ivan's propaganda efforts, Vladimir the Great, the tenth-century ruler of the Rus,[25] was a useful weapon to deploy against the Catholic Poles and Lithuanians who occupied the western regions of what had once been Kyivan Rus. Like Stalin in the twentieth century, and Vladimir Putin in the twenty-first century, Ivan used the Rus as potent symbols to be seized on in the name of Russian expansionism against rivals in the West. Vladimir the Great now became 'the first Russian tsar' and the 'gatherer of the Russian lands'.[26] All this bolstered both a political and a spiritual agenda, since it also enhanced Russia as the 'Third Rome', in succession to Constantinople. Viking origins (though the Norse had long been pushed out of the spotlight) and Orthodox faith were thus intertwined in the emerging myth of 'Holy Rus'. It was a potent image, which would run and run.

When Ivan IV died in 1584, the *Rurikid* dynasty, which claimed descent from the original Viking Age founders of the Rus state, was drawing to its close. His son Fyodor I Ivanovich ruled from 1584 until his death in 1598 but, dying childless, the *Rurikid* dynasty ended with him. Consequently, Russia descended into the infamous 'Time of Troubles'. This was a period of political crisis in Russia, beginning in 1598 and ending in 1613, with the accession of Mikhail/Michael I of the House of Romanov. The memory of it remains vivid in Russian perceptions of history and in the idea that weak leadership leads to chaos in the state. This is a view to which later Russian rulers – tsars, Bolsheviks, Putin – have subscribed. It is a key foundation of the Russian view of autocracy and authoritarianism promoted by later leaders and still a feature of the

Kremlin narrative. The 'little father' (whether tsar or later leader) knows what is best for the nation.

It is fitting that such a ruler as Ivan IV – with this Rus bloodline – should have made so much of the Viking Age history of the Rus state, even though he presented it as an indigenous phenomenon, rather than as a hybrid Norse–Slav one. Little did he know that his dynasty, whose deep story he promoted, had no future.

The matter of the use of the Rus in dynastic propaganda was taken a stage further when the Romanovs emerged as victors after years of civil war in Russia over the right to sit on the throne of the tsar. With no line of descent that connected them to the ancient rulers of Kyivan Rus (so recently promoted by Ivan IV), they had to work overtime to forge a connection. The Romanov dynastic founder, Mikhail/Michael I, had relics of St Vladimir (minus his head) brought from Kyiv to Moscow. The relics were placed in the Dormition Cathedral in the Kremlin and would remain there until 1917, when the Romanov dynasty (then represented by Tsar Nicholas II) would fall from power as a result of the first Russian Revolution (the Bolshevik one would occur later that same year).[27] As well as strengthening the Romanovs' projection of dynastic legitimacy, it also suited the strategic Russian aim of gaining control of Ukraine. And, as we have seen, that culminated in the famous oath sworn by the Cossack *hetman* in 1654.

CHAPTER 12

A PERSISTENT LEGACY, 1654-1783

As we have seen, in 1654 the Ukrainian lands became a Russian protectorate. However, far from bringing stability, this ushered in a new period of violence and turbulence. It also initiated a period that would eventually see the southern lands brought fully under Russian control. The Russian empress, Catherine the Great, finally dissolved the Cossack *hetmanate* between 1764 and 1781. She then annexed Crimea in 1783. It was very much a 'gathering of the Russian lands'. Or that was how it was seen from the vantage point of St Petersburg (the capital of the Russian Empire from 1710 to 1918, being replaced by Moscow, for a short period, between 1727 and 1733 and then again after 1918).

BECOMING PART OF RUSSIA...

Russia's expansion to the south drew it into thirteen years of devastating warfare with Poland and Sweden. In Ukraine, the destruction and chaos caused the period to be known as 'The Deluge' among

Poles and 'The Ruin' among Ukrainians.¹ The conflict with *both* Poland and Sweden was because these nations opposed any increase in Russian power and influence. On the other side, Russia regarded these states as blocking its territorial ambitions. The matter was also complicated by Sweden attacking Poland when it was to the advantage of the Scandinavian nation.

Vilnius and Riga were taken from Poland by Russia in campaigns fought between 1654 and 1656. Taking advantage of Polish difficulties, the Swedes swept south and captured Warsaw and then turned on Lithuania. This resulted in war with Russia between 1656 and 1661, as the Russians attempted to control Swedish expansion. By 1667, all three states were exhausted by the years of warfare. As a result, the Russians and Poles came to terms by the Treaty of Andrusovo. This divided Ukraine between them. Russia took the east of the region, including Kyiv; Poland took the lands to the west. While the treaty officially ended the war, sporadic fighting continued for a decade.² What was clear was that, in the latter part of the seventeenth century, 'Muscovy's military and diplomatic interests remained firmly focused on the south'.³

With Poland weakened, Turkish forces drove into western Ukraine in alliance with the Cossacks of the Zaporozhian Host. By 1670, the Turks had seized large areas of western Ukraine. With the Turks constituting a common enemy, the Russians fielded a large army against them and drove them out of Ukraine. This had been accomplished by 1681. In 1686, Russia signed a Treaty of Eternal Peace (also known as the Treaty of Perpetual Peace) with the Polish–Lithuanian Commonwealth. It was a momentous move as it brought Russia into alliance with the major European powers which were committed to stop Turkish expansion into Europe. As recently as 1683, the Turks had narrowly failed to capture Vienna. But now, the Polish–Lithuanian Commonwealth, the Holy Roman Empire, Venice and Russia united against them. The Russians promised to campaign against the Turks in Crimea.

Back to the 'Treaty of Eternal Peace'. Given that Russia would go on to take part in the three partitions of the Polish–Lithuanian Commonwealth in the eighteenth century (in 1772, 1793 and 1795), which ended the existence of independent Poland and Lithuania for over a century, it should be noted that 'Eternal' can be of shockingly short duration in international diplomacy. After it, it could be commented that 'like the Ukrainians, the Poles were now a nation without a state'.[4]

The Russian expansion into Ukraine (and Poland for that matter) brought it into contact with Western European ideas in art, architecture and religious rituals. The latter were largely derived from Greek culture. Those in Russia who opposed their introduction (self-styled 'Old Believers') regarded the liturgical innovations as evidence of the influence of Antichrist and a sure sign of the imminence of the end of the world.[5] That the Greeks had been overrun by an Islamic army in 1453 was proposed as clear evidence that God had rejected them and their way of doing things (if they differed from Russian practices).

Not for the first time – and not for the last – Ukraine was acting as something of a 'window on the West'.[6] There was, as there is now, intense push-back against this by conservative Russians. One has only to recall how Ukrainian Western associations have been bitterly denounced in Putin's Russia (by both the Kremlin and by extreme Orthodox nationalists) as evidence of everything from 'anti-Christian liberal debauchery' to 'neo-Nazism' to realise that such negative reactions to perceived Western influence have not lost their apocalyptic character. The Old Believer push-back would continue until the accession of the Western-orientated Peter the Great in 1682, after which it was eventually crushed, although it would continue to exist underground.

During the Great Northern War (1700–1721), fought between Tsar Peter the Great of Russia and King Charles XII of Sweden, Ukraine became a battleground once more.[7] The war was fought primarily over access to the Baltic coast, but the Swedes pushed south into Ukraine in the hope of gaining Cossack support (the Cossacks hoped to reassert their independence from Russia, curtailed in 1654) and taking control of vitally needed food stocks (the Russians having destroyed all resources as they retreated through Lithuania). In the end, too few Cossacks rallied, the Russians destroyed food stocks in the south and the Swedes were defeated at Poltava in 1709.

This all proved fatal to any hopes of reviving Ukrainian independence. From the Russian perspective, the Cossack *hetman* state was to be brought firmly under Russian control to ensure that Ukraine would no longer prove to be a weak point through which Western enemies could enter Russia. This anxiety was to echo through later centuries of Russian history, into the present day. The Cossack-run *hetmanate*, ambivalent in its relationship with Russia since 1654, was doomed.

A PERSISTENT LEGACY, 1654–1783

THE END OF THE UKRAINIAN *HETMAN* STATE

Russian control over Ukraine increased during the eighteenth century. In the 1760s, Ukrainian lands of the *hetmanate* were brought under the direct control of Russian miliary governors as Russian provinces. However, the process accelerated during the reign of Empress Catherine II, often called Catherine the Great (reigned 1762–96). Following victory over the Turks in 1774, Russia gained its first Black Sea port at Kherson, along with the Crimean port of Kerch on the Sea of Azov. That same year, Crimea became an independent Tatar state. No longer part of the Ottoman Empire, it was increasingly vulnerable to Russian expansionism.

At the same time, Russia claimed the right to protect the Christian Orthodox subjects in the European provinces of the Turkish Ottoman Empire. This accompanied a major reorientation south and the creation of Russia as a Black Sea power, as well as a Baltic one. Control of the Black Sea coast would both secure its frontier with the Islamic world and ensure that Russia was not solely dependent on access through the Baltic for maritime trade.

The territories north of the Black Sea coast were designated *Novorossiya* (New Russia). This term entered official usage in 1764. The area encompassed by this term expanded following the annexation of the Cossack Zaporozhian lands in 1775. In 1764, the office of *hetman* was abolished and the *hetmanate* ceased to exist as a political unit in 1781.[8]

Two years later, in 1783, Crimea was annexed to the Russian Empire.[9] What had once been independent, or semi-independent, political units on, and north of, the Black Sea coast were now under direct Russian governmental control. From the perspective of the rulers of Russia, 'Great Russia' (Muscovy) and 'Little Russia' (Ukraine) had been reunited. While borders in the south-west of the expanded Russian Empire would continue to shift as Poland was partitioned, the historic lands of the Rus were now basically under one ruler. But that was a ruler based in St Petersburg[10] (and then Moscow from 1918), not in Kyiv. So, did that make it reunification or annexation? On that matter, opinions sharply differ, then as now.

As this 'gathering of the Russian lands' occurred, an intellectual conflict was ignited over the nature of the deep story of the origins of these lands. A 'history war' was about to break out. And it still rages.

THE START OF THE 'HISTORY WAR'

During the eighteenth century, a debate regarding Russian origins occurred which has continued until today.[11] In many ways, it was a period which witnessed the beginning of the writing of Russian history in a modern critical sense. It was often associated with German academics who had come to work in Russia. And that was where things started to get complicated. One of these academics was Gerhard Friedrich Müller (1705–83), who had joined the staff of the St Petersburg Academy of Sciences.[12] This was part of an Enlightenment initiative which sought to apply science and academic rigour to study. In 1749, he had the honour of delivering an oration to the Empress Elizabeth (ruled 1741–62).

It was titled: 'On the Origins of the Russian People and their Name'. And it all went terribly wrong for the German academic in question!

There was nothing historically wrong with Müller's research. Along with several German academics who were studying Russian primary source material (most prominently the *Russian Primary Chronicle*), he concluded that Russian origins were rooted in the Vikings. In his opinion – and it is a reasonable one – the name of the Rus was rooted in *Ruotsi*, a term used by the Finns to describe some of the Swedish adventurers. He was probably correct. At least, his etymology was as likely to be correct as several other competing theories regarding the origins of the name. However, it was then that the wheels came off! He was about to discover that history is often forced to take a back seat to politics and ethnic sensitivities.

Between 1741 and 1743, imperial Russia had been at war again with Sweden. Consequently, it did not go down at all well when Müller attributed the origins of Russia to Swedes. Those Russian academics who read his piece were not about to let a little thing like reasonable evidence get in the way of a patriotic story. Müller suddenly found he was a lightning rod for Russian nationalist sentiments. A committee of scrutiny was set up and he was roundly condemned. His critics accused him of bringing Russia 'into disrepute' by suggesting that Slavs needed foreigners to organise their first state. Müller could have countered that – like it or not – this was exactly what the *Russian Primary Chronicle* claimed.

In contrast to Müller's measured assertion, his chief critic – Mikhail Lomonosov (1711–65) – claimed that the Rus were a Baltic tribe. Furthermore, he stated that they were descended from the Iranian Roxolani tribe, whose origins went back to the Trojan Wars. Faced with a choice of national origins relying on a bunch of Swedish Vikings or the noble Trojans (so prominent in Classical literature), there was just no competition. Vikings were most definitely 'out' (especially Swedish ones). Trojans were 'in'.

After six months of argument, all copies of Müller's oration were seized; he was demoted; and his career never recovered. He would not be the last academic to fall foul of nationalist fantasies in Russia. Or elsewhere for that matter. Undeterred, he wrote a book entitled *Origins of the Russian people and name* (*Origines gentis et nominis Russorum*) in 1761. Wisely, it was published in Germany. The book did not appear in Russian until 1773. This was over ten years after Lomonosov had published his counterargument entitled *Ancient Russian History* in 1760. No prizes for guessing which was more popular in Russia.

Lomonosov was highly honoured for his many achievements. Among these, one could note a lunar crater and a crater on Mars, Lomonosov Bridge in St Petersburg and Lomonosovskaya Station on the Nevsko-Vasileostrovskaya Line of the St Petersburg Metro. Nobody named an underground station or crater after Gerhard Friedrich Müller, although his career certainly 'cratered' after he wrote his oration to Empress Elizabeth.

To be fair to Lomonosov, his later honours were due to his widespread scientific and literary achievements, rather than his venture into fictional national origins derived from the Trojans. Even so, the contrast is extreme. Nobody wanted to hear a German expound what came to be known as the 'Normanist' school of thought on

Russian origins. The term 'Normanist' was derived from the 'northern' origins of the Vikings.

THE BASIS FOR FUTURE DISAGREEMENTS

For the next 250 years, the debate would rumble on and the disagreement in new forms continues today. We shall pick it up again as the argument, in various iterations, resurfaces in different periods of time. As we do so, we will see that those who argue for the Normanist interpretation generally base their views on the information given under year 862 in the *Russian Primary Chronicle* regarding incoming Viking rulers. Alongside this, Arabic sources differentiated the Rus (*ar-Rūs*) and the Slavs (*aṣ-Šaqaliba*), suggesting two different ethnicities were indeed involved in the founding of the ancient state – with the former dominant. In other words, there were incomers who played a key role in its origins. A similar ethnic difference was noted by the Byzantine Emperor Constantine VII Porphyrogenitus, in his book *On the Governance of the Empire* (*De Administrando Imperio*), c.950, which identified the names of the Dnieper cataracts in both Slavic and Rus forms (most of the latter clearly derived from Old Norse).[13] This would also seem to indicate that those who kick-started the formation of the Rus state, and who were its dominant social group at the start, were 'incomers' from Scandinavia. Those that they ruled were Slavs. While both groups merged over the time, the formative period owed its character to Viking settlers (whether warriors or traders).

Against this view, 'anti-Normanists' generally argue in the following terms. The Eastern Slavs did not use the word *Rus* to describe the incoming Vikings; instead they used the word *varyagi* (Varangian) to describe them. A name like *Rus* was used by Greek writers as early as the second century AD for people who were clearly not Scandinavians. In addition to this, Arabic sources (*c.*750) referred to a people called the *Rus* living on the Middle Dnieper about a century before it is currently thought that identifiable Norse activity occurred there. Finally, at least one early source (in the northern area of the assumed Rus lands) referred to the *Rus* as if they were a particular people of the south (probably indigenous and therefore not originating in Scandinavia).[14] In short, this interpretation insists, while there were Norse 'incomers', it was largely an indigenous group of people who formed the state known as Kyivan Rus, with the northerners present but not creating (or dominating) the Kyivan state that emerged in the ninth and tenth centuries. This argument has its merits, but the evidence for a significant Norse impact (in the formative stage) seems indisputable.

These general points are worth rehearsing here as they – alongside others more characteristic of particular periods of time – will underpin much of the to-and-fro of historiographical debate, regarding this issue, over more than 250 years until the modern day. As the events of the twenty-first century remind us, this is not an ivory-tower debate, as it has a direct impact on the outlook and, latterly, the lived experiences of millions of people in Ukraine and Russia. It is history with attitude.

CHAPTER 13

THE ABSORBING OF 'LITTLE RUSSIA', 1783–1917

From the late eighteenth century onwards, Ukraine (along with the Black Sea coastlands) increasingly came under Russian control. While the dissolving of the last vestiges of the Cossack *hetmanate* by Catherine the Great in 1781 was a key moment in this development (followed by annexation of Crimea in 1783), it was a process that had been underway since the seventeenth century. Despite this backstory, what occurred in the late eighteenth century was a key moment in the development of Russian national power. It has been stated, with good reason, that 'Ukraine is key to Russia's imperial pretensions. Without Ukraine, Russia is a regional major power but not a global one.'[1] Much of the history of Russia (later the USSR) and Ukraine, from the seventeenth to the twentieth century, reveals Russian (and then Soviet) awareness of the significance to 'Great Russians' of the lands they came to call 'Little Russia'.

In this time, tsarist authorities attempted to absorb Ukraine into the larger Russian state and to erase areas of difference between these deeply connected, but still significantly different, communities.

This became a key feature of tsarist rule of Ukraine from the late eighteenth century to the Russian Revolution, in February (old-style calendar) 1917.

RETURN OF THE VIKING RUS

During the late eighteenth century, the increasing Russian control of Ukraine accompanied the acceleration of the promotion of the cult of Vladimir the Great, which had earlier been prominently encouraged by Tsar Ivan IV in the sixteenth century and the new Romanov dynasty in the seventeenth. As the royal originator of 'Holy Rus', his cult was without peer as a royal dynastic tool. He was used to promote the myth of a group of nations united into one family. These were: the 'Great Russians' (rooted in the expansion of Muscovy), the 'Little Russians' (those living in Ukraine) and the 'White Russians' (the Belarusians).[2] When his statue was erected in Kyiv in 1853, it was not symbolic of Russian sympathy for Ukrainian identity. Instead, it was an imperial statement of who and what was claimed to unite the empire and it emphasised Ukrainian union with Russia.

Notably, the acceleration of the promotion of Vladimir the Great in the final decades of the eighteenth century saw a revival of the Normanist view of Russia's origins, which we examined in the last chapter. However, in contrast to the earlier verdict, the Germans were now acceptable as the originators of the Russian state because the empress, Catherine the Great (ruled 1762–96), was herself German born.[3] She was keen to Europeanise Russia and, consequently, a Western European, rather than a native Slavic, origin for the nation was now acceptable.[4] It was quite a sea change in opinions. Vikings were back!

This was now the dominant position in the St Petersburg Academy of Science (where it had once been decisively rejected). One of the German academics who was part of this Normanist revival, August Ludwig von Schlözer, went as far as writing the following in a study of the *Russian Primary Chronicle* which was published in 1802:

> They [native Slavs] were people without any leadership, living like wild beasts and birds in their vast forests ... No enlightened European had noticed them or had written about them. There was not a single real town in the whole of the North ... Wild, boorish and isolated Slavs began to be socially acceptable only thanks to the Germans [i.e. the Vikings, who were largely Swedish, actually], whose mission, decreed by fate, was to sow the first seeds of civilization among them.[5]

Hitler – who later wrote: 'Unless other peoples, beginning with the Vikings, had imported some rudiments of organisation into Russian humanity, the Russians would still be living like rabbits'[6] – would have approved of the racist sentiment expressed by von Schlözer. Clearly, by 1802, the mood music in Russia had changed a lot since Gerhard Friedrich Müller had got himself into hot water in 1749 for suggesting that Vikings had founded the first Rus state.

In a bizarre way, this style of manipulating the image of the Viking founders of the Rus nation suited both supporters of tsarist autocracy in the late eighteenth and early nineteenth centuries and the radically racialised ideology of Hitler in the period 1918–45, for similar reasons. For the autocratic apologists, the idea refuted the assertion that the ordinary Russian people could govern themselves. Democracy was, these apologists asserted, never going to work there. As Nikolai Karamzin – a leading Russian writer and historian – noted in his *History of the Russian State* (*Istoriya gosudarstva Rossiyskogo*), published between 1816 and 1826, without external intervention, Russia was (he opined) simply an 'empty space', which was populated by 'wild and warring tribes, living on a level with the beasts and birds'.[7] It was a view identical to that propounded a few years earlier by von Schlözer.

Within such a mindset, what was needed was tough autocratic rule, alongside firm and uncompromising direction. A constitutional monarchy, of the type developing in the United Kingdom at the time, was rejected. Other political ideologies – liberalism, socialism, Marxism, anarchism – that would emerge in Russia during the nineteenth century had even less going for them when viewed from the perspective of exalted autocracy and threatened the established social order in even more alarming ways. In this autocratic view, Russians needed control, whether it was provided by the incoming Viking chieftains of the past or the divine-right-asserting tsars. Much later, in December 1916, Tsarina Alexandra advised her husband – Tsar Nicholas II – that 'Russia loves to feel the whip' because 'it's their nature'.[8]

For Hitler, in contrast, the matter was rooted in biological (bastard-Darwinian) racism, which considered the Slavs as lesser human beings than the Aryan Germans. He was unashamed in asserting that brutal Nazi racialised control was needed in Russia (the USSR by then), from 1941, in order to control its (in his opinion) primitive anarchic peoples and bring the land under proper – and Germanic – order.

While hugely different political systems were united by these demeaning views of the Russian people, they had a lot in common in their contempt for ordinary Russians. And both rooted their views in the mythical origins of the Rus state, as alleged by the *Russian Primary Chronicle* and its story of incoming Norse imposing order onto chaos.

These Normanist views were further elaborated in the nineteenth century by the Russian historian Sergei Solovyov and also in works dealing specifically with the theory by the German-Russian historian-philologist Ernst Eduard Kunik and by the Russian historian and journalist Mikhail Pogodin.[9]

There were even Russian nationalists who put a positive spin on the 'Tatar yoke', traditionally regarded as uniformly negative. According to this view, the resultant Russian isolation from Western Renaissance humanism (with its secularism and individualism) had allowed Russia to 'preserve its Byzantine inheritance, its old Slavonic culture and its Orthodox beliefs'.[10] The first and third of these being rooted in the activities of the tenth-century Norse–Slav rulers of the Viking Age Rus.

The fashion regarding how the Rus should be imagined had certainly shifted; but it would change again in the Russian Empire by the end of the nineteenth century. Before we explore that, it is instructive to see the impact of this new positivity as reflected in tsarist dynastic marriage arrangements. And then, to explore what happened to Ukraine – itself the cradle of the Rus state – in this period.

VIKING ORIGINS AND TSARIST DYNASTIC MARRIAGES

Given that the Normanist position could be construed as demeaning indigenous Slavic culture, a more positive spin on the outlook was attempted at times. Nikolai Karamzin (1766–1826), for example, suggested there was something positive about the Eastern Slavs in that they 'voluntarily had chosen' monarchic state administration (clearly regarded as a good thing by Karamzin) in calling in the foreign Norse rulers. His twelve-volume book *History of the Russian State* (*Istoriya Gosudarstva Rossiyskogo*), compiled between 1816 and 1829, was an apology for tsarist autocracy. As a result, his version of the Normanist approach was, in effect, praising the Slavs for choosing (what he would have regarded as) the necessary and firm hand of monarchs to control them. In this case, Viking ones.[11]

This reflected the ethnic characteristic of the tsarist dynasty which came to power after the death of Peter the Great in 1725 and the eventual extinction of his direct royal line. German royalty then played a major part in later tsarist marriage alliances, and this made the idea of ancient external Germanic influence more acceptable. When Peter the Great's grandson – Peter II – died in 1730 (aged fourteen), the Romanov dynasty in the direct male line came to an end. In the female line, it ended with the death of Empress Elizabeth (Elizaveta) Petrovna in 1762. From then until the Spring Revolution of 1917, Russia was ruled by the dynasty of Holstein-Gottorp-Romanov. While a political dynastic fiction maintained that the throne was still held by the Romanovs, the reality was that German royalty occupied key positions of tsarist power. This started in 1762 with the death of Empress Elizabeth Petrovna. As an unmarried and childless ruler, Elizabeth needed to choose a legitimate heir to secure the Romanov dynasty. In 1742, she selected her nephew Karl Peter Ulrich von Schleswig-Holstein-Gottorp. His parents were Duke Charles Frederick of Holstein-Gottorp in north-west Germany and Grand Duchess Anna Petrovna of Russia. Karl Peter was a grandson of Tsar Peter the Great and a great-grandson of King Charles XI of Sweden. Born in Kiel, Germany, he could barely speak Russian. He eventually ruled Russia as Tsar Peter III.

The tsars of the resulting dynasty traditionally married German princesses. Tsar Peter III (ruled January to July 1762) married Princess Sophia Augustina of Zerb (known to history as Empress Catherine II, the Great, who ruled 1762–96). Both Tsar Peter III and Empress Catherine II had been born in Germany. Their son Tsar Paul I (ruled 1796–1801) married Princess Sophia Dorothea of Württemberg. Their son Tsar Alexander I (ruled 1801–25) married Princess Louisa of Baden. Alexander I's brother Tsar Nicholas I (ruled 1825–55) married Princess Frederica Louisa Charlotte Wilhelmina of Prussia. Their son Tsar Alexander II (ruled 1855–81) married Princess Maximiliana Wilhelmina of Hesse-Darmstadt. His successor, Tsar Alexander III (ruled 1881–94), married Princess Dagmar of Denmark. Finally, their son, the last Russian tsar, Nicholas II (ruled 1894–1917), married Princess Alix of Hesse (who adopted the name Alexandra in Russia).[12] The German connection of the last tsarist dynasty is truly striking and was not lost on contemporary observers. It was often remarked on in a negative way. This was especially so when Russia was locked in a catastrophic war with the German Empire in the First World War (1914–18). That this period saw a further development of the Normanist school of thought regarding the Germanic (i.e. Viking) contribution to Russian origins was clearly no coincidence.

The contemporary German character of the final phase of tsarism was seen in other areas too. At this time, the German population of Russia was no more than 1 per cent of the total population of the Russian Empire. In sharp contrast, Germans made up 57 per cent of officials within the Russian Ministry of Foreign Affairs, 46 per cent in the Ministry of Defence and 62 per cent in the Ministry of Post and Communications. 'These facts help to explain one of the reasons why Russian official circles favoured the Normanist idea, as it could be taken to justify the rule of Germans in the Russian empire and their support for the Germanic origins of the Rus' state.'[13]

All this occurred while Russian control was tightening on the geographical heartland of the original Rus nation.

THE RUSSIFICATION OF UKRAINE

While Kyiv, in the late eighteenth century, might still have the image of a 'New Jerusalem' and a 'City of Glory' in nationalist song and story, the reality fell far short of this. When Catherine the Great visited the settlement, on her way to the newly annexed Crimea in 1787, she was deeply disappointed by what she found there. She commented: 'From the time I arrived I have looked around for a city, but so far I have found only two fortresses and some outlying settlements.'[14] It had not lived up to expectations. The mythical origin city of the nation of the Rus had fallen on hard times indeed. And it would remain so until the 1850s.

What was even more disturbing, from a Ukrainian perspective, was that Russian rule increasingly included activities designed to reduce or erase a recognisably separate Ukrainian identity.

While this had begun in the seventeenth century, it accelerated from the eighteenth century. In 1720, Tsar Peter the Great issued an edict prohibiting printing books in the Ukrainian language. From 1729, all government edicts were in Russian. This was followed, in 1763, when Catherine the Great prohibited lectures in Ukrainian at the Mohyla Academy in Kyiv, and in 1769, the Most Holy Synod of the Russian Orthodox Church prohibited printing in, and using, Ukrainian. From 1832, all Ukrainian schools used Russian and this was reinforced in 1864. In addition, the use of the 'Little Russian' (i.e. Ukrainian) language within the Russian Empire was officially restricted by the Valuev Circular (1863) and banned by the Ems Ukaz (1876). The only exception was the reprinting of historical documents. This also banned the import of Ukrainian publications and the staging of plays and lectures in Ukrainian. Other restrictions followed in the 1880s.[15] All of this occurred at a time of increased Ukrainian national self-consciousness and resistance to tsarist control.

So concerned were the tsarist authorities, under Tsar Nicholas II, to suppress Ukrainian self-awareness that at the centennial of the birth of the Ukrainian poet, writer and ethnographer Taras Shevchenko (died 1861), in 1914, all celebrations of him and his work were banned. Armed imperial police were even stationed at his grave, to prevent any events occurring there to mark the event.

Some imperial restrictions on the use of Ukrainian were relaxed in 1905–07 but only stopped being enforced after the February Revolution in 1917.

THE MATTER OF LANGUAGE

Ukrainian and Russian are very closely related languages. This is because they have a common root. In many ways, language illustrates the complexity of Ukrainian–Russian relations and character (both historical and contemporary). It is a relationship that is not as 'intimate and interchangeable' as contemporary Russian nationalists usually frame it. But, then again, not as 'different and separate' as many Ukrainian nationalists (often wanting to put 'clear blue water' between the two nations and cultures) often argue. Consequently, the deeply connected, but still significantly different, character of the two nations (as illustrated by the languages) defies simplistic nationalist claims. Recent history – especially since 2014 – has only exacerbated the situation and fuelled strong, and often misleading, views on both sides regarding this deeply related issue. And with Ukraine facing an existential threat to its sovereignty since February 2022, and Russia dug into a narrative that insists on a common history and culture being denied by so-called 'Ukrainian Nazis', a reasonable and balanced discussion is hard to achieve. This needs to be borne in mind, as it constitutes much of the mood music behind events since the eighteenth century. The same could be said regarding aspects of connections with Belarus.

There is a common root to these languages. 'A thousand years ago, the language spoken across [what are now] Russian and Ukrainian territories would have been similar, like different dialects of the same language.'[16] But this was subject to significant changes over the ensuing millennium. During this time, for example, 'Ukraine became the eastern part of the Polish–Lithuanian commonwealth, absorbing significant amounts of Polish into its language'.[17] This was just one of the factors that affected the development of language there. And while this was happening, other changes were happening to the north.

The Russian language was also changing. In this case, it 'was shaped by contact with and immigration from areas to the east and the importation of foreign technical and cultural terms from Western European countries like France, Germany and the Netherlands'.[18] As with Ukrainian, these were only some of the factors affecting the linguistic trajectory of the language in the period between the year 1000 and the nineteenth century.

This meant that, by the time imperial Russia took control of Ukraine in the eighteenth century, 'large shifts had emerged both in the languages' vocabularies, as well as in the sounds and grammar'.[19] The two languages had been on the move for eight centuries. In this time, they had remained historically closely related but also notably different, rather like the two communities.

Overall, while sharing a significant amount of grammar, vocabulary, pronunciation and use of the Cyrillic alphabet (with some differences in letters), they are not just dialects of one language.

Rather, they are closely related but different languages. It is relatively easy for speakers of Ukrainian and Russian to learn the other language and they start from a basis of picking up the drift of many conversations in the other language. But this does not make them just versions of one language and nothing like what Vladimir Putin would later (in 2021) describe as representing mere 'regional language peculiarities'. But, back to the nineteenth century.

THE CONTINUED BATTLE FOR THE MEDIEVAL PAST

As the Russian Empire increasingly dominated Ukraine during the nineteenth century, it once again revisited the medieval past. For the Rus of Kyiv had a history to be proud of: 'Ancient, vast, civilised, impeccably European.' Yet the question that hung over this in nineteenth-century Russia was: 'Whose history is it?'[20]

According to the officially approved tsarist narrative (that matured during the nineteenth century), following the Mongol destruction that had devasted Kyiv in the thirteenth century, the people of Kyivan Rus had shifted to the north-east. They had left behind the smoking ruins of their once proud city, the cradle of Orthodoxy.

This framing of events envisaged the transplanting of all that was culturally, ethnically and religiously associated with Orthodox Ukraine of the Rus to Moscow. It was a neat story. In one go, it recognised the great Orthodox state that had come into being under Vladimir the Great, while annexing it, lock, stock and barrel, to

THE ABSORBING OF 'LITTLE RUSSIA', 1783–1917

Muscovy. In short, what eventually grew into the 'Great Russia' of the Moscow-based tsars was the spiritual and literal inheritor of all that was associated with the ancient Rus state. Consequently, what constituted Ukraine in the nineteenth century could be regarded as a people with a 'funny language and quaint provincial ways'. The marvels of Kyivan Rus were nothing to do with them; it had passed to Moscow.[21]

Not surprisingly, this did not go unchallenged in Ukraine itself. There, historians such as Mykhailo Hrushevsky utterly dismissed the Russian appropriation of the Ukrainian past. To such writers, the migration to Moscow was a work of fiction. Either none had gone there or they had soon returned to Kyiv. As Hrushevsky trenchantly wrote: 'The Kievan State, its laws and culture, were the creation of one nationality, the Ukrainian Rus, while the Volodimir-Moscow State [partly named from the Russian city of Vladimir, east of Moscow] was the creation of another nationality, the Great Russian.'[22]

This rebuttal challenged the whole imperial Russian mindset. Far from Moscow representing 'Great Russia', to Kyiv's 'Little Russia', the situation was the other way round! The Moscow-orientated polity should, perhaps, be known as 'Little Ukraine'.[23] Not that such a change in nomenclature was ever going to happen. But the key thing to Hrushevsky was that Kyiv was the source of what constituted contemporary Russian identity. Ukraine was not the poor relation, no matter how much such a narrative suited the imperial government in Moscow and their imperial representatives in Ukraine.

THE VIKING ROLE IS ONCE AGAIN QUESTIONED

We have seen how the Rus came back into favour around the year 1800, as buttresses of the imperial outlook and system. This position was not to remain unchallenged. They would soon find the tide of Russian intellectual fashion flowing against them once more. This renunciation of the Vikings would remain the mood music for most of the nineteenth century.

As the century progressed, Russian nationalist pride pushed back against the Normanist school. Historians and archaeologists began to look for evidence for advanced Slavic culture in the centuries before the year 1000 which were rooted in indigenous developments and not beholden to some external agents. During this period of rising pan-Slavism, which sought to assert a confident view of Slavic achievements (under Russian guidance, of course), the Vikings were most definitely 'out'!

This was the time of the anti-Normanists. For many Russian intellectuals, it was 1749 all over again. For them, the wheel of Russian historiography had turned full circle. The anti-Normanist school of thought was popular in Russia among a group known as the 'Decembrists', a secretive revolutionary movement which arose in the Russian Empire in the first quarter of the nineteenth century. Its activities culminated in an unsuccessful revolt in St Petersburg in December 1825. It was from this failed revolt that the name 'Decembrist' was derived. The Decembrists aimed to abolish serfdom and to establish a constitutional monarchy in the Russian Empire. But they also presented themselves as true Russian patriots (there was also a Ukrainian group) and foreign Vikings did not fit this patriotic approach.

At its most extreme, this anti-Normanist school of thought claimed the Rus (as popularly envisaged) had never existed. Far from being Viking incomers, they were a Slavic people whose name had been recorded as far back as second-century Greek sources. We have seen this argued earlier. Their homeland was in Ukraine and their civilisation 'attained a high level of material culture from their contacts with Hellenic, Byzantine and Asiatic civilisations long before the Vikings had arrived'.[24]

There was no room for the incoming Norse – as claimed by the *Russian Primary Chronicle* – in such a view of the origins of the Russian nation.

In the late nineteenth century, the anti-Normanist school became associated with the work of the Russian historians Stepan Gedeonov, Dmitry Ilovaisky and Vasily Vasilievsky.[25]

THE VIKINGS AND UKRAINIAN NATIONAL AWARENESS IN THE NINETEENTH CENTURY

While the term 'Ukrainian' (to describe the lands around Kyiv) was first recorded in 1187, its general usage to describe the broad region arguably only occurred from the late nineteenth century onwards.[26] Its earlier appearance – in the form *okraina* – was derived from the Slavic word for 'periphery', 'borderland'.[27] It is incorrect to describe it by the term 'Rus–Ukraine' in that early period, as some 21st-century defenders of Ukrainian statehood have asserted in the face of Russian hegemony.[28] Nevertheless, this should not mask the awareness of difference that was present from the Middle Ages onwards. What is particularly interesting is how this sense of Ukrainian identity played out in the Normanist debate about the Rus.

The Normanist theory of Rus origins has frequently failed to achieve traction among Ukrainian historians. In the late eighteenth century, this was seen in the writings of the anonymous author(s) of a work entitled *History of Ruthenians* or *Little Russia* (*Istoriia Rusov*). They argued that the Kyivan Rus state – and the name Rus itself – were both of Slavic origin. Facing Russification policies, this entrenching of *local* culture against *foreign* intervention was in line with assertive Ukrainian cultural identity. The Ukrainians did not need Vikings to sort them out.

This particular strand of the anti-Normanist view can be seen in the work of leading nineteenth-century Ukrainian writers such as Mykhailo Maksymovych, Mykola Kostomarov (the originator of the theory of a Lithuanian origin of Rus) and Volodymyr Antonovych. Such writers either rejected the Viking legend of the Rus – as found in the chronicles – or denied its historical significance in national origins:

> In the early 20th century Mykhailo Hrushevsky contended that the Normanist theory has no historical basis and is simply unnecessary for explicating the origin of the Ukrainian Rus' state. He did not, however, reject the fact that the Varangians contributed in some measure to the creation of the Kyivan empire. The literary scholar Mykhailo Vozniak held similar views, as did Dmytro Bahalii and other historians of Hrushevsky's generation.[29]

AND THEN, IN RUSSIA, THE VIKINGS ARE BACK... A BIT

Despite the rise of anti-Normanism, the northern connection was not entirely abandoned within Russian historiography. This is not surprising, given the German nature of the Romanov dynasty that we explored a little earlier. The continued popularity of aspects of the original Normanist theory was seen in a revival of it in the early twentieth century. This partially plugged into the same idea that foreign intervention was necessary to promote Russian progress. It came at a time of accelerating economic growth, foreign investment and a tsarist elite as keen to stifle or frustrate mass movements (from trade unions to political parties) as tsarist government had been in the past. In a minority of writings, Normanism could be allied to these trends in early twentieth-century Russia, alongside the pan-Slavism being promoted by Tsar Nicholas II in opposition to the power of the kaiser in Germany.

This partial Normanist revival was 'reflected in the works of F. Braun, S. Rożniecki, Aleksei Shakhmatov, K. Tiander, and F. Westberg'.[30] A number of the Normanists left Russia after the 1917 Bolshevik Revolution, which helped strengthen the Normanist outlook in the West.[31] In their writings, the Viking connection became linked to a whole range of historic developments. 'Besides the traditional conception of Norman [Viking] conquest, neo-Normanist theories of Norman [Norse] commercial and ethnic-agrarian colonization, of the social domination of the Slavs by Norman elites, and of continuous domination of the Slavs by foreigners (from the Scythians to the Normans) were presented.'[32]

How this would have developed had the First World War not occurred is anyone's guess. But in the summer of 1914, the guns roared out across Europe and tsarist Russia found itself locked into an existential struggle with Austria–Hungary and Germany. In such a context, an intellectual movement that saw ancient Germanic foreigners as promoters of Russian identity was not going to thrive.

CHAPTER 14

FROM THE RUSSIAN REVOLUTION(S) TO THE 'END OF HISTORY'

In 1917, Russia was convulsed by two revolutions. In February (old-style Russian calendar) 1917, popular protests against shortages caused by the First World War, the huge Russian military losses and the tsarist conduct of the war led to the overthrow of Tsar Nicholas II, the end of the Romanov dynasty and the setting up of a provisional government. In October (old-style Russian calendar) 1917, Russian Communists – initially referred to as Bolsheviks – overthrew this government and began the process of turning Russia into a Communist dictatorship. But first, they had to negotiate an exit from the First World War (achieved with vast territorial losses to Germany in March 1918) and win a civil war against those who opposed their seizure of power.

They also began a process of bringing back under their control nations which had broken free from Russian rule as the tsarist empire disintegrated. This was achieved using the newly formed Red Army and the brutal political police, the Cheka. The latter was the first in an alphabet soup of names for the oppressive Soviet political police, with the KGB being the last iteration when the USSR collapsed in 1991. The secret police legacy is very much apparent in the modern FSB of the Russian Federation.[1]

AN OVERVIEW OF UKRAINE IN THE CONTEXT OF UPHEAVALS, 1917-45

The March 1917 revolution led to Ukraine breaking free from the Russian Empire, but by the end of 1921, it had been brought back into the new Soviet empire by force. In the 1930s, it was antipathy towards Ukrainian nationhood, as well as towards an independent peasantry, that led to the murderous famine visited on Ukraine by Stalin.

The bitter divisions over what constituted Ukrainian nationhood would be fanned by Nazi intervention after 1941, which still echoes in 21st-century politics and in contemporary Russian narratives regarding Ukraine.

At the same time, Galicia saw bitter conflicts between Ukrainians and Poles in a region that was contested as being part of either 'western Ukraine' or 'south-eastern Poland'. It was an area where borders were fluid, clear topographical boundaries lacking, and where the past power politics of now-collapsed empires (Russian and Austro-Hungarian) had seen the imposition of imperial identities, decided in Vienna and St Petersburg, on communities of ethnic complexity which had developed over centuries. In 1918, Polish and Ukrainian partisans clashed there over ownership of land that had once been part of the Austro-Hungarian Empire. Between 1918 and

1939, Ukrainian nationalists, in Polish-administered regions, killed Polish officials in a wave of political assassinations.

When Nazi Germany and its allies invaded Ukraine in the summer of 1941, they both exacerbated existing national rivalries, fears and hatreds and also imposed their own murderous racial policies on the region which killed vast numbers of Jews, Poles, Russians, Ukrainians and others.

As the Germans retreated before the Soviet Red Army in 1944, Russian, Ukrainian and Polish partisan armies fought each other for control of the area. This was only ended after 1945, when 'a wholesale population exchange brought about a crude but effective divorce',[2] as the area was brought into the Ukrainian Soviet Socialist Republic. Poland, losing large swathes of its territory in the east, was compensated with German territory in the west, accompanied by the expulsion of the Germans living there. Not for nothing was a book detailing the history of the great band of territory encompassing Ukraine, Belarus, Poland, western Russia and the eastern Baltic coast, in the period 1933–44, titled *Bloodlands*. These were the areas which witnessed the greatest numbers of deaths during Stalin's Collectivisation campaigns of the early 1930s against peasants and Hitler's 'Final Solution' against Jews (also frequently now known as the Holocaust) and other racial and ethnic groups slated for Nazi destruction in the 1940s.[3]

UKRAINE IN THE AFTERMATH OF THE 1917 REVOLUTIONS

Reflecting on the devastation of the Russian Civil War, 1918–21, the Russian writer Boris Pasternak commented: 'Those days justified the ancient saying that "man is a wolf to man".'⁴ It was a time of horrors. 'Red' (Bolshevik) and 'White' (anti-Bolshevik) atrocities were accompanied by other atrocities committed by 'Greens' (peasants resisting both sides), whose less-organised violence could still rival the others in the manner of the horrific deaths they dealt out to those regarded as their enemies.

The number of Russians who died as a result of the First World War was somewhere in the region of 1.8 million soldiers and 2 million civilians.⁵ In comparison, the war-related death toll in the Russian Civil War amounted to about 1.5 million combatants and 8 million civilians.⁶ The latter figure includes deaths caused by war-related famine and disease, which killed huge numbers. The total number who died in this civil war may have been as high as about 12 million.⁷ This included as many as 300,000 Jews murdered in pogroms.⁸

A wide range of different groups opposed the Bolsheviks (the 'Reds'). These included nationalists and other conservatives ('Whites'); other left-wing groups (Mensheviks, Socialist Revolutionaries); while 'Green' (or 'Black') armies of peasants resisted both 'Reds' and 'Whites'. Some of the 'Green/Black' forces were anarchists, such as the Ukrainian fighters of the Revolutionary Insurrectionary (or Insurgent) Army of Ukraine, led by Nestor Makhno.

Overall, there were also a bewildering variety of nationalists – in places such as Ukraine, Finland, the Baltic States and the Caucasus – who were fighting for national independence. In Ukraine, the Germans intervened in 1918 to try to establish a Ukrainian right-wing nationalist client state (the *hetmanate*), which initially acted in line with German interests.

General Denikin led the (White) Armed Forces of South Russia. He was successful at first, and even advanced to within 150 miles of Moscow, but was forced to retreat in 1920. Following this, Denikin resigned and was replaced by Baron Wrangel, who was unable to regain the initiative. By the end of 1920, all that remained of his army was evacuated from Crimea by the British and French navies. Although nationalists succeeded in Finland and the Baltic States, elsewhere they were defeated by the Reds and their lands brought into the emerging Communist USSR.

THE HUMAN COST IN UKRAINE

Ukraine was affected by a Bolshevik policy of 'Decossackisation' in 1919. The Cossacks, as we saw in earlier chapters, lived in the regions bordering the Black and Caspian Seas and had a tradition of relative independence, in return for military service to the tsarist government. Although their independence reduced as the powers of central government increased through the nineteenth and early twentieth centuries, their military role continued and their martial abilities were extensively utilised by the tsars in the Russian army and in the suppression of revolutionary unrest. They also had a reputation for brutal antisemitism.[9]

In southern Russia, many Cossacks supported the White forces and formed the core of their armies. In January 1919, the Secret Resolution of the Central Committee of the Bolshevik Party called for 'mass terror against rich Cossacks, who should be exterminated and physically eliminated to the last'.[10] It was class war against a whole civilian population. In the Don region, in February and

March, the Red Army killed 8,000 Cossack hostages.[11] In June, the Cheka killed several thousand more Cossacks through the use of special revolutionary tribunals, called *troiki*. Many others were held in concentration camps of the early Gulag system. In late October and early November 1920, a second phase of Decossackisation saw the deportation of 17,000 Cossacks to work as forced labourers in the mines of the Donets Basin. Cossack power was broken.

Other class-based actions by the Cheka marked the Red occupation of areas of Ukraine in 1919, before a temporary Red withdrawal in the face of a White advance. Hundreds of middle-class hostages were seized against the payment of massive fines and large numbers massacred. In Odessa, Kyiv and Kharkov, deliberate humiliations were carried out by which middle-class women were forced to clean public toilets and military camps, where rape was frequent. Before withdrawing from Kharkov, in June 1919, the Cheka executed up to 1,000 middle-class hostages. Up to 2,000 were similarly shot in Odessa in June and August. In Kyiv, about 3,000 hostages were killed by the Cheka during the period February to August of that year.

As this Red Terror occurred, racially motivated pogroms also took place in Ukraine and Belarus between 1919 and 1921 – overwhelmingly at the hands of White forces, Ukrainian nationalists and peasant Greens – which claimed the lives of 150,000 Jewish civilians.[12]

As the civil war drew to its close, the killing intensified as White forces withdrew and civilian supporters (or those perceived as supporters) were left behind. In Crimea, the Cheka were responsible for the deaths of 50,000 people in six weeks between mid-November and the end of December 1920.[13]

Ukraine was finally brought fully into the emerging USSR, by force, by the end of 1921. Consequently, the Ukrainian Soviet Socialist Republic was one of the constituent republics of the Soviet Union between 1922 and 1991.

THE CRUSHING OF UKRAINIAN NATIONHOOD

During the 1920s, there was a brief period when Russian pressure on Ukrainian culture and language reduced. In 1923, a policy termed 'indigenisation' was announced. This included the promotion of native languages in education, publishing, the workplace and government. The idea was to reconcile national cultures with Soviet power. It accompanied recruitment of a cadre of trained new Soviet leaders and administrators from the indigenous populations of the newly minted USSR. 'In Ukraine this program inaugurated a decade of rapid Ukrainization and cultural efflorescence.'[14] It is this approach that Vladimir Putin refers to when he claims that 'modern Ukraine is entirely the product of the Soviet era'.[15]

This policy was not to last. As Stalin rose to supreme power in the USSR, in the late 1920s and early 1930s, Ukrainian nationhood and cultural independence was restricted and then crushed as an expression of so-called 'bourgeoise nationalism'. This saw an approach by which, 'as with many other Soviet republics, Ukraine was effectively colonized by Moscow, a relationship carried over from the pre-revolutionary era of tsarist imperial Russia. Its wealth and population were exploited for the benefit of the ruling Russian class.'[16] Processes of history were once more coming full circle.

In the late 1920s, Stalin launched a series of Five-Year Plans (starting in 1928). The aim was the break-neck expansion of industry and catching up with the advanced Western industrial powers in just ten years. This was accompanied by a policy of Collectivisation in the countryside, which crushed peasant independence, at the same time as securing grain supplies for the cities and the Red Army and providing grain to export in return for much-needed foreign hard currency to buy industrial machinery.

It was not just a reorganisation of farming but the imposition of class war with a death toll running into millions. For many Communist Party members and for many workers in the towns, this was a settling of scores with the *temnyia muzhiki* (dark/primitive peasants), which was long overdue and carried out with extreme ruthlessness.

It was a political victory that came at a huge cost to agriculture in the USSR. In response to the assault on their freedom, many peasants chose to destroy crops and livestock rather than hand them over to the new collective farms. Farm animals were destroyed in vast numbers. Between 1929 and 1931, about 160 million cattle, 45 million pigs and 330 million sheep were slaughtered.[17]

All agricultural areas suffered terribly. Across the USSR, about 5.7 million people died because of the hurried Collectivisation campaigns.[18] Some historians think that the final death toll might have been as high as 7 million.[19] Worst hit was Ukraine, where this time of mass starvation is remembered as the Holodomor (extermination by hunger).

The fact that this suffering struck Ukraine with such force was due to more than the area simply being the breadbasket of the nation. It was also an attempt to crush Ukrainian national independence once and for all. Ukrainian nationalists had almost succeeded in forming an independent state after March 1917, until defeated by the Red Army and the Cheka. This independent Ukrainian cultural outlook had continued to irritate Soviet authorities after then. As a result, Ukraine soon felt the full force of the Soviet police state in a brutal assault on its culture, as well as its farming system.

In November 2008, the Verkhovna Rada (Ukrainian Parliament) defined the Holodomor as a deliberate 'act of genocide against the Ukrainian people'.[20] That claim has not gone unchallenged within Russia, where some Russian historians have asserted that, if it was to be regarded as 'an intentional act of genocide against the Ukrainian peasantry', then it was 'no less a genocide against the Russian peasantry'.[21]

However, there was clearly a particular ferocity in the focus on Ukraine (along with other assaults on its distinctive culture). This inevitably leaves one with the impression that, within the wider horrors perpetrated by Collectivisation, there was something particularly anti-Ukrainian about large parts of it too. Even if the claim that what occurred in Ukraine constituted 'genocide' is rejected, what took place there looks like something *approaching* 'culturicide'. It is clear that Ukraine and its culture were to be utterly crushed. It may not have aimed at destroying Ukrainians as *an ethnic group*, but it was clearly intended to destroy the 'Ukrainian civic nation'.[22]

Grain was taken by force from Ukraine, even as people there starved, and cannibalism broke out. Desperate peasants flooded into the Ukrainian cities searching for food. In response, the Soviet police arrested thousands of starving orphan children and left them to die in prison. Many Ukrainian religious and political leaders were executed at the same time. Modern estimates suggest that the death toll in the Holodomor was about 3.3 million, of which about 3 million were Ukrainians and the rest other ethnic groups living in Ukraine.[23] The Ukrainian death toll surpassed that of any other nationality in the USSR.

As the tide began flowing strongly against Ukrainian nationhood, an undercurrent was increasingly flowing against the role of Vikings in the formation of the state of the Kyivan Rus.

THE VIKINGS BECOME EVEN MORE UNACCEPTABLE

The Soviets inherited the nineteenth-century Slavophile emphasis on rejecting external forces taking the credit for Russian developments. It became ever more problematic to reference Germanic origins in the aftermath of the carnage of the First World War, the rise of the Nazis after 1933 and then the experiences of the Great Patriotic War (1941–45), when the USSR suffered terribly as the result of another German invasion of the Motherland. Germanic Vikings, in such circumstances, remained 'out'!

This trend was allied with the urge to downplay the significance of Ukraine as a nation and annex its achievements to Russia. As we have seen, while expressions of Ukrainian national culture were

FROM THE RUSSIAN REVOLUTION(S) TO THE 'END OF HISTORY'

allowed some respite in the 1920s, the political tide turned against this after 1928 (as Stalin became the dominant player within the Soviet political elite). From 1932, any support for Ukrainian cultural expression was officially terminated, in favour of Russification. This official policy was murderously applied as the 1930s progressed and Collectivisation and the Stalinist Great Terror occurred. Both Vikings and Ukrainians were out in the cold. What became ethno-archaeology was highly politicised and subject to the same kind of Communist Party manipulation as every other aspect of Soviet life. And in this approach to the past, there was no place for a separate Ukrainian identity. This had huge implications for the Normanist debate and the role of the Norse in the formation of the ancient Rus nation.

Although, in the 1920s, the Normanist outlook could still be identified in the writings of the famous Soviet Russian historians Mikhail Pokrovsky and Alexander Presniakov, this radically changed once Stalin became entrenched in power from the late 1920s onwards. Though a Georgian, he was no friend to the minority nationalities of the USSR. Rather, he exemplified the worst excesses of what can be described as Great Russian chauvinism. He was also antagonistic towards ideas of foreign influence on the lands that were part of the USSR. Alongside this, he promoted the standard Marxist line that all major developments in history and culture were products of economic factors which drove change and decided the relationships between classes. The idea of Vikings decisively changing Russian history went rapidly off the historiographical agenda in the Soviet Union. 'According to Soviet historians, the Kyivan state emerged in consequence of the evolution of economical and social conditions, it was the work of Slavs exclusively, foreign elements played no noteworthy role in this process.'[24]

Consequently, during the 1930s, it was anti-Normanist views that gained official approval. These views (reflecting the new Stalinist orthodoxy) could be found in the works of Soviet historians, such as Boris Grekov, Vladimir Mavrodin, Arseny Nasonov and Mikhail Tikhomirov; expressed by the Soviet archaeologists Mikhail Artamonov and Boris Rybakov; and found in the work of the literary scholar Dmitry Likhachev. These views were acceptable to the party line and this approach denounced the Normanist theory as unscientific.[25] Normanism was no longer acceptable within the fusion of Communism and Russian nationalism which flourished under Stalin. 'In the 1930s, Soviet scholars started a contra-attack against the Norman "claims". The Norman theory was pronounced as politically harmful because it denied the capability of Slavic peoples to create an independent state.'[26]

This anti-Normanist position could also take the – classically Marxist – stance that the Rus were a *politico-social* group that emerged from the Slavic population due to economic (*not ethnic*) factors.[27]

However, it should be noted that this did not necessarily mean that all involved in producing this historiography were Stalinist in inclination. For example, Likhachev was incarcerated by the Soviet authorities in 1928. After time in prison, he was sent to the concentration camp on the Solovetsky Islands in the White Sea and then, from 1931, he was one of the slave workers toiling on the construction of the Stalin White Sea–Baltic Canal. He survived and died in 1999. The threat of imprisonment in the Gulag system hung over the heads of all academics in the USSR of Josef Stalin.

The key point was that the Viking originators of the Rus state had no place within the intellectual framework of Stalin's Russia. Neither did Normanism find adherents in Ukraine in this period. Most Soviet Ukrainian historians in the 1920s and 1930s agreed with the anti-Normanist positions that had been articulated by the distinguished Ukrainian historian Mykhailo Hrushevsky, by the influential academic Dmytro Bahalii and by the historian of the Ukrainian church Volodymyr Parkhomenko.[28] It should be remembered that for these Ukrainian scholars, as for others in the Soviet period (especially under Stalin), 'it was rather dangerous to be a Normanist'.[29]

Hrushevsky proposed 'the existence of Rus' in southern lands already before the first Scandinavian-Rus' duke ... with his brothers came to this world'.[30] In other words, he thought that a Slavic people called the 'Rus' existed before the Viking arrival in the Kyiv area. As a result, he considered the Norman theory unnecessary to understand the emergence of the Rus but 'admitted a certain influence of the Varangian military organization upon the unification process of old Rus' lands under the power of Kyiv'.[31] Several other scholars, then and since, have similarly suggested that the Rus were actually a Slavic people and that any Norse contribution to their society was limited.

There is some justification in balancing Norse cultural influence with the rapidly developing Slavic nature of the Rus state by the eleventh century, but totally writing off Norse influence (as some have done) is a step too far.

While an anti-Normanist position was in line with Stalinist orthodoxy, this did not mean that all who stood by it were in favour with the Soviet government, as we have earlier seen regarding Likhachev. Hrushevsky, for example, came under increasing pressure (including secret police surveillance) for alleged Ukrainian nationalist sympathies. This included attempts by the secret police to identify him as a major figure in an invented counter-revolutionary organisation titled the 'Ukrainian National Centre'. Though arrested and exiled to Moscow, he survived this aggressive attention, although most of his students and colleagues were purged and died for their alleged subversive opinions.[32] He died in 1934, apparently of natural causes.

Those who were slow to recognise the change in the political mood music were soon in deep trouble, as those around Hrushevsky discovered to their cost. However, things could be a little more complex elsewhere. Some historians of what has been termed the 'Ukrainian state school' accepted some aspects of Normanist theory. A number were active in 'Western Ukrainian' historiography. This is a reminder that this area of Ukraine was part of Poland in the period 1918–39. As a result, they were away from the Stalinist pressures which were brought to bear on historians in the USSR. These included the historians Stepan Tomashivsky (died 1930), at Cracow University, and Myron Korduba (died 1947), at the University of Warsaw and later Lviv University, among others.[33]

THE EXPERIENCE OF UKRAINE IN THE GREAT PATRIOTIC WAR, 1941–45

There is a graphic and revealing scene in the 2001 film *Enemy at the Gates* which tells the story of a duel between Soviet and German snipers in the ruins of Stalingrad in 1942. In the scene in question, the Germans repeatedly send a succession of wireman out to repair a telephone line cut by the Soviets. The Soviet snipers kill them, one after the other. After the latest German wireman dies, one of the snipers (played by Jude Law) remarks how strange it is that German officers keep sending infantrymen to their deaths in this predictable way. His companion remarks: 'They don't give a shit about telephone guys. I mean, it's like us with the Ukrainians.'[34]

Alongside other areas of the western USSR, Ukraine suffered terribly in the war. By the end of November 1941, all of Ukraine was under German occupation. Some Ukrainians initially welcomed the Germans as liberators. Especially in Galicia (in the west), some assumed that Germany, a bitter enemy of Poland and the USSR, would support Ukrainian nationalist aspirations. Stepan Bandera and Yaroslav Stetsko – leaders of one of the factions (OUN-B) within the Organization of Ukrainian Nationalists (OUN) – supported the creation of an independent Ukraine, allied to the Third Reich.

Such Ukrainian nationalists were rapidly disappointed. Galicia was transferred administratively to German-occupied Poland, Bukovina was ceded to Romania and Romania took control over the area between the Dniester and Southern Buh rivers. This became the province of Transnistria, with its capital at Odessa. The remainder of the nation became the *Reichskommissariat Ukraine*. Both Bandera and Stetsko were arrested by the Gestapo.

The German occupation of Ukraine was complex, and its reverberations continue into modern times. An estimated 1.5 million Ukrainian Jews were murdered, most infamously at Babi Yar

(Ukrainian: Babyn Yar), near Kyiv. Here, nearly 34,000 Jews were murdered in just two days. The Ukrainian population generally was destined for slave status under the Nazi 'New Order'. About 2.2 million Ukrainians were taken to Germany as forced *Ostarbeiters* (eastern workers). Overall, between 5 and 7 million Ukrainians died in 1941–45.

A disturbing fact is that the mass killings of Jews was assisted at times by significant numbers of Ukrainians (antisemitism was prevalent among many of the Ukrainian population, as in Poland and elsewhere in Europe); while other Ukrainians served as mercenary guards in Nazi extermination camps located in Nazi-occupied Poland. Those responsible for assisting in Nazi genocide against the Jews in Ukraine itself included local Ukrainian nationalists from the OUN militias, members of the Ukrainian Insurgent Army (UPA – see below) and the Auxiliary Police (which was under SS command).[35] Many men transferred directly from the militias to the Auxiliary Police. These 'Ukrainian police rounded up Jews for deportation to death camps and for mass executions in the general vicinity of the ghettos'.[36] In addition, many Ukrainians fought in the 14th Waffen Grenadier Division of the SS (1st Galician).

From 1942, the nationalist Ukrainian Insurgent Army (UPA) fought both the Germans and partisans loyal to the USSR. In September 1944, Bandera and Stetsko were released by the Germans, who regarded them now as potential allies in resisting the advancing Red Army. The Nazis allowed the establishment of a 'Ukrainian National Army' and a 'Ukrainian National Committee'. Members of OUN-B and the UPA were also responsible for massacres of thousands of Poles.

By the end of October 1944, all of Ukraine was once more under Soviet control. This was accompanied by the crushing of Ukrainian aspirations for independence from the USSR. The UPA – led by Roman Shukhevych (killed 1950) – carried out military operations against Soviet troops until the early 1950s. Bandera escaped to West Germany, where he was murdered by the KGB in 1959. Stetsko died in Germany in 1986.

Putin's unjustifiable framing of *all* modern Ukrainian nationalists as neo-Nazi 'Banderites' is based on the historical collaboration of many Ukrainian nationalists with the Nazis, their involvement in ethnic-based atrocities during the world war, their resistance to the Red Army and by the presence of *some* modern neo-Nazis among the groups opposing Russian interference in Ukraine before the 2022 invasion. The terrible complexity of twentieth-century history lies behind this modern caricature, designed as it is to accuse all 21st-century supporters of Ukrainian national independence of being neo-Nazis.

UKRAINE IN THE AFTERMATH OF WAR AND VICTORY

After the 1945 victory, Ukraine continued to be a republic within the multi-ethnic Soviet state. It was a state which – despite the horrors that Ukraine had experienced since 1917 – claimed to balance national identities with an overarching Soviet character. This perspective influenced the way that the deep story of the Rus was presented.

In the aftermath of the appalling carnage of war, any idea of the

USSR or its predecessor, tsarist Russia, being in any way beholden to the West, let alone to a Germanic culture (i.e. the Vikings), was totally off the table. Any scholar in the USSR who made such a claim was in serious trouble.[37] Buoyed by the victory over the Nazis, what we might call 'Late Stalinism' (Stalin died in 1953) was more nationalist than ever.

Soviet archaeologists were funded to find the evidence for a recognisably ancient 'Slavic homeland', which could be viewed as the predecessor of the mighty war-winning USSR. This 'Slavic homeland' was eventually defined as stretching (east–west) from the River Volga to the River Elbe and (south–north) from the Aegean and Black Sea to the Baltic. This 'ancient homeland' was conveniently similar to the Soviet sphere of influence that Stalin claimed for the USSR after 1945.[38]

In sharp contrast to Western academics, who were increasingly promoting the idea of ethnic groups being 'modern intellectual constructions, invented categories imposed on complex social groups',[39] post-war Soviet scholars presented ethnic groups as 'primordial entities defined by biology'.[40] Given that Marxist orthodoxy insisted that society was the superstructure above an economic substructure, and that culture was simply the outworking of class conflict and class consciousness, the Late Stalinist commitment to immutable biological origins of historical ethnic/culture groups was surprising, to say the least. And it left no room for the Norse in this Slavosphere.

After Stalin's death in 1953, Ukrainian cultural identity was allowed limited expression, so long as loyalty to the Communist system was maintained. In 1954, the celebration of the 'reunification'

FROM THE RUSSIAN REVOLUTION(S) TO THE 'END OF HISTORY'

(as it was and is still presented in Russia) of Ukraine with Russia in 1654 emphasised the common Rus status (minus intruding Norse) of the two peoples. It was then that Crimea was transferred from the Russian Soviet Federative Socialist Republic to Ukraine. It would remain part of Ukraine until it was annexed by the Russian Federation of Putin in 2014.

Leonid Brezhnev, a Ukrainian, served as leader of the Soviet Union from 1964 to 1982. While Communist control remained paramount, in many ways Ukrainian culture initially experienced a relative relaxation of control unparalleled since the 'Ukrainisation' phase in the 1920s. However, during the 1970s, a reaction against 'bourgeois nationalism', accompanied by a celebration of 'the great Russian people', again became pronounced. This was part of the return to repression of dissidence that was a feature of the Late Soviet period. Russification was once again on the agenda. At the same time, economic performance deteriorated and, in April 1986, the worst nuclear accident in history occurred at Chernobyl, northwest of Kyiv. The USSR was failing.

After 1986, Mikhail Gorbachev's policies of *perestroika* (restructuring) and *glasnost* (openness) led to increased expressions of Ukrainian national sentiment. In May and June 1988, the millennium of the Christian conversion of the Rus was celebrated as part of a religious revival. The ancient Rus and the end of the USSR had become entangled!

Three and a half years after this, the USSR collapsed. Following a failed hardline coup against Gorbachev in August 1991, Ukraine's Parliament – meeting in emergency session – declared the full independence of Ukraine. On 1 December 1991, Ukraine voted overwhelmingly for independence. By the end of the year, the USSR was no more.

THE END OF HISTORY?

With the end of the USSR, it looked as if the ideological framework that had shaped Europe – and much of the world – since 1945 was over. Some optimistically proclaimed that it was 'the end of history'.[41] Liberal democracy had apparently triumphed. But was this really true? Would even older histories now assert themselves? The reality, which emerged after 1991, would eventually deflate the Western triumphalism that marked the end of the Cold War. As this occurred, the Rus would, once more, make a comeback.

CHAPTER 15

AN INDEPENDENT UKRAINE AND THE RETURN OF THE VIKINGS!

A key part of the contested relationship between Russia and Ukraine since 1991 – and especially since 2000 – has been the mining of the 'deep story' of 'Holy Rus' by Russian nationalists, to both challenge the legitimacy of Ukrainian independence and provide an alternative narrative to that presented by Western liberal democracy. In this, the ancient history has been weaponised. The Rus are back and have been deployed in the propaganda of an increasingly assertive and aggressive Russian state under Vladimir Putin. From Vladimir the Great to Vladimir Putin, history is being deployed to both assert 'true Russian' identity and undermine the legitimacy of Ukraine.

FROM 1991 TO 2000

Just under a decade separates the gaining of Ukrainian independence in 1991 from the accession of Vladimir Putin as President of the Russian Federation at the end of 1999. These were eventful years for the new nation of Ukraine.

In 1991, Crimea was (once again) made an autonomous republic within the Soviet Union, but, with the formal dissolution of the USSR, in December 1991, Crimea passed to the newly independent Ukraine. Ethnic Russians constituted a majority of the population in Crimea, and there was a short-lived independence (from Ukraine) movement in 1994.

Again in 1991, Russia, Belarus and Ukraine signed the Belovezha Accords in December, declaring the end of the USSR and proclaiming the Commonwealth of Independent States (CIS) in its place (officially established later by the Alma-Ata Protocol). Estonia, Latvia and Lithuania chose not to participate in the CIS, Georgia withdrew in 2008 following war with Russia, and Ukraine formally ended its participation in CIS statutory bodies in 2018 (although it had stopped participating in the organisation in 2014, following the Russian annexation of Crimea).

In 1994–96, Ukraine gave up its nuclear weapons and the Budapest Memorandum of 1994, signed by Russia, Ukraine, Britain and the US, promised that none of these nations would use force or threats against Ukraine; all would respect its sovereignty and existing borders.

As early as 1995, the Russian Council on Foreign and Defense Policy issued a report entitled 'Russia and NATO'. It stated that NATO expansion could lead to the 'first serious crisis in relations between Russia and the West since the end of the Cold War'.[1] Two years later, the Russian policy assessment 'National Security Concept of the Russian Federation 1997' stated that any future enlargement of NATO to the east was unacceptable because it represented a threat to Russian national security.²

VLADIMIR PUTIN AND UKRAINE

In 2002, at the European Political Community summit held in Prague, Putin (President of the Russian Federation since the end of 1999) stated that Russia's interests were not affected by good relations between Ukraine and NATO. This attitude did not last and 'the story of contemporary Ukraine is largely the story of its attempts to define a new future for itself in Europe and Russia's attempts to obstruct this new direction'.³

In 2004, the Orange Revolution (mass protests) occurred in Ukraine, following credible allegations of (Russian-backed) electoral interference. As a result, the presidential elections were rerun. Several years of political turbulence followed. But Moscow clearly saw this as a failure to dictate the course of Ukrainian politics. Earlier, in 2003, a similar event – the Rose Revolution – had led to a non-violent change of government in Georgia, which ended the rule of Soviet-era politicians there and a transition to a more democratic government. Russia accused the US of orchestrating the event.

The relationship of Russia and the West was souring, and the possible future of Ukraine was at the centre of this. In 2007, at the Munich Conference on Security Policy, Putin explicitly blamed the US for using military force in the international arena; and he criticised NATO and the European Union for using force against other countries without the passing of a UN Security Council resolution. He was particularly opposed to the US-led invasion of Iraq in 2003 but was also more widely critical of what he saw as US- and NATO-led interventionism. In addition, Putin stated that Russia would not use military force without UN approval. However, this was with the caveat that Russia's self-defence would justify use of force outside of such a restriction. This 'self-defence' argument was used to validate Russian aggression against Ukraine in 2022.

In 2008, the NATO Bucharest Summit invited Albania and Croatia to begin accession talks with NATO. Regarding former Soviet-controlled nations: the Czech Republic, Hungary and Poland had joined NATO in 1999; Bulgaria, Estonia, Latvia, Lithuania, Romania, Slovakia and Slovenia joined in 2004. The summit also reaffirmed the commitment to keeping NATO's door open to any European democracy willing and able to assume the responsibilities and obligations of membership. It further welcomed Ukraine's and Georgia's Euro-Atlantic aspirations for membership and agreed that these countries would eventually become members of NATO. This crossed a 'red line' as far as Moscow was concerned (especially after the eastward enlargements of NATO in 1999 and 2004). 'We will do all we can to prevent Ukraine's and Georgia's accession into NATO and to avoid an inevitable serious exacerbation of our relations with both the alliance and our neighbours,' was the response of the Russian Foreign Minister Sergei Lavrov.[4] Other senior Russians concurred: 'Russia will take unambiguous action toward ensuring its interests along its borders. These will not only be military steps, but also steps of a different character,' was the verdict of General Yuri Baluyevsky, Chief of the General Staff of the

Russian Federation (as reported by the Interfax news agency).[5] At the same time, the Russia polling agency Levada Center indicated that 74 per cent of the Russian population thought that Ukrainian membership of NATO would pose a threat to Russian national security interests[6] (77 per cent thought this regarding Georgia). The shape of a future conflict was emerging.

In 2013–14, bloody street protests in Kyiv (called the Euromaidan protests) culminated in the overthrow of pro-Russian Ukrainian President Viktor Yanukovych (who had halted Ukraine developing closer ties with Western Europe, primarily the 'association agreement' with the EU, after intense pressure from Moscow). This was also called the Revolution of Dignity by those organising it. Yanukovych fled to Moscow.

After this failure to control the direction of Ukrainian travel, Russia seized Crimea and encouraged breakaway Russian-speaking states in the Donbas in 2014. In the run-down Donbas towns – heavily Russian in terms of linguistics and ethnic awareness and struggling economically – dissatisfaction with Kyiv was growing long before Russia openly intervened there. To start with, this seemed unlikely to lead to breaking away from Ukraine until it was fanned by active Russian intervention and Putin's encouraging (and arming) of pro-Russian militias.[7] The region was the Ukrainian version of the US 'rustbelt' and 'flyover states', but one whose disillusionment and dissatisfaction combined with ethnic and linguistic characteristics which emphasised their differences from Kyiv and the western regions. The Minsk Agreements (2014–15) failed to end conflict in the Donbas or Russia's intervention in the area.

In 2019, Volodymyr Zelensky was elected President of Ukraine. Zelensky's main promise during the presidential election campaign had been to stop the conflict with Russia. Putin clearly underestimated Zelensky's political gravitas. The two Presidents met face to face in the Normandy Format Summit in December, but any brief hopes of de-escalation soon faded. Russia continued to infiltrate the Donbas and Zelensky worked against the influence of pro-Russian oligarchs in Ukraine by blocking their TV channels. And he increased moves towards NATO and the EU. In response, in 2020, NATO granted Ukraine 'Enhanced Opportunity Partner' status and Russia conducted a large military exercise, called Zapad-2021, as a rehearsal for a possible invasion of Ukraine.

Tensions increased further in 2021, when Russia deployed around 100,000 troops near the Ukrainian border, accusing the West of creating an anti-Russian Ukrainian state which purportedly threatened Russia both ideologically and strategically. Putin repeated the alleged strategic threat this posed in speeches in February 2022, emphasising the importance of Ukraine's geographical position to Russia and the supposed threat posed by the West.

In February 2022, Russia (opposing the increasingly close relationship between Ukraine and NATO and the EU) recognised the breakaway Donbas republics and invaded Ukraine.

PUTIN AND THE ANCIENT RUS

Vladimir Putin has become increasingly fixated on the great Rus ruler, Vladimir the Great. In 2009, Putin visited the grave of the Russian fascist thinker and historian Ivan Ilyin (died 1954 in

Switzerland and reinterred in Russia in 2005). He went in the company of ultra-nationalist Tikhon Shevkunov, then an *archimandrite* (an honorific title for a respected senior monk) of the Russian Orthodox Church. Later, in October 2023 – having been Metropolitan of Pskov and Porkhov since 2018 – Shevkunov was transferred to head the diocese of annexed Crimea.[8]

> At the gravesite [in 2009], Shevkunov blessed Putin and suggested that his role was in the near future to fulfil the eternal cycle of the Kyivan Rus' state forged by Vladimir the Great in AD 987 [988]. In 2012, Putin suggested as much to the Russian Parliament. In the following year, 2013, in Kyiv, he even proclaimed that the union of Ukraine and Russia was blessed by God and would take place on the authority of the Lord. Then, in 2014 the annexation of Crimea followed, to be finally 'crowned' with the ongoing 2022 Ukrainian war.[9]

The erection of the statue of Vladimir the Great in Moscow in 2016 (see Chapter 1) vividly underscored Putin's determination to identify with the ancient Viking–Slav rulers of the Rus in his campaign to undermine the concept of Ukrainian independence.

In February 2022, the lethal nature of this contested origin myth was vividly displayed when the Russia of Vladimir Putin invaded the nation which claimed its origins in the mixed Norse–Slav community of Vladimir (Ukrainian: Volodymyr) the Great in the tenth century. The previous summer, Putin had issued a version of 'history' which claimed that Ukraine did not constitute a separate people or nation. Then, in February 2024, Putin treated the US conservative political commentator Tucker Carlson to a tour of Russian history which further developed this narrative.

Many historical ingredients went into the lethal cocktail of competing national identities that was bloodily unleashed on Ukraine in 2022, but the Vikings of the East certainly were (and are) there too. And this is clear from Putin's own words.

'ON THE HISTORICAL UNITY OF RUSSIANS AND UKRAINIANS'

On 12 July 2021, Putin published a very revealing 5,000-word essay. In it, he laid out his version of the history of Russia and Ukraine. It was entitled 'On the Historical Unity of Russians and Ukrainians'. He wrote:

> The wall that has emerged in recent years between Russia and Ukraine, between the parts of what is essentially the same historical and spiritual space, to my mind is our great common misfortune and tragedy. These are, first and foremost, the consequences of our own mistakes made at different periods of time. But these are also the result of deliberate efforts by those forces that have always sought to undermine our unity …
>
> Russians, Ukrainians, and Belarusians are all descendants of Ancient Rus, which was the largest state in Europe. Slavic and other tribes across the vast territory – from Ladoga, Novgorod, and Pskov to Kiev and Chernigov – were bound together by one language (which we now refer to as Old Russian), economic ties,

the rule of the princes of the Rurik dynasty, and – after the baptism of Rus – the Orthodox faith. The spiritual choice made by St Vladimir, who was both Prince of Novgorod and Grand Prince of Kiev, still largely determines our affinity today.[10]

There was no reference to the Normanist debate in Putin's excursion through Russian and Ukrainian history in 2021, but the generally Slavic focus of his deep dive into origins suggests that – if prompted on the question – he would have adopted the anti-Normanist stance. Putin's view of the past was characterised, at this point, by ethnic homogeneity. No Western influences were allowed to creep in (or be invited in) when it came to conceptualising the origins of the Rus.

However, by 2024, his exploration of Russian origins had become more expansive. This is curious given the fact that this was two years after he had launched the invasion of Ukraine and was now openly at odds with the West. Nevertheless, during his conversation with Tucker Carlson in Moscow, on 6 February 2024, the origin myth which Putin promulgated was straight out of the *Russian Primary Chronicle*:

> The Russian state started gathering itself as a centralized statehood, and it is considered to be the year of the establishment of the Russian state, in 862 when the townspeople of Novgorod invited a Varangian prince, Rurik, from Scandinavia to Reign …
>
> In 882 Rurik's successor Prince Oleg, who was actually playing the role of regent and Rurik's young son because Rurik had died

by that time, came to Kiev. He ousted two brothers who apparently had once been members of Rurik's squad, so Russia began to develop with two centers of power, Kiev and Novgorod.[11]

The Normanist stance was clear in Putin's statement. We might ask: Why the change from a focus on ethnic homogeneity in 2021 to a specific reference to the *incoming* of a *foreign* ruling elite in 2024? The 'princes of the Rurik dynasty' were namechecked in his 2021 essay but without mentioning their crucial geographical origins. In short, a shift in tone occurred between the 2021 essay and the Carlson interview in 2024.

We might conjecture that this was because the subtext had altered between 2021 and 2024, and this allowed the *foreign* Vikings of the Rus to achieve their place within the lecture that Putin delivered to his US visitor. In 2021, the mood music was Russian ethnic unity triumphing over – in Putin's view – the artificial divisions of modern borders which had severed the 'Little Russians' (Ukrainians) from the 'Great Russians' (those living in the Russian Federation). Mention of Scandinavian incomers hardly worked within that agenda. However, by 2024, Putin was claiming Russia as the true repository of 'Western traditional values', which he asserted had been abandoned by liberal Western societies and their cosmopolitan elites. Within this narrative, the Norse founders of the Rus state could be made to play a part in underscoring how far Russia is historically a part of the European mainstream; a mainstream from which Western liberals have (in the Putinist worldview) deviated. This is where the historical Rus meet modern 'culture wars'.

There is good reason for suggesting this as the causal factor for the explicit part *foreign Vikings* played in the 2024 lecture that Putin delivered to Carlson. And this reason can be discovered in yet another Putin reflection on history and modern society that he delivered four months after the interview with Carlson. On 7 June 2024, during Putin's Q&A with the academic Sergei Karaganov at the St Petersburg International Economic Forum (SPIEF), he made some revealing remarks concerning the relationship of Russia with Europe, in the context of the ongoing conflict with the West over the Russian war against Ukraine. In the Q&A, Karaganov pressed Putin to agree that Russia ought to reorientate towards Siberia and Asia. In contrast to such a suggested reorientation, Putin emphasised the ongoing rootedness of Russia as a European nation (as envisaged by Putin): 'As for the elements of European culture, it is not we who are losing those genes, and elements of European culture, but that part of Europe called "Western".'[12]

In such a view of contemporary developments, an anchoring of the origins of the Rus in the ancient Norse rulers gained some traction and was politically useful.

THE CORE OF THE PUTIN WORLDVIEW

The Putinist narrative was (and is) simple: it is not Russia that has turned its back on its 'European' character, rather it is Europe (with its alleged 'liberal globalist' agenda) that has abandoned its historic culture and its role.

This outlook became increasingly stated within extreme Russian nationalist circles after 2014. In that year, as Russian-backed rebels sought to establish a separate political identity in the eastern Ukrainian region of the Donbas, one Russian Orthodox priest claimed that Ukrainian forces, and those supporting them in the West, were seeking 'the establishment of planetary Satanic rule'. In addition, he claimed: 'What's occurring here is the very beginning of a global war. Not for resources or territory, that's secondary. This is a war for the destruction of true Christianity, Orthodoxy.' He then further castigated the West in apocalyptic terms: 'They are intentionally hastening the reign of Antichrist.' In contrast to this, he asserted, any Russian-backed militia member who was seeking to wrest the Donbas from Ukrainian control 'is also a monastic, but wages not an inner war with the spirits of evil, but an outer one'.[13] This outlook spread among the most extreme nationalists within the Russian Orthodox community. It challenges the West's 'liberal democratic values', claiming that critics of the Putin regime oppose the values of 'Holy Russia', and denounces many features of modern Western society (such as LGBTQ+ rights).[14] Those Russian nationalists who hold these views have claimed that war with Ukraine (regarded as a proxy of the West) will eventually lead to the creation of a revitalised Russian Orthodox national community and the end of Russian spiritual decay.[15]

Within such a negative take on contemporary culture in the West, a Russian rootedness in a wider historic European movement of people (as epitomised by the originators of the Rurik dynasty) has been made to play a part. A celebration of this foreign Viking origin has been used to assert both the historic European character (and connectedness) of Russia and its particular Christian Orthodox nature. This is then contrasted with the current nature of Western Europe, which is condemned as liberal, secular, divided and detached from its traditional Christian character and morality.

The 'Holy Rus' status was spelled out to Carlson, in 2024, in terms immediately familiar to modern Russian Orthodox nationalists; and the event referred to is familiar from our exploration of tenth-century developments in the Kyivan state. In Putin's words:

> The next very significant date in the history of Russia was 988. This was the baptism of Russia when Prince Vladimir, the great-grandson of Rurik, baptized Russia and adopted orthodoxy or eastern Christianity. From this time, the centralized Russian state began to strengthen. Why? Because of the single territory integrated economic size, one and the same language, and after the baptism of Russia, the same faith and rule of the prince. The centralized Russian state began to take shape.[16]

This recalled Putin's lengthy essay on Russian and Ukrainian history from 2021. In that essay, he was at pains to stress how, despite later decline, the unity of the Rus people was maintained: 'Later, like other European states of that time, Ancient Rus faced a decline of central rule and fragmentation. At the same time, both the nobility and the common people perceived Rus as a common territory, as their homeland.'[17]

While this unity showed itself in an original common language, it was also rooted in religious faith, which takes us back to the conversion of Vladimir the Great in the tenth century. 'Most importantly, people both in the western and eastern Russian lands spoke the same language. Their faith was Orthodox. Up to the middle of the 15th century, the unified church government remained in place.'[18]

For Putin, this character of the Rus then passed to the rulers of Moscow. Putin could not, of course, ignore the role played by Lithuania, but it was – in his view – Moscow that was the true inheritor of what constituted the Rus heritage:

> Both Lithuanian Rus and Moscow Rus could have become the points of attraction and consolidation of the territories of Ancient Rus. It so happened that Moscow became the center of reunification, continuing the tradition of ancient Russian statehood. Moscow princes – the descendants of Prince Alexander Nevsky – cast off the foreign yoke and began gathering the Russian lands.[19]

Consequently, in the Putinist narrative, what happened in the seventeenth century and after was not a Russian *imposition* but a Russian *restoration* of what constituted Rus geographical identity. It was 'gathering the Russian lands'. There were echoes of this in how Putin framed his annexation of eastern Ukraine and the war to bring Ukraine under Russian control. This constituted yet another 'gathering [of] the Russian lands'. His account of the seventeenth-century expansion of the power of Muscovy provided him with an opportunity to deploy a term which, by its nature, undermined Ukrainian claims to national separate identity. This asserted that Ukraine was, and is, 'Little Russia':

> The Russian state incorporated the city of Kiev [in 1686] and the lands on the left bank of the Dnieper River, including Poltava region, Chernigov region, and Zaporozhye. Their inhabitants

AN INDEPENDENT UKRAINE

were reunited with the main part of the Russian Orthodox people. These territories were referred to as '*Malorossia*' (Little Russia).[20]

Later, to Carlson in 2024, Putin further defined the seventeenth century as the key point at which the Ukrainian population under Polish domination (termed by him as 'this part of the Russian lands that is now called Ukraine') were finally reunited with the Rus Motherland. This event occurred, he told Carlson, in 1654. The matter was further resolved, in Putin's view, when 'under the rule of Catherine the Great, Russia reclaimed all of its historical lands, including in the south and west. This all lasted until the revolution.'[21] Then – in 1917 – Putin stated that things began to go badly wrong for the united Russian peoples and lands.[22] But more of that later.

For any modern observer who might be thinking of the way Ukrainian culture and separateness had developed since the thirteenth-century Mongol invasions, Putin focused on this in 2021 and harnessed the name of this alleged independent state, in order to refute the very idea of its distinctiveness:

> The name 'Ukraine' was used more often in the meaning of the Old Russian word '*okraina*' (periphery), which is found in written sources from the 12th century, referring to various border territories. And the word 'Ukrainian', judging by archival documents, originally referred to frontier guards who protected the external borders.[23]

In short, Putin asserted that Ukraine as an entity (separate to Muscovy) never existed and the modern proponents of such a view are out of step with the realities of history. For those who might object that, in reality, Ukraine has a persistent self-awareness of itself as separate from Moscow–Russia, Putin had a ready answer. It was all the fault of the Bolsheviks and their policies, as they were applied after the Russian Revolution of October 1917. Reading what comes next in his essay, one could be forgiven for forgetting that Putin had been an officer in the Soviet political police, the KGB, and a loyal upholder of the Communist world view that the Kremlin promulgated across the USSR prior to its collapse. Clearly, since then, Putin has both reinvented himself and his world view. And in this reinvented self and outlook, it was the Bolsheviks (whom Putin had loyally served until 1991) who were to blame for the emergence of the idea that Ukraine is a nation separate from Russia:

> In 1922, when the USSR was created, with the Ukrainian Soviet Socialist Republic becoming one of its founders, a rather fierce debate among the Bolshevik leaders resulted in the implementation of Lenin's plan to form a union state as a federation of equal republics. The right for the republics [including Ukraine] to freely secede from the Union was included in the text of the Declaration on the Creation of the Union of Soviet Socialist Republics and, subsequently, in the 1924 USSR Constitution. By doing so, the authors planted in the foundation of our statehood the most dangerous time bomb, which exploded the moment the safety mechanism provided by the leading role of the CPSU [Communist Party of the Soviet Union] was gone, the party itself collapsing from within [culminating, in 1991, with the end of the USSR].[24]

AN INDEPENDENT UKRAINE

This assertion is rather curious. If Ukrainian national identity is a fiction and 'Ukrainians' (so-called 'Little Russians') have been longing since the thirteenth century to be restored to the Motherland, why did tsarist authorities spent so much time, money and effort between 1800 and 1914 on Russification, which was designed to stamp out a Ukrainian cultural consciousness that (apparently) did not exist? One wishes that this conundrum had been addressed in some of Putin's perambulations through history. What one does get from his writings is the sense that it was this Bolshevik promotion of (in his view, artificial) Ukrainian identity which – when the USSR finally collapsed – was responsible for the fact that (in Putin's words): 'A "parade of sovereignties" followed [the collapse of the USSR]. On 8 December 1991, the so-called Belovezh Agreement on the Creation of the Commonwealth of Independent States was signed, stating that "the USSR as a subject of international law and a geopolitical reality no longer existed".'

Out of this situation, the republic of Ukraine emerged. To the chagrin of Putin, this meant that the 'artificially inflated statelet' of Ukraine (as he viewed it) continued to exist, even when the Soviet regime – which allegedly had created this Frankensteinian political entity – had collapsed. It was this which caused Putin to angrily conclude:

> Therefore, modern Ukraine is entirely the product of the Soviet era. We know and remember well that it was shaped – for a significant part – on the lands of historical Russia. To make sure of that, it is enough to look at the boundaries of the lands reunited with the Russian state in the 17th century and the territory of the

Ukrainian SSR [Soviet Socialist Republic] when it left the Soviet Union [in 1991].[25]

The whole process, as presented by the author of 'On the Historical Unity of Russians and Ukrainians', occurred because 'the Bolsheviks treated the Russian people as inexhaustible material for their social experiments'. As part of this Soviet political laboratory, the Bolsheviks 'dreamt of a world revolution that would wipe out national states'. When it came to the sacred territory of Holy Rus, their policies were responsible for 'chopping the country into pieces'. For Putin, the end product was undeniable: 'One fact is crystal clear: Russia was robbed, indeed.'[26] What had started with the establishment of the Viking dynasty of Rurik had been spiritually transformed by the conversion of Vladimir the Great and had developed into the mighty state of Holy Kyivan Rus and had been traduced by the Bolsheviks between 1922 and 1991 and then by Ukrainian nationalists after 1991. However, what Vladimir the Great had started, and what (in Putin's view) had later been trashed by the Bolsheviks and by Ukrainian nationalists, will be reinstated by Vladimir Putin. The Kremlin agenda was and is clear: Ukraine will be united with Russia. The once-unified nation, which had been created by the Viking Age rulers of the Rus, will be restored.

There was, he opined, only one legitimate path forward, since the 'true sovereignty of Ukraine is possible only in partnership with Russia'. This arises out of 'spiritual, human and civilizational ties formed for centuries'. It is a 'kinship [that] has been transmitted from generation to generation', vividly revealed 'in the blood ties that unite millions of our families' and capable of being condensed into five dramatic words: 'For we are one people.'²⁷ In 2024, Putin unpackaged this a little more for Tucker Carlson when he bitterly stated that 'everything that Russia had generously bestowed on Ukraine was dragged away by the latter'.²⁸

Given what was unleashed on the people of Ukraine in February 2022, the conclusion Putin reached in his 2021 essay is particularly striking: 'Russia has never been and will never be "anti-Ukraine". And what Ukraine will be – it is up to its citizens to decide.'²⁹ As long, it seems, that their decision is validated by the Kremlin of Putin. And in that contested identity, the Eastern Vikings remain in the mix.

EPILOGUE

BACK TO THE FUTURE? WHERE NEXT FOR THE 'DEEP STORY' OF THE RUS?

A number of modern Ukrainian historians, such as Pyotr Tolochko (died 2024), Mykhailo Braychevsky, Mykola Kotlyar, Volodymyr Baran and others, have argued that the debate over the Normanist origins of the Rus state has become largely irrelevant in the light of emerging archaeological evidence for the early formation of states in the vicinity of the River Dnieper/Dnipro (around Kyiv), and also in Galicia and Volhynia, well before there were any literary references to Norse arrival in the area. This suggests that, whatever contribution the foreign Vikings made to these states, they did not cause them to develop.[1] While they contributed to their character, they were only one of a number of factors that fed into the formation of these communities and their interactions with their neighbours. And a Slavic character soon predominated.

However, this may be going too far in writing the Vikings out of Ukrainian and Russian history...

THE RUS ROOTS OF A DEEP STORY

The reality is that the roots of both nations (and their deep stories) *are* intertwined in the early medieval past. And these origins lie in the activities of Viking traders, raiders and settlers who first travelled the river systems of the Volga, Dnipro/Dnieper and other waterways, in the 300 years after 750. For – while not being the only actors in that historical drama – they played a crucial part in the functioning of trade routes which linked the Caspian, Black Sea and Mediterranean to the Baltic and Scandinavia. From that emerged the Rus and, in time, the Norse–Slav state which eventually became an Orthodox people in the late tenth century. The part played by Eastern Vikings was a vital aspect of that process.

The fact that their role in the contested deep story of both Ukraine and Russia is still debated is testimony to their impact on history and the way that (even when misconstrued) it is used to frame modern identities.

What is clear is that Ukraine is not simply a subdivision of Russia, lacking legitimate aspirations to sovereignty and independence, as Russian nationalists insist. Rather, it has its own particular history, character and culture. But it is not as different as some Ukrainian nationalists assert. Ukraine and Russia are deeply connected (and conflicted). This is rooted in old history, much of it in the Rus.

Nevertheless, however intertwined their pasts have been, it remains the fundamental right of a people to decide their own future. This Ukraine did in 1991 and that has been violently opposed by the Putin regime and extreme Russian nationalists. In addition, complex historical relations (including, arguably, the failure by Kyiv to sufficiently engage with a minority who felt greater affinity with Russia) does not justify or excuse the violent invasion of a neighbouring state, as carried out by Russia in 2014 and culminating in outright invasion in 2022.

What is beyond dispute is that it has been an extraordinary journey from 750 to the third decade of the twenty-first century. It is a journey which connects the world of Vladimir the Great with the world of Vladimir Putin. And the journey is far from over. For it is rooted in an origin that has a contested legacy. What started in the age of Viking longships now continues in the age of drone- and cyber-warfare, tanks and ballistic missiles. The story of the Vikings in the East goes on.

NOTES

A NOTE ABOUT SPELLINGS
1. '"Kyiv" or "Kiev" – Here's why the difference is political,' https://www.cbc.ca/news/world/cbc-pronunciation-kyiv-ukraine-crisis-explainer-1.6371766 (accessed April 2024).

INTRODUCTION
1. Zbigniew Brzezinski, 'The Premature Partnership', *Foreign Affairs* (1 March 1994). See also: Mykola Bielieskov, 'Russian victory in Ukraine would leave Europe at Putin's mercy', https://www.atlanticcouncil.org/blogs/ukrainealert/russian-victory-in-ukraine-would-leave-europe-at-putins-mercy/ (accessed August 2024).
2. Denys Yurchenko, 'Russian Strategic Culture and the War in Ukraine', https://www.fpri.org/article/2024/07/russian-strategic-culture-and-the-war-in-ukraine/ (accessed August 2024).
3. James Roberts and Martyn Whittock, *Trump and the Puritans: How the Evangelical Religious Right Put Donald Trump in the White House* (London: Biteback, 2020).
4. Arlie Russell Hochschild, *Strangers in Their Own Land: Anger and Mourning on the American Right* (New York and London: New Press, 2018).
5. Martyn Whittock, *Mayflower Lives: Pilgrims in a New World and the Early American Experience* (New York: Pegasus Books, 2019).
6. Roberts and Whittock, *Trump and the Puritans*.
7. Martyn Whittock, *The Secret History of Soviet Russia's Police State* (London: Robinson, 2020).
8. Martyn Whittock, *The End Times, Again?* (Eugene, OR: Cascade Books, 2021).
9. Martyn Whittock, *Apocalyptic Politics* (Eugene, OR: Cascade Books, 2022).
10. Martyn Whittock, *American Vikings: How the Norse Sailed into the Lands and Imaginations of America* (New York: Pegasus Books, 2023).

CHAPTER 1: GO EAST!
1. Angus A. Somerville and R. Andrew McDonald (eds), *The Viking Age: A Reader* (Toronto: University of Toronto Press, 2014), p. 290.
2. For the extraordinary North American dimension that connects Norse exploration of eleventh-century North America with January 6th at the US Capitol, see: Whittock, *American Vikings*.

3   Neil Bermel, 'Ukraine war: "vranyo" – Russian for when you lie and everyone knows it, but you don't care', https://theconversation.com/ukraine-war-vranyo-russian-for-when-you-lie-and-everyone-knows-it-but-you-dont-care-181100 (accessed April 2024). The pithy definition was earlier quoted by John Sipher and referred to in this article.
4   Orysia Lutsevych, 'Myth 12: "Crimea was always Russian"', https://www.chathamhouse.org/2021/05/myths-and-misconceptions-debate-russia/myth-12-crimea-was-always-russian (accessed April 2024).
5   Ibid.
6   Ibid.
7   This should not be interpreted as Ukraine giving up a usable independent nuclear deterrent, since the access codes to the weapons in question, which were located on Ukrainian soil, were kept in Moscow.
8   International Republican Institute, 'Public Opinion Survey Residents of the Autonomous Republic of Crimea May 16–30 2013', https://www.iri.org/sites/default/files/2013%20October%207%20Survey%20of%20Crimean%20Public%20Opinion,%20May%2016-30,%202013.pdf (accessed April 2024).
9   Ye Bobrov, 'Проблемы жителей Крыма [Problems of residents of Crimea]', Members' Blogs, Council under the President of the Russian Federation on Civil Society Development and Human Rights, 22 April 2014, http://president-sovet.ru/members/blogs/bobrov_e_a/problemy-zhiteley-kryma (accessed April 2024).
10 Paul Coyer, 'Putin's Holy War and the Disintegration of the "Russian World"', https://www.forbes.com/sites/paulcoyer/2015/06/04/putins-holy-war-and-the-disintegration-of-the-russian-world/?sh=51619ca285b4 (accessed April 2024).
11 Melik Kaylan, 'The Real Reason Why Putin Gave a History Lesson to Tucker Carlson', https://www.forbes.com/sites/melikkaylan/2024/02/10/the-real-reason-why-putin-gave-a-history-lesson-to-tucker-carlson/?sh=727f79763b79 (accessed April 2024).
12 Raymond Ian Page, *Reading the Past: Runes* (London: British Museum Publications, 1987), p. 23.
13 Ibid, p. 30.
14 Somerville and McDonald (eds), *The Viking Age*, p. 290.
15 Ibid.
16 Ibid.
17 Gary Dean Peterson, *Vikings and Goths: A History of Ancient and Medieval Sweden* (Jefferson, NC: McFarland, 2016), p. 230.
18 For a succinct overview of the expedition, see: Kim Hjardar and Vegard Vike, *Vikings at War* (Oxford: Casemate, 2016), p. 367.
19 Dorothy Whitelock (ed.), *English Historical Documents, Volume I, c.500–1042* (London: Eyre Methuen, 1979), p. 180; compare the information found in Manuscript A, also called the *Parker Chronicle*, with Manuscript E, the Laud or *Peterborough Chronicle*, of the *Anglo-Saxon Chronicle*.
20 Gwyn Jones, *A History of the Vikings* (Oxford: Oxford University Press, 2002), pp. 75–6.
21 Martyn Whittock and Hannah Whittock, *The Viking Blitzkrieg: AD 789–1098* (Stroud: History Press, 2013), p. 25.
22 Neil Price, 'Novgorod, Kiev and their Satellites', in Mogens Herman Hansen (ed.), *A Comparative Study of Thirty City-state Cultures: An Investigation* (Copenhagen: Kongelige Danske Videnskabernes Selskab, 2000), p. 267.
23 Whittock and Whittock, *The Viking Blitzkrieg*, p. 26.
24 Martyn Whittock, 'The saint at the heart of the war in Ukraine', https://www.christiantoday.com/article/the.saint.at.the.heart.of.the.war.in.ukraine/138286.htm (accessed April 2024).
25 See Whittock, *American Vikings*.
26 'Viking Runes at Hagia Sophia', https://www.atlasobscura.com/places/viking-runes-at-hagia-sophia (accessed April 2024).

NOTES

27 Whittock and Whittock, *The Viking Blitzkrieg*, p. 26.
28 Jones, *A History of the Vikings*, pp. 76–7.
29 Ibid., p. 76.
30 Martyn Whittock, 'Vikings: When the hammer met the cross', *Church Times* (26 October 2018), https://www.churchtimes.co.uk/articles/2018/26-october/features/features/vikings-when-the-hammer-met-the-cross (accessed April 2024).
31 Ibid.
32 Martyn Whittock and Hannah Whittock, *Norse Myths and Legends* (London: Robinson, 2017), p. 1.
33 For an overview of the use of the term 'Viking' and the names used by others to describe them, see: Martin Arnold, *The Vikings: Culture and Conquest* (London: Hambledon Continuum, 2006), pp. 7–8. See also: Somerville and McDonald (eds), *The Viking Age*, p. xiii.
34 Martyn Whittock and Hannah Whittock, *Tales of Valhalla* (New York: Pegasus Books, 2018), p. 2.
35 C. Balbirnie, 'The Vikings at home', *BBC History Magazine* (September 2012), volume 13, number 9, p. 25.

CHAPTER 2: EVIDENCE FOR VIKINGS IN THE EASTERN BALTIC: TRADE AND SETTLEMENT

1 Technically, at this period, we should really refer to this complex of territories in Central Europe as 'the Empire' or 'the Roman Empire'. Dating from the crowning of Charlemagne by Pope Leo III in 800, this revived the Roman title of 'emperor' in Western Europe, although it gained a more stable and long-lasting foundation on the crowning of Otto I as emperor in 962. It was not until 1157 that the term 'Holy' was first used and it was only after 1254 that the form 'Holy Roman Empire' came into use. Nevertheless, there is some justification in using the term before these dates, if only to indicate which institution is being referred to and to avoid confusion with the earlier Roman Empire and the Eastern Roman Empire (the Byzantine).
2 The date of the start of Harald Fairhair's reign is uncertain. Various dates between 860 and 880 have been suggested. Even his death (though usually dated as being in 930) has, by some historians, been placed as late as 940. The most detailed account of his life is found in the much later saga written by Snorri Sturluson, *Heimskringla*, although he also features in a number of other Icelandic sagas. See: Somerville and McDonald (eds), *The Viking Age*, pp. 434–9.
3 For a succinct overview of Viking Age Scandinavia, see: John Haywood, *The Penguin Historical Atlas of the Vikings* (London: Penguin, 1995), pp. 28–33; see also: Angelo Forte, Richard Oram and Frederik Pedersen, *Viking Empires* (Cambridge: Cambridge University Press, 2005), pp. 7–53.
4 Haywood, *The Penguin Historical Atlas of the Vikings*, p. 32.
5 See ibid., p. 100, for a brief outline of the roots of these terms.
6 Florin Curta, *Eastern Europe in the Middle Ages 500–1300, Volume 1* (Leiden and Boston: Brill, 2019), p. 268.
7 Daniel Weiss, 'Hoards of the Vikings: Evidence of trade, diplomacy, and vast wealth on an unassuming island in the Baltic Sea', https://archaeology.org/issues/january-february-2017/features/sweden-gotland-viking-wealth/ (accessed April 2024).
8 Martyn Whittock and Hannah Whittock, *The Vikings: From Odin to Christ* (Oxford: Lion, 2018), p. 143.
9 Helen Appleton, '*Ohthere and Wulfstan*', https://ora.ox.ac.uk/objects/uuid:b856b3a9-45fd-429f-8cf4-826501e81df5/files/m7047cbce4871d6853ea4e9fe28cd25f5 (accessed November 2024).
10 Francis Young, 'Lithuania and Britain: an entwined history', https://drfrancisyoung.com/2020/06/17/lithuania-and-britain-an-entwined-history/ (accessed April 2024).
11 Ibid.
12 Curta, *Eastern Europe in the Middle Ages 500–1300, Volume 1*, p. 270.

13 Ibid.
14 Ibid., p. 269–270.
15 Ibid., p. 269, note 94.
16 Unlike the city, this Russian region never changed its name back to St Petersburg.
17 Weiss, 'Hoards of the Vikings'.
18 'The Vikings in the East', https://www.asncvikingage.com/vikings-east (accessed April 2024).
19 Curta, *Eastern Europe in the Middle Ages 500–1300, Volume 1*, p. 272–3.
20 Ibid., p. 273.
21 Weiss, 'Hoards of the Vikings'.
22 Rory Naismith, *Early Medieval Britain, c.500–1000* (Cambridge: Cambridge University Press, 2021), p. 57.

CHAPTER 3: VIKINGS OF THE RIVERS

1 'Rus–Vikings in the East', https://the-past.com/review/museum/rus-vikings-in-the-east/ (accessed April 2024).
2 Ibid.
3 Ibid.
4 Ibid.
5 It was this that led Cat Jarman to title her exploration of the Eastern Vikings: *River Kings: The Vikings from Scandinavia to the Silk Roads* (London: William Collins, 2021).
6 'Volga River', https://www.britannica.com/place/Volga-River (accessed April 2024).
7 Stefan T. Possony, 'European Russia's Inland Waterways – Past, Present, and Future', *US Naval Institute Proceedings* (August 1947), vol. 73/8/534, https://www.usni.org/magazines/proceedings/1947/august/european-russias-inland-waterways-past-present-and-future (accessed April 2024).
8 Ibid.
9 Orlando Figes, *The Story of Russia* (London: Bloomsbury, 2022), p. 20.
10 Doug Simms, 'The Early Period of Sámi History, from the Beginnings to the 16th Century', https://www.laits.utexas.edu/sami/dieda/hist/early.htm (accessed April 2024).
11 Helena Hals, 'The cultural contact between the Norse and Sámi is key to our understanding of Viking Age Society', https://www.scandinavianarchaeology.com/the-cultural-contact-between-the-norse-and-sami-is-key-to-our-understanding-of-viking-age-society/ (accessed April 2024)
12 Ibid.
13 Sirpa Aalto and Veli-Pekka Lehtola, 'The Sami Representations Reflecting the Multi-Ethnic North of the Saga Literature', *Journal of Northern Studies*, 11(2), 2017, p. 23.
14 Curta, *Eastern Europe in the Middle Ages 500–1300, Volume 1*, p. 282.
15 Neil Price, 'The Little-Known Role of Slavery in Viking Society', https://www.smithsonianmag.com/history/little-known-role-slavery-viking-society-180975597/ (accessed April 2024). See Neil Price, *Children of Ash and Elm: A History of the Vikings* (New York: Basic Books, 2020).
16 'Rus–Vikings in the East'.
17 Ibid.
18 See: Tatjana N. Jackson, 'Ladoga as a Gateway on the Road from the Varangians to the Greeks: Icelandic Sagas on Security Measures, Eleventh–Thirteenth Centuries', in Sari Nauman et al. (eds), *Baltic Hospitality from the Middle Ages to the Twentieth Century* (London: Palgrave Macmillan, 2022), pp. 63–84.
19 'The Vikings in the East'.
20 'Dangerous journeys to Eastern Europe and Russia', https://en.natmus.dk/historical-knowledge/denmark/prehistoric-period-until-1050-ad/the-viking-age/expeditions-and-raids/dangerous-journeys-to-eastern-europe-and-russia/ (accessed April 2024).
21 Ibid.

NOTES

22 Ibid.
23 Christoph Kilger, 'Long distance trade, runes and silver: a Gotlandic perspective', in Laila Kitzler Åhfeldt et al. (eds), *Relations and Runes: The Baltic Islands and Their Interactions During the Late Iron Age and Early Middle Ages* (Visby: Riksantikvarieämbetetp, 2020), p. 51.
24 Ibid., p. 50.
25 'Runestone G280 Commemorating a Death in the Dnieper Rapids', https://varangians01.omeka.net/items/show/149 (accessed April 2024).
26 Kilger, 'Long distance trade, runes and silver: a Gotlandic perspective', p. 52.
27 'Rus–Vikings in the East'.
28 Weiss, 'Hoards of the Vikings'.
29 'Rus–Vikings in the East'.
30 See: Anne Stalsberg, 'Women as actors in North European Viking Age trade', in Ross Samson (ed.), *Social Approaches to Viking Studies* (Glasgow: Cruithne, 1993).
31 Jarman, *River Kings*, pp. 147–8.

CHAPTER 4: EAST MEETS WEST IN THE WORLD OF THE GODS AND GODDESSES

1 Whittock, *American Vikings*, p. 15.
2 Aalto and Lehtola, 'The Sami Representations Reflecting the Multi-Ethnic North of the Saga Literature', pp. 14–15.
3 For modern translations of these, see: Snorri Sturluson, *Edda*, Anthony Faulkes (ed. & trans), (London: Everyman, 1987) – often known as the *Prose Edda* – and *The Poetic Edda*, Carolyne Larrington (trans) (Oxford: Oxford University Press, 1996).
4 *Skaldic* poetry is one of the two main forms of Old Norse poetry and is a highly complicated poetic form usually reserved for writing historical or praise poems.
5 For an overview of the Norse saga literature, see: Margaret Clunies Ross, *The Cambridge Introduction to the Old Norse-Icelandic Saga* (Cambridge: Cambridge University Press, 2010).
6 Whittock and Whittock, *Norse Myths and Legends*, p. 206.

CHAPTER 5: THE CREATION OF THE RUS STATE

1 *The Russian Primary Chronicle Laurentian Text*, Samuel Cross and Olgerd Sherbowitz-Wetzor (trans and eds) (Cambridge, MS: Mediaeval Academy of America, 1953), p. 59.
2 Quoted in: Jarman, *River Kings*, p. 225.
3 Anna Reid, *Borderland: A Journey Though the History of Ukraine* (London: Weidenfeld & Nicolson, 2022), p. 6.
4 Whittock and Whittock, *The Vikings*, p. 145.
5 Ibid.
6 Serhii Plokhy, *The Gates of Europe* (London: Penguin, 2016), p. 25.
7 Curta, *Eastern Europe in the Middle Ages 500–1300, Volume 1*, p. 287.
8 Plokhy, *The Gates of Europe*, p. 26.
9 Reid, *Borderland*, p. 6–7.
10 Curta, *Eastern Europe in the Middle Ages 500–1300, Volume 1*, p. 289.
11 Plokhy, *The Gates of Europe*, p. 26.
12 Whittock and Whittock, *The Vikings*, p. 146.
13 Ibid., p. 147.
14 Ibid.
15 Curta, *Eastern Europe in the Middle Ages 500–1300, Volume 1*, p. 279.
16 Ibid.
17 Ibid.
18 Reid, *Borderland*, p. 6.
19 Ibid., p. 7.
20 Curta, *Eastern Europe in the Middle Ages 500–1300, Volume 1*, p. 292, note 86.
21 Ibid., p. 296.

CHAPTER 6: TO THE 'GREAT CITY': THE LURE OF CONSTANTINOPLE

1. Richard E. Sullivan, 'Charlemagne Holy Roman emperor [747?–814]', https://www.britannica.com/biography/Charlemagne/Military-campaigns (accessed May 2024).
2. 'Dangerous journeys to Eastern Europe and Russia'.
3. Ibid.
4. Thomas S. Noonan, 'Scandinavians in European Russia', in Peter Sawyer (ed.), *The Oxford Illustrated History of the Vikings* (Oxford: Oxford University Press, 1999), p. 150.
5. Curta, *Eastern Europe in the Middle Ages 500–1300, Volume 1*, p. 291.
6. Joshua J. Mark, 'Kievan Rus', https://www.worldhistory.org/Kievan_Rus/ (accessed May 2024).
7. Curta, *Eastern Europe in the Middle Ages 500–1300, Volume 1*, p. 291.
8. Noonan, 'Scandinavians in European Russia', p. 149.
9. Curta, *Eastern Europe in the Middle Ages 500–1300, Volume 1*, p. 292.
10. Noonan, 'Scandinavians in European Russia', p. 149.
11. 'The Vikings in the East'.
12. Ibid.
13. Noonan, 'Scandinavians in European Russia', p. 149.
14. Curta, *Eastern Europe in the Middle Ages 500–1300, Volume 1*, p. 292.
15. Constantine Porphyrogenitus, *De Administrando Imperio* [*On the Administration of the Empire*], Greek text edited by Gyula Moravcsik, English text translated by Romilly J. H. Jenkins, rev. ed. (Cambridge, MS: Harvard University Press, 2009), p. 31.
16. Curta, *Eastern Europe in the Middle Ages 500–1300, Volume 1*, p. 297 and note 105.
17. Plokhy, *The Gates of Europe*, p. 30.

CHAPTER 7: THE MAKING OF 'HOLY RUS'

1. Coyer, 'Putin's Holy War and the Disintegration of the "Russian World"'.
2. Ian Blanchard, *Mining, Metallurgy and Minting in the Middle Ages* (Stuttgart: Franz Steiner Verlag, 2001), p. 562.
3. 'Silver shortage: true or false', http://islamicceramics.ashmolean.org/Samanids/shortage.htm (accessed May 2024).
4. See: Curta, *Eastern Europe in the Middle Ages 500–1300, Volume 1*, p. 294.
5. *The Russian Primary Chronicle Laurentian Text*, p. 86.
6. See: Curta, *Eastern Europe in the Middle Ages 500–1300, Volume 1*, p. 296.
7. Robert Ferguson, *The Hammer and the Cross* (London: Penguin, 2010), pp. 129–31, gives a good account of the events in one of the well-known traditions.
8. Andrzej Poppe, 'Two Concepts of the Conversion of Rus' in Kievan Writings', *Proceedings of the International Congress Commemorating the Millennium of Christianity in Rus'-Ukraine 1988–1989* (1989), vol. 12/13, p. 488.
9. Ferguson, *The Hammer and the Cross*, p. 131.
10. 'Rus–Vikings in the East'.
11. Michele Colucci, 'The Image of Western Christianity in the Culture of Kievan Rus', *Proceedings of the International Congress Commemorating the Millennium of Christianity in Rus'-Ukraine 1988–1989* (1989), vol. 12/13, pp. 576–86.
12. Raymond Ian Page, *Chronicles of the Vikings* (London: British Museum Press, 1995), p. 84.
13. Noonan, 'Scandinavians in European Russia', p. 151.
14. Ibid.
15. Page, *Chronicles of the Vikings*, p. 101.
16. Whittock and Whittock, *The Vikings*, p. 156.

CHAPTER 8: VIKINGS ON CAMELS

1. 'The Vikings in the East'.
2. Ibid.

NOTES

3 James Graham-Campbell, *The Viking World* (London: Frances Lincoln, 2001), pp. 108–9.
4 Ibid., p. 109.
5 It should be noted that the modern term 'Silk Roads' is applied to a range of different trade routes which crossed Eurasia, connecting eastern Asia with Western Europe. It was not one routeway, nor a formalised one.
6 'Dangerous journeys to Eastern Europe and Russia'.
7 Graham-Campbell, *The Viking World*, p. 109.
8 Weiss, 'Hoards of the Vikings'.
9 Ibid.
10 Ibid.
11 Haywood, *The Penguin Historical Atlas of the Vikings*, map, p. 107.
12 Weiss, 'Hoards of the Vikings'.
13 Ibid.
14 Probably written between 844 and 848.
15 Wladyslaw Duczko, *Viking Rus: Studies on the Presence of Scandinavians in Eastern Europe* (Leiden: Brill, 2004), p. 22.
16 Charlotte Hedenstierna-Jonson and Neil Price, 'Iron Age Scandinavia and the Silk Roads: a new frontier', *The Historian* (Spring 2024), Issue 161, p. 38.
17 Noonan, 'Scandinavians in European Russia', p. 147.
18 Ibid., p. 148.
19 Ibid.
20 Albert Stanburrough Cook, 'Ibn Fadlān's Account of Scandinavian Merchants on the Volga in 922', *Journal of English and Germanic Philology*, Vol. 22, No. 1 (January 1923), pp. 55–6.
21 Ibid.
22 The following extracts are adapted from the translation by Cook and used with permission from Jessalynn Bird at Saint Mary's College, Notre Dame, Indiana, US, https://human.libretexts.org/Courses/Saint_Mary's_College_(Notre_Dame_IN)/Humanistic_Studies/Ahmad_ibn_Fadlan_and_the_Rus_(Vikings) (accessed March 2025).
23 Haywood, *The Penguin Historical Atlas of the Vikings*, p. 107.
24 'The Vikings in the East'.

CHAPTER 9: A NEW SLAV STATE AND THE LAST HURRAH OF THE VIKINGS

1 'The Vikings in the East'.
2 'Rus–Vikings in the East'.
3 'The Vikings in the East'.
4 Katherine Holman, *The A to Z of the Vikings* (Lanham, MD, Plymouth: Scarecrow Press, 2003), p. 196.
5 Whittock and Whittock, *The Vikings*, p. 154.
6 Ibid., p. 155.
7 Ibid., p. 156.
8 Page, *Chronicles of the Vikings*, p. 84.
9 Ibid., p. 87.
10 Anne-Sofie Gräslund and Linn Lager, 'Runestones and the Christian Missions', in Stefan Brink and Neil Price (eds), *The Viking World* (Abingdon: Routledge, 2008), p. 634.
11 Page, *Chronicles of the Vikings*, p. 85.
12 Whitelock (ed.), *English Historical Documents, Volume I, c.500–1042*, p. 312.
13 Most notably explored in: Gabriel Ronay, *The Lost King of England: The East European Adventures of Edward the Exile* (Woodbridge: Boydell Press, 1989).
14 Martyn Whittock and Hannah Whittock, *1016 & 1066: Why the Vikings Caused the Norman Conquest* (Ramsbury: Robert Hale, 2016), p. 96. See also: Ronay, *The Lost King of England*.
15 Whittock and Whittock, *1016 & 1066*, p. 96.
16 Ibid., pp. 96–7.

17 Ibid., p. 97.
18 Figes, *The Story of Russia*, p. 30.

CHAPTER 10: THE ECLIPSING OF KYIVAN RUS: THE CALAMITOUS THIRTEENTH CENTURY

1 Figes, *The Story of Russia*, pp. 31–2.
2 William of Rubruck, *The Mission of Friar William of Rubruck: His Journey to the Court of the Great Khan Möngke, 1253-1255*, trans. Peter Jackson, with David Morgan (London: Hakluyt Society, 1990), pp. 182–3. See also: Michal Biran, 'Encounters Among Enemies: Preliminary Remarks on Captives in Mongol Eurasia', *Archivun Eurasia Medii Aevi* (2015), 21, pp. 27–42.
3 For an examination of Mongol behaviour seen through the lens of modern ideas about genocide, see: Timothy May, 'Mongol Genocides of the Thirteenth Century', in Ben Kiernan et al. (eds), *The Cambridge World History of Genocide, Volume 1* (Cambridge: Cambridge University Press, 2023), pp. 498–522.
4 Rebecca Joyce Frey, *Genocide and International Justice* (New York: Facts On File, 2009), p. 106, note 2.
5 Ibid.
6 Ibid.
7 'Mongol Empire: Origin Story, Military Invasions, Rise, and Fall', https://worldhistoryedu.com/mongol-empire-origins-military-conquests-rise-and-fall/ (accessed July 2024).
8 Qamar Adamjee and Stefano Carboni, 'The Legacy of Genghis Khan', https://www.metmuseum.org/toah/hd/khan1/hd_khan1.htm (accessed July 2024).
9 Ibid.
10 Figes, *The Story of Russia*, p. 35.
11 Reid, *Borderland*, p. 11.
12 Plokhy, *The Gates of Europe*, p. 51.
13 Reid, *Borderland*, p. 11.
14 Ibid.
15 'The Tale of Batu's Capture of Ryazan', https://www.rusliterature.org/the-tale-of-batus-capture-of-ryazan/ (accessed July 2024).
16 Marie Favereau, *The Horde: How the Mongols Changed the World* (Cambridge, MS: Belknap Press of Harvard University Press, 2021), p. 202.
17 Plokhy, *The Gates of Europe*, p. 51.
18 Reid, *Borderland*, p. 12.
19 Lawrence Langer, 'Muscovite Taxation and the Problem of Mongol Rule in Rus', *Russian History*, vol. 34, nos. 1–4 (2007), p. 116.
20 Ibid., p. 110.
21 Figes, *The Story of Russia*, pp. 38–9.
22 Plokhy, *The Gates of Europe*, pp. 49–50.
23 Ibid., p. 50.
24 Ibid., p. 53.
25 Ibid., p. 50.
26 Figes, *The Story of Russia*, pp. 41–2.
27 Plokhy, *The Gates of Europe*, p. 54.
28 Figes, *The Story of Russia*, p. 32.
29 Ibid., p. 33.
30 And this is admitted by those who reject simple ideas of Kyivan–Muscovy continuity. See: Figes, *The Story of Russia*, pp. 32–3.

CHAPTER 11: CONTESTED LANDS, 1300-1654

1 Reid, *Borderland*, pp. 13–14.
2 Figes, *The Story of Russia*, p. 3.

3 Reid, *Borderland*, p. 18.
4 Adam Zamoyski, *The Polish Way* (London: John Murray, 1987), p. 164.
5 Alisa Ballard Lin, 'The Cossacks, Ukraine's Paradigmatic Warriors', https://origins.osu.edu/read/cossacks-ukraines-paradigmatic-warriors (accessed July 2024).
6 Ibid.
7 Reid, *Borderland*, p. 31.
8 Shane O'Rourke, *The Cossacks* (Manchester: Manchester University Press, 2007), p. 82.
9 Reid, *Borderland*, p. 33.
10 'Tucker Carlson Interviews Vladimir Putin Transcript', www.rev.com/blog/transcripts/tucker-carlson-interviews-vladimir-putin-transcript (accessed July 2024).
11 Langer, 'Muscovite Taxation and the Problem of Mongol Rule in Rus', p. 101.
12 Ibid., p. 102.
13 Ibid.
14 See: Donald Ostrowski, 'The Growth of Muscovy (1462–1533)', in Maureen Perrie (ed.), *The Cambridge History of Russia, Vol. 1 From Early Rus to 1689* (Cambridge: Cambridge University Press, 2006).
15 See: ibid.
16 See: ibid.
17 The date of the expulsion of the Poles from Moscow – 4 November – was chosen by Vladimir Putin in 2005 as the Day of National Unity.
18 While Ivan IV was the first grand prince to be crowned 'tsar', the title had been used occasionally by his predecessors Ivan III (ruled 1462–1505) and Vasily III (ruled 1505–33).
19 Figes, *The Story of Russia*, pp. 57–8.
20 Ibid. The carvings on the throne illustrated scenes taken from the early sixteenth-century document *The Tale of the Princes of Vladimir*.
21 'Stalin on the Film Ivan the Terrible', the record of the conversation with Eisenstein based on Grigoriy Maryamov, *Kremlevskii tsenzor* (Moscow, 1992), pp. 84–92, https://soviethistory.msu.edu/1943-2/the-cult-of-leadership/the-cult-of-leadership-texts/stalin-on-the-film-ivan-the-terrible/ (accessed June 2024).
22 Ibid.
23 Ibid.
24 Ibid.
25 Figes, *The Story of Russia*, p. 7.
26 Ibid.
27 Ibid.

CHAPTER 12: A PERSISTENT LEGACY, 1654–1783

1 Reid, *Borderland*, p. 36.
2 Carol Stevens, *Russia's Wars of Emergence 1460–1730* (London: Taylor & Francis, 2013), p. 168.
3 Ibid., p. 180.
4 Reid, *Borderland*, p. 39.
5 Figes, *The Story of Russia*, p. 101.
6 A role and phrase traditionally associated with the later city of St Petersburg on the Baltic.
7 For an examination of this war, see: Anna Sofie Schøning et al. (eds), *1716 – The Great Northern War: New Perspectives* (Odense, Denmark: University Press of Southern Denmark, 2018); Stephen L. Kling (ed.), *Great Northern War Compendium* (St Louis, MO: THGC, 2015).
8 See: Nancy Shields Kollmann, *The Russian Empire 1450–1801* (Oxford: Oxford University Press, 2017), p. 111.
9 See: ibid., p. 292.
10 Russian capital from 1710 to 1918, with a brief period (1727–33) when it relocated back to Moscow.
11 A succinct account of the controversy that follows can be found in: Figes, *The Story of Russia*, pp. 14–16.

12 For his role in a wider context, see: Harun Yilmaz, *National Identities in Soviet Historiography: The Rise of Nations Under Stalin* (London: Taylor & Francis, 2015), p. 57.
13 Roman Zakharii, 'The Historiography of Normanist and Anti-Normanist theories on the origin of Rus': A review of modern historiography and major sources on Varangian controversy and other Scandinavian concepts of the origins of Rus", MPhil thesis, University of Oslo, 2002, https://www.duo.uio.no/bitstream/handle/10852/26680/7245.pdf?sequence=2 (accessed June 2024), p. 19.
14 Ibid., p. 25.

CHAPTER 13: THE ABSORBING OF 'LITTLE RUSSIA', 1783-1917

1 Yurchenko, 'Russian Strategic Culture and the War in Ukraine'.
2 Figes, *The Story of Russia*, p. 7.
3 Regarding Russian royal titles: from 1721, the official titles of Russian rulers were 'emperor' (Russian: император, *imperator*) and 'empress' (Russian: императрица, *imperatritsa*) or 'empress consort'. Technically, the last Russian ruler titled 'tsarina' was Eudoxia Lopukhina (died 1731, but effectively divorced in 1698), who was the first wife of Peter the Great. Alexandra Feodorovna (aka Alicia/Alix of Hesse), who was the wife of the last emperor, Nicholas II, was the last Russian empress. However, in English-language works, the terms 'tsar' and 'tsarina' are commonly used for Russian rulers from the late eighteenth century to 1917.
4 Figes, *The Story of Russia*, p. 16.
5 August Ludwig von Schlözer, quoted in Zena Harris and Nonna Ryan, 'The Inconsistencies of History: Vikings and Rurik', *New Zealand Slavonic Journal* (2005), vol. 38, pp. 105–30.
6 Quoted in: Jarman, *River Kings*, p. 225.
7 Nikolai Karamzin, *Istoriia gosudarstva rossiiskogo*, 3 vols (St Petersburg, 1842–1843), vol 1, p. 43.
8 Edmund A. Walsh, *The Fall of the Russian Empire: The Story of the Last of the Romanovs and the Coming of the Bolsheviks* (Rockville, MD: Wildside Press, 2009), p. 116.
9 Oleksander Ohloblyn, 'Normanist Theory', https://www.encyclopediaofukraine.com/display.asp?linkpath=pages%5CN%5CO%5CNormanisttheory.htm (accessed June 2024).
10 Figes, *The Story of Russia*, p. 48.
11 Zakharii, 'The Historiography of Normanist and Anti-Normanist theories on the origin of Rus", p. 21.
12 Ibid., p. 22.
13 Ibid.
14 Michael Hamm, *Kiev: A Portrait 1800–1917* (Princeton, NJ: Princeton University Press, 1993), p. 18.
15 These prohibited education in Ukrainian at private schools, in theatres, in official institutions and christening using Ukrainian names. In 1892, a further edict prohibited translation from Russian to Ukrainian and, in 1895, the tsarist Main Administration of Publishing prohibited printing of children's books in Ukrainian.
16 Neil Bermel, 'Ukrainian and Russian: how similar are the two languages?', https://theconversation.com/ukrainian-and-russian-how-similar-are-the-two-languages-178456 (accessed May 2024).
17 Ibid.
18 Ibid.
19 Ibid.
20 Reid, *Borderland*, p. 12.
21 Ibid.
22 Michael [Mykhailo] Hrushevsky, 'The Traditional Scheme of "Russian" History and the Problem of the Rational Organization of the History of the East Slavs', 1903, reprinted in English in *Slavistica: Proceedings of the Institute of Slavistics of the Ukrainian Free Academy of Sciences* (1966), No. 55, Winnipeg, pp. 8–9.
23 Reid, *Borderland*, p. 13.

NOTES

24 Figes, *The Story of Russia*, p. 17.
25 Ohloblyn, 'Normanist Theory'.
26 Reid, *Borderland*, p. 13.
27 Figes, *The Story of Russia*, p. 3.
28 Ibid.
29 Ohloblyn, 'Normanist Theory'.
30 Ibid.
31 Sina Maria Dubowoj, *A Historiographical Analysis of Gottlieb Siegfried Bayer's (1694-1738) De Varagis: The Varangian Theory in Russian History* (Madison, WI: University of Wisconsin–Madison, 1974), pp. 113, 124.
32 Figes, *The Story of Russia*, p. 3.

CHAPTER 14: FROM THE RUSSIAN REVOLUTION(S) TO THE 'END OF HISTORY'

1 See: Whittock, *The Secret History of Soviet Russia's Police State*.
2 Reid, *Borderland*, p. 40.
3 Timothy Snyder, *Bloodlands: Europe Between Hitler and Stalin* (London: Vintage, 2011).
4 Quoted in: Angela Livingstone, *Landmarks of World Literature, Pasternak: Doctor Zhivago* (Cambridge: Cambridge University Press, 1989), p. 31.
5 Quoted in: Gary Sheffield, *A Short History of the First World War* (London: One World, 2014), pp. 129–30. These figures are in line with most readily available sources. However, much higher figures are sometimes suggested.
6 Whittock, *The Secret History of Soviet Russia's Police State*, p. 41.
7 Evan Mawdsley, *The Russian Civil War* (New York: Pegasus Books, 2007), p. 287. See also: Robert W. Thurston, *Life and Terror in Stalin's Russia, 1934-1941* (New Haven and London: Yale University Press, 1996), p. 2, who suggests a death toll somewhere in the region of 7–10 million (1917–20), before casualties from famine and disease (after 1921) are added to the total.
8 Martin McCauley, *The Rise and Fall of the Soviet Union* (London and New York: Routledge, 2013), p. 57.
9 In the modern Russian state, 'Cossack' nationalist militias have been employed as auxiliaries alongside local police forces, and at the Sochi Olympic Winter Games, in 2014, gained a reputation for brutality and suppression of protesters expressing dissent, including physical assault on the 'Pussy Riot' punk collective group. Other modern Cossacks have been used to police gay rights rallies and in promoting and enforcing Russian nationalist and socially conservative sentiments.
10 Nicolas Werth, 'Crimes and Mass Violence of the Russian Civil Wars (1918–1921)', http://www.sciencespo.fr/mass-violence-war-massacre-resistance/en/document/crimes-and-mass-violence-russian-civil-wars-1918-1921 (accessed October 2024).
11 Vladimir N. Brovkin, *Behind the Front Lines of the Civil War* (Princeton, NJ: Princeton University Press, 1994), pp. 103–5; Peter Holquist, '"Conduct merciless, mass terror": Decossackization on the Don, 1919', in *Cahiers du Monde russe* (1997), number 38 (1–2), pp. 127–62.
12 Antisemitic atrocities also occurred elsewhere. An additional 2,200 (mostly Jews) fell victim to one action alone by the Whites at Yekaterinburg, in July 1919.
13 Brovkin, *Behind the Front Lines of the Civil War*, pp. 346–9.
14 Oleksa Eliseyovich Zasenko et al., 'Ukraine in the interwar period', https://www.britannica.com/place/Ukraine/Ukraine-in-the-interwar-period (accessed September 2024).
15 Extracted from Vladimir Putin, 'On the Historical Unity of Russians and Ukrainians' (12 July 2021), via the International Criminal Court Legal Tools Database, https://www.legal-tools.org/doc/tt382m/pdf (accessed September 2024). Also available on www.kremlin.ru.
16 Orysia Lutsevych and Jon Wallace, 'Ukraine–Russia Relations', https://www.chathamhouse.org/2021/11/ukraine-russia-relations (accessed May 2024).
17 For a more detailed breakdown see: Alec Nove, *An Economic History of the USSR* (London: Penguin, 1989), p. 176.

18 Michael Ellman, *Socialist Planning* (Cambridge: Cambridge University Press, 1989), p. 196.
19 William. D. Rubinstein, *Genocide* (Abingdon: Routledge, 2014), p. 203.
20 Stanislav Kulchytskyi, 'Holodomor in Ukraine 1932-1933: An Interpretation of Facts,' in Christian Noack, Lindsay Janssen, Vincent Comerford (eds), *Holodomor and Gorta Mór: Histories, Memories and Representations of Famine in Ukraine and Ireland* (London & New York: Anthem Press, 2012), p. 19.
21 Stanislav Kulchytskyi, 'Holodomor in Ukraine 1932-1933: An Interpretation of Facts', p. 20.
22 A point made as early as 1983, by the historian James Mace, at a conference held in Montreal, Canada, dedicated to the Ukrainian Famine.
23 Snyder, *Bloodlands*, p. 53.
24 Zakharii, 'The Historiography of Normanist and Anti-Normanist theories on the origin of Rus", pp. 92–3.
25 Ohloblyn, 'Normanist Theory'.
26 Zakharii, 'The Historiography of Normanist and Anti-Normanist theories on the origin of Rus", p. 93.
27 Ibid., p. 97.
28 Ohloblyn, 'Normanist Theory'.
29 Zakharii, 'The Historiography of Normanist and Anti-Normanist theories on the origin of Rus", p. 21.
30 Mykhailo Hrushevsky, *Istoriya Ukrayiny Rusy* (*History of Ukraine-Rus'*), in 10 Volumes (Lemberg/Lviv: Shevchenko Scientific Society, 1895–1933), Vol. 1, p. 624.
31 Zakharii, 'The Historiography of Normanist and Anti-Normanist theories on the origin of Rus", p. 21.
32 Oleksander Ohloblyn and Lubomyr Wynar, 'Hrushevsky, Mykhailo', https://www.encyclopedia ofukraine.com/display.asp?linkpath=pages%5CH%5CR%5CHrushevskyMykhailo.htm (accessed June 2024).
33 Zakharii, 'The Historiography of Normanist and Anti-Normanist theories on the origin of Rus", p. 21.
34 https://www.youtube.com/watch?v=Vv_IWJrDeFs (accessed June 2024).
35 John-Paul Himka, 'The Organization of Ukrainian Nationalists, the Ukrainian Police, and the Holocaust,' *Seventh Annual Danyliw Research Seminar in Contemporary Ukrainian Studies, sponsored by the Chair of Ukrainian Studies* (20–22 October 2011), University of Ottawa, p. 3.
36 John-Paul Himka, 'The Organization of Ukrainian Nationalists, the Ukrainian Police, and the Holocaust,' p. 4.
37 Figes, *The Story of Russia*, p. 17.
38 Ibid.
39 Ibid., p. 18.
40 Ibid.
41 Francis Fukuyama, *The End of History and the Last Man* (New York: Free Press, 1992).

CHAPTER 15: AN INDEPENDENT UKRAINE AND THE RETURN OF THE VIKINGS!
1 Elias Götz, 'Explaining Russia's Opposition to NATO Enlargement: Strategic Imperatives, Ideas, or Domestic Politics?' in Daniel Hamilton, Kristina Spohr (eds), *Open Door: NATO and Euro-Atlantic Security after the Cold War* (Washington DC: Johns Hopkins University Press, 2019), pp. 481–500.
2 Ibid.
3 Orysia Lutsevych, Jon Wallace, 'Ukraine-Russia Relations,' https://www.chathamhouse.org/2021/11/ukraine-russia-relations (accessed May 2024).
4 Deutsche Welle, 'Talking Tough', https://www.dw.com/en/russia-talks-tough-in-response-to-natos-eastward-expansion/a-3261078 (accessed August 2024).
5 Ibid.

NOTES

6. Interfax, 'Russians see Ukraine and Georgia joining NATO as a threat to country's security – poll', https://www.interfax.ru/russia/7061 (accessed August 2024).
7. See: Christopher Miller, *The War Came to Us: Life and Death in Ukraine* (London: Bloomsbury, 2023), for an insider view of the complexity of Ukraine before 2014 and the impact of accelerating Russian intervention since then.
8. 'Russian Bishop Known as "Putin's Confessor" Named Head of Crimea Diocese', *Moscow Times*, 12 October 2023, https://www.themoscowtimes.com/2023/10/12/russian-bishop-known-as-putins-confessor-named-head-of-crimea-diocese-a82746 (accessed October 2024).
9. Karen Schousboe, 'Putin and his Medieval Worldview: Putin's Orthodox worldview calls for him to play the leading role in the reenactment of the medieval Kyivan Rus', https://www.medieval.eu/putin-and-his-medieval-worldview/ (accessed August 2024).
10. Extracted from Putin, 'On the Historical Unity of Russians and Ukrainians'.
11. 'Tucker Carlson Interviews Vladimir Putin Transcript'.
12. Mark Galeotti, 'Putin's Q&A at the St Petersburg International Economic Forum (SPIEF), 7 June 2024, in conversation with Sergei Karaganov', *In Moscow's Shadows* podcast, 9 June 2024, https://podcasts.apple.com/gb/podcast/in-moscows-shadows/id1510124746?i=1000658332796 (accessed June 2024).
13. Coyer, 'Putin's Holy War and the Disintegration of the "Russian World"'.
14. Whittock, *Apocalyptic Politics*, pp. 173–4.
15. See: Dmitry Shlapentokh, 'The Time of Troubles in Alexander Dugin's Narrative', https://www.cambridge.org/core/journals/european-review/article/time-of-troubles-in-alexander-dugins-narrative/CAF11EDE51F7C4016D541CD40A096C61 (accessed June 2024).
16. 'Tucker Carlson Interviews Vladimir Putin Transcript'.
17. Extracted from Putin, 'On the Historical Unity of Russians and Ukrainians'.
18. Ibid.
19. Ibid.
20. Ibid.
21. 'Tucker Carlson Interviews Vladimir Putin Transcript'.
22. Although Putin does admit that there had been people demanding concessions to Ukrainian national identity since the nineteenth century.
23. Extracted from Putin, 'On the Historical Unity of Russians and Ukrainians'.
24. Ibid.
25. Ibid.
26. Ibid.
27. Ibid.
28. 'Tucker Carlson Interviews Vladimir Putin Transcript'.
29. Extracted from Putin, 'On the Historical Unity of Russians and Ukrainians'.

EPILOGUE: BACK TO THE FUTURE? WHERE NEXT FOR THE 'DEEP STORY' OF THE RUS?

1. Zakharii, 'The Historiography of Normanist and Anti-Normanist theories on the origin of Rus'', p. 21.

INDEX

Abbasid Caliphate 15, 34, 63, 115, 118, 124
ibn Abdallah, Yakut 122, 123
Adam of Bremen 142, 143
Aesir 58–60, 62, 63, 64
Alexander of Tver 160
Algirdas, Grand Duke 165, 167, 168
Alma-Ata Protocol 230
Al-Ya'qūbī 76
American Vikings xx
Ancient Russian History 188
Anglo-Saxon Chronicle 17, 143
Annals of St Bertin 76
Apocalyptic Politics xx
ARC (Autonomous Republic of Crimea) 5, 6
Asgard (Asagarth) 59, 62
Askold and Dir 72, 73, 90
Austro-Hungarian Empire 210
austrvegr 3
autocephalous 10, 161

Baghdad 2, 44, 77, 115, 118–22, 124, 151
Bandera, Stepan 223, 224, 225
baptism of the Rus 107–8, 178
Basil II, Emperor 106, 131
Batu Khan 153, 154, 155
Belarus xxi, 18, 28, 36, 37, 39, 47, 53, 166, 201, 211, 214, 230
Belovezha Accords 230
Birka 39, 47, 49, 89, 96
Black Sea 18, 37, 42, 47, 48, 62, 100, 142, 185
 coast 53, 185, 86, 91, 186, 191
 fleets 5, 6
 trade 54, 67, 72, 77, 79, 90, 93, 250

Bloodlands 211
Bolsheviks 41, 179, 180, 207, 209, 212, 213, 244–6
Book of Roads and Kingdoms, The 120
Brezhnev, Leonid 227
Budapest Memorandum 6, 230
Bulgar/Bulgars 77, 101, 105, 112, 116–18, 121, 123–4, 130
Byzantine Empire 18, 28, 31, 37, 43, 48, 63, 83, 85–6, 92–3, 100–103, 110, 140, 145, 175
Byzantium 86, 106

Carlson, Tucker 9, 172, 236–9, 241, 243, 247
Caspian Sea 13, 16, 18–19, 31, 36–42, 47, 54, 100–104, 213
 battles 115, 128–9
Catalogue of Norwegian Kings 112, 135
Catherine II, Empress (Catherine the Great) 5, 177, 181, 185, 191, 192, 197, 198, 199, 243
Charlemagne 23, 87
Charles XII, King of Sweden 184
Cheka, the 209, 214, 217
Chingiz Khan (Genghis Khan) 149–54, 176
Christianity 87, 104, 105, 107
 conversion to xxi, 11, 12, 58, 82, 83, 86, 96, 102
 Orthodox 9, 82, 88, 103, 105, 159
Church of the Tithes 103, 108
Circle of the World 61
Cnut, King of Denmark 141
Cold War 7, 8, 228, 230
collateral succession 144, 145
Collectivisation 211, 216, 217, 219

colonial perspective 69, 70
Commonwealth of Independent States (CIS) 230
Communist Party 216, 219, 244
Constantine VII, Emperor 49, 50, 75, 95, 131, 189
Constantine VIII, Emperor 131
Constantine IX Monomachos, Emperor 137, 138, 176
Constantinople 10, 14–19, 40, 42, 76, 81, 83, 85–97, 100, 104, 110, 135–9
    decline and fall 145, 163, 170
    ecumenical patriarchate 162
    Viking raid on 90
conversion 11, 58, 88, 91, 99, 100, 102, 103–9, 119
Cossacks, the 167, 170, 171, 180, 182, 184, 213, 214
Crimea 4–8, 16, 78, 91, 94, 108, 227
    annexation of 5, 8, 99, 162, 181, 185, 191, 198, 230, 233, 235
Cumans/Polovtsy 148
Cyrillic alphabet 110, 201

Danegeld 102
Danilovich, Ivan I 160, 161
Decembrists 204
'Decossackisation' 213, 214
'deep story/stories' xviii, xix, xx, 1, 3, 9, 11, 67, 88, 99, 108, 163, 165, 178, 186, 229, 249–51
Denikin, General 213
Denmark 12, 17, 23–7, 29, 31, 65, 117
Derevlians 74, 81
al-Din, Rashid 151
dirham 31, 32, 34, 35, 54, 57, 77, 102, 104, 111, 119, 121, 125
Dmitry Donskoy 173
Dnieper, River 42, 47–53, 71–2, 94, 104, 107, 116, 131–2, 168, 170, 242, 249, 250
Dniester, River 53, 223
Don, River 62, 63, 90, 170, 173, 213
Donbas, the 162, 233, 234, 240
Dorset, England 17, 29, 37, 39

Eastern Roman Empire 14, 85
Edgar Ætheling 142, 143
Edmund Ironside 141
Edward Ætheling (Edward the Exile) 141, 142, 143
Eisenstein, Sergei 177, 178
End Times, Again?, The xx
Enemy at the Gates 222, 223
England 23, 24, 27
Erik Bloodaxe 25

EU (European Union) 3, 7, 231, 233, 234
euhemerised 63
Euromaidan 3, 4, 233

ibn Fadlan, Ahmad 54, 77, 119, 122–6, 128, 130
Finns 33, 34, 112, 187
first Russian Revolution 180, 209
First World War 166, 198, 208, 209, 212, 218
Five Year Plans 216
France 17, 110, 201
FSB 210
Fukuyama, Francis 7
Futhark, the 12

Gaimar, Geoffrey 142, 143
Galicia 210, 223, 224, 249
Galicia–Volhynia 157, 158
Garthariki xv, 63, 78, 85
Genghis Khan (Chingiz Khan) 149–54, 176
Georgia 14, 129, 230–33
Gnezdovo 49, 51, 69, 71, 74
Godwinson, Harold 143
Golden Horde, the 152, 153, 155, 156, 159, 160, 172
Gorbachev, Mikhail 227
Gorm, King 24
Gormsson, Harald Bluetooth 25
Götar, the 26
Gotland 20, 29, 30, 35, 40, 47, 52–4, 57, 73, 101, 118
Grand Princes of Kyiv 133
'Great City', the 83, 85–7, 89, 91, 95, 104, 154, 157
Great Northern War 184
Great Patriotic War 218, 222–5
'Great Russia' 186, 191, 192, 203, 219, 227, 238, 243
Great Schism of 1054 110
Great Terror, the 219
'Greek fire' 16, 94, 129
Gripsholm Castle, Sweden 13

Haakon the Good 25
Hagia Sophia 19, 105, 111
Hanseatic League 145
Harald Fairhair, King 25, 65
Haraldr 1, 12, 13
Haraldsson, King Olaf (St Olaf) 134, 136, 142
Hardrada, King Harald 134–9
Hastings, Battle of 135, 143, 144
Hedeby 30, 47, 49, 89
Henry III, Emperor 142
hetmanate 181, 184, 185–6, 191, 212
History of Ruthenians 206

INDEX

History of the English 142
History of the Russian State 194, 196
Hitler, Adolf 69, 193, 194, 211
hoards 35, 54, 101
Holodomor, the 217, 218
Holstein-Gottorp-Romanov dynasty 197
Holy Roman Empire 23, 183
'Holy Rus' 11, 70, 88, 99–113, 122, 154, 163, 166, 179, 192, 229, 241, 246
'Holy Russia' xxi, 240
House of Romanov 179, 180, 192, 196, 197, 207, 209
Hrushevsky, Mykhailo 203, 206, 221, 222
Hungary 24, 110, 141, 142, 143, 149, 150, 154, 208, 232

Iceland 2, 16, 25, 37, 38, 61, 63, 79
Igor (Ingvar) 80, 81, 94, 96
Ilyin, Ivan 234
Ingvar the Far-Travelled 13, 14, 15, 16, 102, 129
Innocent IV, Pope 155
Ireland 19, 20, 37
Islamic caliphate 2, 54, 86, 116
Ivan IV Vasilyevich, Tsar (Ivan the Terrible) 174, 175, 176, 177, 178, 179, 180, 192

jarls of Lade 25
John of Worcester 141, 142, 143
Jonsson, Kenneth 36

Kalka, River 149
Karaganov, Sergei 239
Karamzin, Nikolai 194, 196
KGB 210, 225, 244
khagan 76, 121, 128
Khazars, the 72, 76, 77, 81, 90, 105, 115, 121, 123, 128, 129
Khmelnytsky, Bodhan 171, 172
ibn Khordadbeh, Abu'l Qasim 77, 119, 120
Kostomarov, Mykola 206
Kunik, Ernst Eduard 195
Kyivan Rus 110, 112, 113, 133, 135, 139, 143, 144, 167
  conversion of 99, 103–9, 169
  end of the state 153–9, 175
  foundation stages of the state 75
  grand prince 121, 175
  legacy 162–4
  state 67, 72–8, 79, 99, 103, 111, 131, 132, 190, 206, 218, 246

Lavrov, Sergei 232
Laws of Edward the Confessor 143

Life of Kartli 14
Likhachev, Dmitry 220, 222
Listven, Battle of 132
Lithuania 158, 160, 167, 168, 169, 174, 182–4, 230, 242
'little green men' 3, 4
'Little Russia' 10, 168, 172, 186, 191–208, 242
Lomonosov, Mikhail 187, 188
Louis the Pious 76

Mayflower Lives xx
Metropolitans of Kiev 10, 161
Michael I, Tsar 179, 180
Michael IV, Emperor 137
Michael V, Emperor 135, 137
Miklagarðr 15, 85, 89
Minsk Agreements 233
Mongols, the (Tatar) 73, 146, 148–60, 162–5, 167
Müller, Gerhard Friedrich 186, 187, 188
Murfatlar 53
Muscovy 158–60, 162–3, 165, 172–5, 176, 182, 186, 192, 203, 242–3

names, Finnish 81
names, Norse to Slavic 80, 81
nationalism 8, 215, 220, 227
NATO (North Atlantic Treaty Organization) 4, 7, 230–34
Navalny, Alexei 7
Nazi Germany 211, 218
Neva, River 47, 116
Nevsky, Alexander 156, 160, 242
Nicholas II, Tsar 180, 194, 197, 199, 207, 209
Normandy 17, 79, 80
Normandy Format Summit 234
Normanist/anti-Normanist 188, 189, 192, 193, 195, 196, 198, 204–7, 219–22, 237, 238, 249
Norse gods from the East 61–5
Norse mythology 20, 57, 58–61, 64, 65
Norway 17, 21, 23, 25, 27, 33, 44, 65, 111, 112, 134–6, 138, 142
Novgorod 39, 42, 45, 48, 50, 51, 54, 70–75, 78, 92, 111–12, 145, 147, 174
Novgorod First Chronicle 72
Novgorod princes 73, 160
Novorossiya 185

Odesa/Odessa 6
Odin 58, 63–5
Odoacer 87
okraina 167, 205, 243

Old Believers 183, 184
Old Norse 18–22, 28, 48, 61–3, 71, 79–81, 102, 112, 134, 139, 143, 189
Oleg (Helgi) 73, 74, 80, 92, 93
Olga (wife of Igor) 81, 96, 103, 104
On the Governance of the Empire 50, 75, 189
Orange Revolution 231
Origins of the Russian people and name 188
Orosius, Paulus 30
Orthodox Christianity 9, 82, 88, 103, 105, 159

Paris, Matthew 143, 151
Pasternak, Boris 211, 212
patriarch 10, 11, 90, 161, 162
Pechenegs 53, 82, 95
Perun 82, 107
Peter III, Tsar 197
Peter the Great, Tsar 177, 184, 196, 197, 199
Philotheus 88
Photios I 90, 91
pilgrimage 140
Poetic Edda 61
Pogodin, Mikhail 195
Poland 30, 33, 35, 110, 168–9, 176, 181–3, 186, 211, 223, 224, 232
Polish–Lithuanian Commonwealth 158, 168, 170, 182, 183, 201
'polite people, the' 4
Porphyrogenita, Princess Anna 106
Price, Neil 46
Prose Edda 61
Putin, Vladimir 1, 6–11, 74, 78, 167, 215, 225, 229, 250, 251
  fixation on Vladimir the Great 234, 235
  'On the Historical Unity of Russians and Ukrainians' 11, 236–47
  Ukraine 231–4
  worldview 184, 239–47

Qur'an 88

Razi, Amin 130
Red Army 166, 209, 210, 211, 214, 216, 217, 224, 225
Revolution of Dignity 3, 233
Rhos, the 18, 76
Roger of Howden 143
Romanov dynasty 179, 180, 192, 196, 197, 207, 209
Rome 23, 86, 87, 88, 110
Romulus Augustus, Emperor 87

runestones 1, 12–16, 68, 128, 138, 139, 140
  Ed 112, 113
  Ingvar 129
  Pilgårds (G280) 52
  Sjonhem cemetery 53
  Sjusta 111
  Skepptuna
  Sö 179 13, 14, 15
  U 1143 15
  Ulunda 113
Rurik (*Rorik*) 70–73, 80
Rurikid dynasty 71, 73, 77, 82, 179, 238, 240, 246
Rus, the *see also* Kyivan Rus
  map of Rus lands ix
  Slavic culture 78–83
  state 68–72
  Varangian 69, 72, 100
Russian Civil War 41, 211, 212
Russian Federation 1, 5–7, 9, 29, 41, 97, 99, 108, 166, 210, 227, 230–33, 238
Russian Orthodox Church 10, 161, 162, 199, 235
Russian Orthodoxy 8, 9, 10, 161, 163
Russian Primary Chronicle 68, 70–74, 78, 81, 90, 93, 95, 99, 103–4, 108–9, 187, 189, 193, 195
Russification 198–200, 206, 219, 227, 245
Russkaya Pravda 110
ibn Rusta, Ahmad 77, 118
Ruthenian 166, 168, 169
Ruthenian Uniate Church 169
van Ruysbroeck, Willem 149, 154

Saga of Ingvar the Far-Travelled 14, 15
Saga of the People of Laxárdalur 43
sagas 48, 61–2, 78, 112, 135
St Petersburg 181, 186, 188, 193, 204, 210, 239
Sámi, the 44, 45, 60, 112
von Schlözer, August Ludwig 193, 194
Second Rome 163
Secret History of Soviet Russia's Police State, The xx
Serkland 1, 12, 13, 15, 63, 112, 116, 128, 138
Sevastopol 5, 6
Seven Books of History Against the Pagans 30
Shevchenko, Taras 200
Shevkunov, Tikhon 235
silk 43, 89, 94, 95, 96, 104, 118, 129, 155
  lands 116–17
  roads 116, 117, 118, 119, 120
Skötkonung, Olaf 26, 134
Skylitzes, John 54–5
Slav state 131, 132

INDEX

slavery 43, 46, 77, 118
slaves 3, 14, 31, 32, 118, 119, 126, 128, 156
Slavic culture 28, 78–83, 196, 204
'Slavic homeland' 226
sledges 51–2
Solovyov, Sergei 195
Stalin, Josef 177, 178, 179, 210, 211, 215, 216, 219–23, 226
Stamford Bridge, Battle of 135
Staraya Ladoga 33, 34, 36, 48, 50–54, 69, 71, 116
Stetsko, Yaroslav 223, 224, 225
Sturluson, Snorri 61–5, 18
Svear, the 26, 65
Svyatoslav I 81, 82, 131, 133
Sweden 15, 18, 26–9, 37, 47, 54, 65, 78, 101, 112, 129, 138, 140, 181–2, 187

Tale of Bygone Years 68
Tale of the Destruction of Ryazan by Batu 154
'Tatar yoke, the' 155, 156, 157, 158, 195
Thietmar of Merseburg, Bishop 106, 107
Third Rome 163, 179
Time of Troubles 175, 177, 179
Timur (Tamerlane) 151, 174
trade routes 47, 54, 78, 89–91, 100–104, 117, 145, 155, 156, 250
Treaty of Andrusovo 182
Treaty of Eternal Peace 182, 183
Treaty of Pereyaslav 165
Trinity Chronicle 173
Trump and the Puritans xviii, xx
Trump, Donald xviii, xix, xx
Truso 30, 31, 32, 33, 34, 69
Tryggvason, King Olaf 134

Ukraine
    after 1917 revolutions 211–18
    contested lands 165–7
    German occupation 223, 224
    Great Patriotic War 222–5
    independence 227, 228, 229–34
    language 200–202
    nationhood 210, 215–18
    okraina 167, 205, 243
    post-war 225–8
    Putin and 231–4
    Russian invasion 11, 234
    Russification of 198–200, 219
Ukrainian Insurgent Army (UPA) 224, 225
Ukrainian Orthodox Church 10
Ukrainian Soviet Socialist Republic 211, 215, 244

Uppsala 15, 26, 46, 65
USSR 5, 109, 166, 178, 191, 195, 210, 213, 215–16, 218–20, 222–8, 230, 244–5

Vanir 58, 59, 63, 64
Varangian 92, 132–4, 137, 139, 190, 221, 237
    guard 19, 28, 113, 144
    Rus, the 69, 72, 100
Vasily IV, Tsar 73
Vikings 9–12
    becoming the Rus 68–72
    conquest of England 141
    definition 17–22
    deities 58–61
    evidence of 23–38
    movement East 28, 29, 30
    rivers 39–55
    Scandinavia 24–7
    ships 49, 50
Viking–Slav xxi, 18, 67, 112, 162, 175, 235
Vistula, River 30, 31
Vladimir the Great 99–100, 103–9, 131–4, 161–3, 175–6, 179, 192, 202, 229, 234, 241, 246, 251
Vladimir–Suzdal 157
Volga, River 34, 37, 40–42, 47, 54, 63, 90, 102, 116–24, 159, 226, 250
Volkhov, River 33, 42, 48
Voyages of Ohthere and Wulfstan 30
vranyo 4

Wallachians 53
William of Malmesbury 143
Wolin 33
Wrangel, Baron 213

Yanukovych, Victor 3, 233
Yaroslav the Wise 110, 111, 112, 132, 134, 139, 144, 145
Yeke Monggol Ulus 150
Yngling dynasty 26, 65
Ynglinga Saga 61, 62, 63, 64, 65

Zamoyski, Adam 170
Zaporozhian Sich 170, 182, 185
Zelensky, Volodymyr 234
Zeno, Emperor 87